John Gerard

What was the Gunpowder Plot?

The Traditional Story Tested by Original Evidence

John Gerard

What was the Gunpowder Plot?
The Traditional Story Tested by Original Evidence

ISBN/EAN: 9783744749466

Printed in Europe, USA, Canada, Australia, Japan

Cover: Foto ©Andreas Hilbeck / pixelio.de

More available books at **www.hansebooks.com**

WHAT WAS THE GUNPOWDER PLOT?

THE TRADITIONAL STORY TESTED BY
ORIGINAL EVIDENCE

BY

JOHN GERARD, S.J.

LONDON
OSGOOD, McILVAINE & CO.
45, ALBEMARLE STREET, W.
1897

PREFACE.

THE following study of the Gunpowder Plot has grown out of the accidental circumstance that, having undertaken to read a paper before the Historical Research Society, at Archbishop's House, Westminster, as the day on which it was to be read chanced to be the 5th of November,[1] I was asked to take the famous conspiracy for my subject. It was with much reluctance that I agreed to do so, believing, as I then did, that there was absolutely nothing fresh to say upon this topic, that no incident in our annals had been more thoroughly threshed out, and that in regard of none, so far, at least, as its broader outlines are concerned, was the truth more clearly established.

When, however, I turned to the sources whence our knowledge of the transaction is derived, and in particular to the original documents upon which it is ultimately based, I was startled to find how grave were the doubts and difficulties which suggested themselves at every turn, while, though slowly and gradually, yet with ever gathering force, the conviction forced itself upon me, that, not merely in its details is the traditional story unworthy of credit, but that all the evidence points to a conclusion fundamentally at

[1] 1894.

variance with it. Nothing contributed so powerfully to this conviction as to find that every fresh line of reasoning or channel of information which could be discovered inevitably tended, in one way or another, towards the same result. In the following pages are presented to the reader the principal arguments which have wrought this change of view in my own mind.[1]

I cannot pretend to furnish any full or wholly satisfactory answer to the question which stands upon the title-page. The real history of the Plot in all its stages we shall, in all probability, never know. If, however, we cannot satisfy ourselves of the truth, it will be much to ascertain what is false; to convince ourselves that the account of the matter officially supplied, and almost universally accepted, is obviously untrue, and that the balance of probability lies heavily against those who invented it, as having been the real plotters, devising and working the scheme for their own ends.

Neither have I any wish to ignore, or to extenuate, the objections which militate against such a conclusion, objections arising from considerations of a general character, rather than from any positive evidence. Why, it may reasonably be asked, if the government of the day were ready to go so far as is alleged, did they not go further? Why, being supremely anxious to incriminate the priests, did they not fabricate unequivocal evidence against them, instead of satisfying themselves with what appears to us far from conclusive? Why did they encumber their tale with incidents, which, if they did not really occur, could serve

[1] Some of these have been partially set forth in a series of six articles appearing in *The Month*, December 1894—May, 1895.

only to damage it, inasmuch as we, at this distance of time, can argue that they are impossible and absurd? How is it, moreover, that the absurdity was not patent to contemporaries, and was not urged by those who had every reason to mislike and mistrust the party in power?

Considerations such as these undoubtedly deserve all attention, and must be fully weighed, but while they avail to establish a certain presumption in favour of the official story, I cannot but think that the sum of probabilities tells strongly the other way. It must be remembered that three centuries ago the intrinsic likelihood or unlikelihood of a tale did not go for much, and the accounts of plots in particular appear to have obtained general credence in proportion as they were incredible, as the case of Squires a few years earlier, and of Titus Oates somewhat later, sufficiently testify. It is moreover as difficult for us to enter into the crooked and complex methods of action which commended themselves to the statesmen of the period, as to appreciate the force of the cumbrous and abusive harangues which earned for Sir Edward Coke the character of an incomparable pleader. On the other hand, it appears certain that they who had so long played the game must have understood it best, and, whatever else may be said of them, they always contrived to win. In regard of Father Garnet, for example, we may think the evidence adduced by the prosecution quite insufficient, but none the less it in fact availed not only to send him to the gallows, but to brand him in popular estimation for generations, and even for centuries, as the arch-traitor to whose machinations the whole enterprise was due.

In the case of some individuals obnoxious to the government, it seems evident that downright forgery was actually practised.

The question of Father Garnet's complicity, though usually considered as the one point in connection with the Plot requiring to be discussed, is not treated in the following pages. It is doubtless true that to prove the conspiracy to have been a trick of State, is not the same thing as proving that he was not entangled in it; but, at the same time, the first point, if it can be established, will deprive the other of almost all its interest. Nevertheless, Father Garnet's case will still require to be fully treated on its own merits, but this cannot be done within the limits of such an inquiry as the present. It is not by confining our attention to one isolated incident in his career, nor by discussing once again the familiar documents connected therewith, that we can form a sound and satisfactory judgment about him. For this purpose, full consideration must be given to what has hitherto been almost entirely ignored, the nature and character of the man, as exhibited especially during the eighteen years of his missionary life in England, during most of which period he acted as the superior of his brother Jesuits. There exist abundant materials for his biography, in his official and confidential correspondence, preserved at Stonyhurst and elsewhere, and not till the information thus supplied shall have been duly utilized will it be possible to judge whether the part assigned to him by his enemies in this wild and wicked design can, even conceivably, represent the truth. It may, I trust, be possible at no distant date to attempt this work, but it is not possible now, and to introduce this topic into our present discussion would only confuse the issue which is before us.

Except in one or two instances, I have judged it advisable, for the sake of clearness, to modernize the spelling of documents quoted in the text. In the notes they are usually given in their original form.

I have to acknowledge my indebtedness in many particulars to Mr. H. W. Brewer, who not only contributes valuable sketches to illustrate the narrative, but has furnished many important notes and suggestions, based upon his exhaustive knowledge of ancient London. I have to thank the Marquis of Salisbury for permission to examine MSS. in the Hatfield collection, and his lordship's librarian, Mr. Gunton, for information supplied from the same source. Through the courtesy of the Deputy-Keeper of the Public Records, every facility has been afforded me for consulting the precious documents contained in the "Gunpowder Plot Book." The Dean of Corpus Christi College, Oxford, has kindly given me access to an important MS. in the College Library; and I have been allowed by the Rector of Stonyhurst to retain in my hands Father Greenway's MS. history of the Plot during the whole period of my work. The proprietors of the *Daily Graphic* have allowed me to use two sketches of the interior of " Guy Faukes' Cellar," and one of his lantern, originally prepared by Mr. Brewer for that journal.

CONTENTS.

CHAP.   **PAGE**

I. THE STATE OF THE QUESTION 1

Disclosure of the Plot—Arrest of Guy Faukes—Flight of his associates—Their abortive insurrection—Their fate—The crime charged on Catholics in general—Garnet and other Jesuits proclaimed as the ringleaders—Capture of Garnet—Efforts to procure evidence against him—His execution—Previous history of the Plot as traditionally narrated; Proceedings and plans of the conspirators—Manner of the discovery.

Reasons for suspecting the truth of this history—Previous plots originated or manipulated by the government—Suspicious circumstances respecting the Gunpowder Plot in particular—Essential points of the inquiry.

II. THE PERSONS CONCERNED 19

Robert Cecil, Earl of Salisbury—His character variously estimated—Discreditable incidents of his career—Contemporary judgments of him—His unpopularity—His political difficulties largely dissipated in consequence of the Plot.

His hatred of and hostility towards the Catholics—Their numbers and importance—Their hopes from King James, and their disappointment—The probability that some would have recourse to violence—The conspirators known as men likely to seek such a remedy—Their previous history—Difficulties and contradictions in regard of their character.

CHAP.		PAGE
III.	THE OPINION OF CONTEMPORARIES AND HISTORIANS	42

The government at once suspected of having contrived or fomented the Plot—Persistence of these suspicions, to which historians for more than a century bear witness—No fresh information accounts for their disappearance.

IV.	THE TRADITIONAL STORY	54

The old House of Lords and its surroundings—House hired by the conspirators—They attempt to dig a mine beneath the Peers' Chamber—Difficulties and improbabilities of the account—The "Cellar" hired—Its position and character—The gunpowder bought and stored—Further problems concerning it—The conspirators' plans—Contradictions respecting them—Their wild and absurd character—Impossibility of the supposition that the proceedings escaped the notice of the government.

V.	THE GOVERNMENT INTELLIGENCE DEPARTMENT	93

Evidence that the government were fully aware of what was in progress—Various intelligence supplied to them—Cecil's uneasiness on account of the spread of Catholicity, and the king's communication with the pope—His evident determination to force on James a policy of intolerance—He intimates that a great move is about to be made, and acknowledges to information concerning the conspirators and their schemes—His political methods illustrated.

VI.	THE "DISCOVERY"	114

Importance of the letter received by Lord Monteagle—Extraordinary prominence given to it—Monteagle's character—He receives the letter—Suspicious circumstances connected with its arrival—It is shown to Cecil—Hopeless contradictions of the official narrative as to what followed

CONTENTS.

| CHAP. | | PAGE |

—Impossibility of ascertaining what actually occurred—The French version of the story—The conduct of the government at variance with their own professions—Their inexplicable delay in making the discovery—They take no precautions against the recurrence of danger—The mystery of the gunpowder—Incredibility of the official narration.

VII. PERCY, CATESBY, AND TRESHAM 147

Probability that the government had an agent among the conspirators—Suspicious circumstances regarding Percy—His private life—His alleged intercourse with Cecil — His death.

Catesby and Tresham likewise accused of secret dealings with Cecil—Catesby's falsehood towards his associates and Father Garnet—Tresham's strange conduct after the discovery—His mysterious death.

Alleged positive evidence against the government.

VIII. THE GOVERNMENT'S CASE 163

A monopoly secured for the official narrative, which is admittedly untruthful—Suspicions suggested by such a course, especially in such a case—The confessions of Faukes and Winter, on which this narrative is based, deserve no credit—Nor does the evidence of Bates against Greenway—Indications of foul play in regard of Robert Winter—The case of Owen, Baldwin and Cresswell; assertions made respecting them of which no proof can be produced—Efforts to implicate Sir Walter Raleigh and others—Falsification of evidence—The service of forgers employed.

Catholic writers have drawn their accounts from the sources provided by the government.

CHAP.		PAGE
IX. THE SEQUEL		209

Cecil well informed as to the real nature of the conspiracy, and apprehends no danger from it—At once turns it to account by promoting anti-Catholic legislation—Honour and popularity resulting to him—Ruin of the Earl of Northumberland—Cecil's manifesto—His alleged attempt to start a second plot.

The popular history of the Plot, and how it was circulated—Singular suitability of the Fifth of November for the "Discovery."

Summary of the argument.

APPENDIX A.	NOTES ON THE ILLUSTRATIONS	235
APPENDIX B.	SIR EVERARD DIGBY'S LETTER TO SALISBURY	245
APPENDIX C.	THE QUESTION OF SUCCESSION	249
APPENDIX D.	THE SPANISH TREASON	251
APPENDIX E.	SITE OF PERCY'S LODGING	251
APPENDIX F.	ENROLMENT OF CONSPIRATORS	252
APPENDIX G.	HENRY WRIGHT THE INFORMER	254
APPENDIX H.	MONTEAGLE'S LETTER TO KING JAMES	256
APPENDIX I.	EPITAPH ON PETER HEIWOOD	258
APPENDIX K.	THE USE OF TORTURE	259
APPENDIX L.	MYTHS AND LEGENDS OF THE PLOT	260
APPENDIX M.	MEMORIAL INSCRIPTIONS IN THE TOWER	264
APPENDIX N.	GUY FAUKES' PUBLISHED CONFESSION	268
INDEX		279

LIST OF ILLUSTRATIONS.

		PAGE
1.	Medal Commemorative of the Gunpowder Plot	*Title-page*
2.	The Gunpowder Plot. I.	*Frontispiece*
3.	,, ,, ,, II.	90
4.	,, ,, ,, III.	215
5.	,, ,, ,, IV.	227
6.	,, ,, ,, V.	229
7.	Discovery of the Gunpowder Plot	136
8.	Monteagle and Letter	115
9.	Arrest of Faukes	125
10.	Guy Faukes' Lantern	139
11.	Group of Conspirators	3
12.	Thomas Percy	149
13.	Houses of Parliament in 1605	56-7
14.	Ground Plan of the Same	59
15.	House of Lords in 1807	61
16.	Interior of House of Lords, 1755	97
17.	Interior of "Cellar"	71
18.	Arches from "Cellar"	75
19.	Vault under Painted Chamber	73
20.	Cell adjoining Painted Chamber	83
21.	Facsimile of part of Winter's Confession, Nov. 23	168
22.	Signatures of Faukes and Oldcorne	173
23.	Facsimile of part of Faukes' Confession of Nov. 9	199

"Quis hæc posteris sic narrare poterit, ut facta non ficta esse videantur?"

"Ages to come will be in doubt whether it were a fact or a fiction."

Sir Edw. Coke on the trial of the Conspirators.

WHAT WAS THE GUNPOWDER PLOT?

CHAPTER I.

THE STATE OF THE QUESTION.

ON the morning of Tuesday, the 5th of November, 1605, which day was appointed for the opening of a new Parliamentary session, London rang with the news that in the course of the night a diabolical plot had been discovered, by which the king and legislature were to have been destroyed at a blow. In a chamber beneath the House of Lords had been found a great quantity of gunpowder, and with it a man, calling himself John Johnson, who, finding that the game was up, fully acknowledged his intention to have fired the magazine while the royal speech was being delivered, according to custom, overhead, and so to have blown King, Lords, and Commons into the air. At the same time, he doggedly refused to say who were his accomplices, or whether he had any.

This is the earliest point at which the story of the Gunpowder Plot can be taken up with any certainty. Of what followed, at least as to the main outlines, we are sufficiently well informed. Johnson, whose true name was presently found to be Guy, or Guido, Faukes,[1] proved, it is true, a most obstinate and unsatisfactory witness, and obstinately refused to give any evidence which might incriminate others. But the actions of his confederates quickly supplied the information which he withheld. It was known that the "cellar" in which the powder was found, as well as a house adjacent, had been hired in the name of one Thomas Percy, a Catholic gentleman, perhaps a kinsman, and certainly a dependent, of the Earl of Northumberland. It was now discovered that he and others of his acquaintance had fled from London on the previous day, upon receipt of intelligence that the plot seemed at least to be suspected. Not many hours later the fugitives were heard of in Warwickshire, Worcestershire, and Staffordshire, the native counties of several amongst them, attempting to rally others to their desperate fortunes, and to levy war against the crown. For this purpose they forcibly seized cavalry horses[2] at Warwick, and arms at Whewell Grange, a seat of Lord Windsor's. These violent proceedings having raised the country behind them, they were pursued by the sheriffs with what forces could be got together, and finally brought to bay at Holbeche, in Staffordshire, the residence of one Stephen Littleton, a Catholic gentleman.

There proved to have been thirteen men in all who had undoubtedly been participators in the treason. Of these Faukes, as we have seen, was already in the

[1] So he himself always wrote it.

[2] Also described as "Great Horses," or "Horses for the great Saddle."

hands of justice. Another, Francis Tresham, had not fled with his associates, but remained quietly, and without attempting concealment, in London, even going to the council and offering them his services; after a week he was taken into custody. The eleven who either betook themselves to the country, or were already there, awaiting the issue of the enterprise, and

THE CONSPIRATORS, FROM A PRINT PUBLISHED AT AMSTERDAM.

prepared to co-operate in the rising which was to be its sequel, were Robert Catesby, Thomas Percy, Robert and Thomas Winter, John and Christopher Wright, John Grant, Robert Keyes, Ambrose Rokewood, Sir Everard Digby, and Thomas Bates. All were Catholics, and all, with the exception of Bates, Catesby's servant, were "gentlemen of blood and name," some of them, notably Robert Winter, Rokewood, Digby, and Tresham, being men of ample fortune.

On Friday, November 8th, three days after the discovery, Sir Richard Walsh, sheriff of Worcestershire, attacked Holbeche. Catesby, Percy, and the two Wrights were killed or mortally wounded in the assault. The others were taken prisoners on the spot or in its neighbourhood, with the exception of Robert Winter, who, accompanied by their host, Stephen Littleton, contrived to elude capture for upwards of two months, being at last apprehended, in January, at Hagley Hall, Worcestershire. All the prisoners were at once taken up to London, and being there confined, were frequently and diligently examined by the council, to trace, if possible, farther ramifications of the conspiracy, and especially to inculpate the Catholic clergy.[1] Torture, it is evident, was employed with this object.

Meanwhile, on November 9th, King James addressed to his Parliament a speech, wherein he declared that the abominable crime which had been intended was the direct result of Catholic principles, Popery being "the true mystery of iniquity." In like manner Chichester, the Lord Deputy in Ireland, was informed by Cecil, Earl of Salisbury, his Majesty's Secretary of State, that the Plot was an "abominable practice of Rome and Satan,"[2] while the monarch himself sent word to Sir John Harington that "these designs were not formed by a few," that "the whole legion of Catholics were consulted," that "the priests were to

---

[1] "The great object of the Government now was to obtain evidence against the priests."—GARDINER, *History of England*, i. 267. Ed. 1883.

[2] See his despatch in reply. *Irish State Papers*, vol. 217, 95. Cornwallis received Cecil's letter on November 22nd.

pacify their consciences, and the Pope confirm a general absolution for this glorious deed."[1]

Then follows an interval during which we know little of the course of events which were proceeding in the seclusion of the council-room and torture-chamber; but on December 4th we find Cecil complaining that he could obtain little or no evidence against the really important persons: "Most of the prisoners," he writes,[2] "have wilfully forsworn that the priests knew anything in particular, and obstinately refuse to be accusers of them, yea, what torture soever they be put to."

On January 15th, 1605-6, a proclamation was issued declaring that the Jesuit fathers, John Gerard, Henry Garnet, and Oswald Greenway, or Tesimond, were proved to have been "peculiarly practisers" in the treason, and offering a reward for their apprehension. On the 21st of the same month Parliament met, having been prorogued immediately after the king's speech of November 9th, and four days later an Act was passed for the perpetual solemnization of the anniversary of the projected crime, the preamble whereof charged its guilt upon "Many malignant and devilish papists, jesuits, and seminary priests, much envying the true and free possession of the Gospel by the nation, under the greatest, most learned, and most religious monarch who had ever occupied the throne."[3]

In consequence of this Act, was introduced into the Anglican liturgy the celebrated Fifth of November service, in the collect of which the king, royal family,

---

[1] See Harington's account of the king's message, *Nugæ Antiquæ*, i. 374.
[2] To Favat. (Copy) Brit. Mus. MSS. Add. 6178, fol. 625.
[3] Statutes: Anno 3° Jacobi, c. 1.

nobility, clergy, and commons are spoken of as having been " by Popish treachery appointed as sheep to the slaughter, in a most barbarous and savage manner, beyond the examples of former ages ;" while the day itself was marked in the calendar as the " Papists' Conspiracy."

It will thus be seen that the Powder Plot was by this time officially stigmatized as the work of the Catholic body in general, and in particular of their priests ; thus acquiring an importance and a significance which could not be attributed to it were it but the wild attempt of a few turbulent men. As a natural corollary we find Parliament busily engaged upon measures to insure the more effectual execution of the penal laws.[1]

On January 27th the surviving conspirators, Robert and Thomas Winter, Faukes, Grant, Rokewood, Keyes, Digby, and Bates,[2] were put upon their trial. In the indictment preferred against them, it was explicitly stated that the Plot was contrived by Garnet, Gerard, Greenway, and other Jesuits, to whose traitorous persuasions the prisoners at the bar had wickedly yielded. All were found guilty, Digby, Robert Winter, Grant, and Bates being executed at the west end of St. Paul's Church, on January the 30th, and the rest on the following day in Old Palace Yard.

[1] This work was taken in hand by the Commons, when, in spite of the alarming circumstances of the time, they met on November 5th, and was carried on at every subsequent sitting. The Lords also met on the 5th, but transacted no business. *Journals of Parliament.*

[2] Tresham had died in the Tower, December 22nd. Although he had not been tried, his remains were treated as those of a traitor, his head being cut off and fixed above the gates of Northampton (*Dom. James I.* xvii. 62.)

On the very day upon which the first company suffered, Father Garnet, whose hiding-place was known, and who had been closely invested for nine days, was captured, in company with another Jesuit, Father Oldcorne. The latter, though never charged with knowledge of the plot, was put to death for having aided and abetted Garnet in his attempt to escape. Garnet himself, being brought to London, was lodged first in the Gatehouse and afterwards in the Tower.

As we have seen, he had already been proclaimed as a traitor, and "particular practiser" in the conspiracy, and had moreover been officially described as the head and front of the treason. Of the latter charge, after his capture, nothing was ever heard. Of his participation, proofs, it appeared, still remained to be discovered, for on the 3rd of March Cecil still spoke of them as in the future.[1] In order to obtain the required evidence of his complicity, Garnet was examined three-and-twenty times before the council, and, in addition, various artifices were practised which need not now be detailed. On the 28th of March, 1606, he was brought to trial, and on May 3rd he was hanged at St. Paul's. The Gunpowder Conspirators were thenceforth described in government publications as "Garnet, a Jesuit, and his confederates."

Such is, in outline, the course of events which followed the discovery of November 5th, all circum-

---

[1] "That which remaineth is but this, to assure you that ere many daies you shall hear that Father Garnet . . . is layd open for a principall conspirator even in the particular Treason of the Powder."—*To Sir Henry Bruncard, P. R. O. Ireland*, vol. 218, March 3rd, 1605-6. Also (Calendar) *Dom. James I.* xix. 10.

stances being here omitted which are by possibility open to dispute.

It will probably be maintained, as our best and most circumspect historians appear to have assumed, that we are in possession of information enabling us to construct a similar sketch of what preceded and led up to these events,—whatever obscurity there may be regarding the complicity of those whose participation would invest the plot with the significance which has been attributed to it. If it were indeed but the individual design of a small knot of men, acting for themselves and of themselves, then, though they were all Catholics, and were actuated by a desire to aid the Catholic cause, the crime they intended could not justly be charged upon the body of their co-religionists. It would be quite otherwise if Catholics in general were shown to have countenanced it, or even if such representative men as members of the priesthood were found to have approved so abominable a project, or even to have consented to it, or knowingly kept silence regarding it. Of the complicity of Catholics in general or of their priesthood as a body there is no proof whatever, nor has it ever been seriously attempted to establish such a charge. As to the three Jesuits already named, who alone have been seriously accused, there is no proof, the sufficiency of which may not be questioned. But as to the fact that they who originated the Plot were Catholics, that they acted simply with the object of benefiting their Church, and that the nation most narrowly escaped an appalling disaster at their hands, can there be any reasonable doubt? Is not the account of their proceedings, to be read in any work on the subject, as absolutely certain as anything in our history?

This account is as follows. About a year after the accession of James I.,[1] when it began to be evident that the hopes of toleration at his hands, which the Catholics had entertained, were to be disappointed, Robert Catesby, a man of strong character, and with an extraordinary power of influencing others, bethought him in his wrath of this means whereby to take summary vengeance at once upon the monarch and the legislators, under whose cruelty he himself and his fellows were groaning. The plan was proposed to John Wright and Thomas Winter, who approved it. Faukes was brought over from the Low Countries, as a man likely to be of much service in such an enterprise. Shortly afterwards Percy joined them,[2] and somewhat later Keyes and Christopher Wright were added to their number.[3] All the associates were required to take an oath of secrecy,[4]

---

[1] In Lent, 1603-4. Easter fell that year on April 8th.

[2] "About the middle of Easter Term."—*Thomas Winter's declaration*, of November 23rd, 1605.

[3] "Keyes, about a month before Michaelmas."—*Ibid.* About Christopher Wright there is much confusion, Faukes (November 17th, 1605) implying that he was introduced before Christmas, and Thomas Winter (November 23rd 1605) that it was about a fortnight after the following Candlemas, *i.e.*, about the middle of February.

[4] The form of this oath is thus given in the official account: "You shall swear by the blessed Trinity, and by the Sacrament you now propose to receive, never to disclose directly or indirectly, by word or circumstance, the matter that shall be proposed to you to keep secret, nor desist from the execution thereof until the rest shall give you leave." It is a singular circumstance that the form of this oath, which was repeated in official pub-

and to confirm it by receiving Holy Communion.[1]

These are the seven "gentlemen of blood and name," as Faukes describes them, who had the main hand in the operations which we have to study. At a later period six others were associated with them, Robert Winter, elder brother of Thomas, and Grant, both gentlemen of property, Bates, Catesby's servant, and finally, Rokewood, Digby, and Tresham, all rich men, who were brought in chiefly for the sake of their wealth, and were enlisted when the preparations for the intended explosion had all been completed, in view of the rising which was to follow.[2]

Commencing operations about the middle of December, 1604, these confederates first endeavoured to dig a mine under the House of Lords, and after-

---

lications, with an emphasis itself inexplicable, occurs in only one of the conspirators' confessions, viz., the oft-quoted declaration of T. Winter, November 23rd, 1605. This—as we shall see, a most suspicious document—was one of the two selected for publication, on which the traditional history of the plot depends. Curiously enough, however, the oath, with sundry other matters, was omitted from the published version of the confession.

[Published in the "King's Book:" copy, or draft, for publication, in the Record Office: original at Hatfield. Copy of original Brit. Mus. Add. MSS., 6178, 75.]

[1] T. Winter says: "Having upon a primer given each other the oath of secrecy, in a chamber where no other body was, we went after into the next room and heard mass, and received the blessed Sacrament upon the same."—*Declaration*, November 23rd, 1605.

[2] Digby was enlisted "about Michaelmas, 1605;" Rokewood about a month before the 5th of November. Tresham gives October 14th as the date of his own initiation. *Examination*, November 13th, 1605.

wards hired a large room, described as a cellar, situated beneath the Peers' Chamber, and in this stored a quantity of gunpowder, which Faukes was to fire by a train, while the King, Lords, and Commons, were assembled above.

Their enemies being thus destroyed, they did not contemplate a revolution, but were resolved to get possession of one of the king's sons, or, failing that, of one of his daughters, whom they would proclaim as sovereign, constituting themselves the guardians of the new monarch. They also contrived a "hunting match" on Dunsmoor heath, near Rugby, which was to be in progress when the news of the catastrophe in London should arrive; the sportsmen assembled for which would furnish, it was hoped, the nucleus of an army.

Meanwhile, as we are assured—and this is the crucial point of the whole story—the government of James I. had no suspicion of what was going on, and, lulled in false security, were on the verge of destruction, when a lucky circumstance intervened. On October 26th, ten days before the meeting of Parliament, a Catholic peer, Lord Monteagle, received an anonymous letter, couched in vague and incoherent language, warning him to absent himself from the opening ceremony. This document Monteagle at once took to the king's prime minister, Robert Cecil, Earl of Salisbury, who promptly divined its meaning and the precise danger indicated, although he allowed King James to fancy that he was himself the first to interpret it, when it was shown to him five days later.[1]

---

[1] This is clear from a comparison of Cecil's private letter to Cornwallis and others (Winwood, *Memorials*, ii. 170), with

Not for four other days were active steps taken, that is, till the early morning of the fatal Fifth. Then took place the discovery of which we have already heard.

Such is, in brief, the accepted version of the history, and of its substantial correctness there is commonly assumed to be no room for reasonable doubt. As Mr. Jardine writes,[1] "The outlines of the transaction were too notorious to be suppressed or disguised; that a design had been formed to blow up the Parliament House, with the King, the Royal Family, the Lords and Commons, and that this design was formed by Catholic men and for Catholic purposes, could never admit of controversy or concealment." In like manner, while acknowledging that in approaching the question of Father Garnet's complicity, or that of other priests, we find ourselves upon uncertain ground, Mr. Gardiner has no hesitation in declaring that "the whole story of the plot, as far as it relates to the lay conspirators, rests upon indisputable evidence."[2]

Nevertheless there appear to be considerations, demanding more attention than they have hitherto received, which forbid the supposition that, in regard of what is most vital, this official story can possibly be true; while the extreme care with which it has obviously been elaborated, suggests the conclusion that it was intended to disguise facts, to the concealment of which the government of the day attached supreme importance.

As has been said, the cardinal point of the tale, as

the official account published in the *Discourse of the manner of the Discovery of the Gunpowder Plot.*
[1] *Criminal Trials*, ii. 3.
[2] *History of England*, i. 269 (1883).

commonly told, is that the Plot was a secret and dangerous conspiracy, conducted with so much craft as to have baffled detection, but for a lucky accident; that the vigilance of the authorities was completely at fault; and that they found themselves suddenly on the very brink of a terrible catastrophe of which they had no suspicion.[1] If, on the contrary, it should appear that they had ample information of what was going on, while feigning absolute ignorance; that they studiously devised a false account of the manner in which it came to their knowledge; and that their whole conduct is quite inconsistent with that sense of imminent danger which they so loudly professed—the question inevitably suggests itself as to whether we can rely upon the authenticity of the opening chapters of a history, the conclusion of which has been so dexterously manipulated.

A French writer has observed[2] that the plots undertaken under Elizabeth and James I. have this feature in common, that they proved, one and all, extremely opportune for those against whom they were directed. To this law the Gunpowder Plot was no exception. Whatever be the true history of its origin, it certainly placed in the hands of the king's chief minister a most effective weapon for the enforcement of his favourite

---

[1] "We had all been blowne up at a clapp, if God out of His Mercie and just Reuenge against so great an Abomination, had not destined it to be discovered, though very miraculously, even some twelve Houres before the matter should have been put in execution."—*Cecil to Cornwallis*, November 9th, 1605. Winwood, *Memorials*, ii. 170.

[2] M. l'Abbé Destombes, *La persécution en Angleterre sous le règne d'Elizabeth*, p. 176.

policy, and very materially strengthened his own position. Without doubt the sensational manner of its "discovery" largely contributed to its success in this respect; and if this were ingeniously contrived for such a purpose, may it not be that a like ingenuity had been employed in providing the material destined to be so artistically utilized?

There can be no question as to the wide prevalence of the belief that previous plots had owed their origin to the policy of the statesmen who finally detected them, a belief witnessed to by Lord Castlemaine,[1] who declares that "it was a piece of wit in Queen Elizabeth's days to draw men into such devices," and that "making and fomenting plots was then in fashion; nor can it be denied that good grounds for such an opinion were not lacking. The unfortunate man Squires had been executed on the ridiculous charge that he had come over from Spain in order to poison the pommel of Queen Elizabeth's saddle. Dr. Parry, we are informed by Bishop Goodman, whose verdict is endorsed by Mr. Brewer,[2] was put to death by those who knew him to be guiltless in their regard, they having themselves employed him in the business for which he suffered. Concerning Babington's famous plot, it is absolutely certain that, whatever its origin, it was, almost from the first, fully known to Walsingham, through whose hands passed the correspondence between the conspirators, and who assiduously worked the enterprise, in order to turn it to the destruction of the Queen of Scots. As to Lopez, the Jewish physician, it is impossible not to concur in the verdict

---

[1] *Catholique Apology*, third edition, p. 403.
[2] Goodman's *Court of King James*, i. 121.

that his condemnation was at least as much owing to political intrigue as to the weight of evidence.[1] Concerning this period Mr. Brewer says: "The Roman Catholics seem to have made just complaints of the subtle and unworthy artifices of Leicester and Walsingham, by whom they were entrapped into the guilt of high treason. 'And verily,' as [Camden] expresses it, there were at this time crafty ways devised to try how men stood affected; counterfeit letters were sent in the name of the Queen of Scots and left at papists' houses; spies were sent up and down the country to note people's dispositions and lay hold of their words; and reporters of vain and idle stories were credited and encouraged."[2] Under King James,[3] as Bishop Goodman declares, the priest Watson was hanged for treason by those who had employed him.[4]

It must farther be observed that the particular Plot which is our subject was stamped with certain features more than commonly suspicious. Even on the face of things, as will be seen from the summary already given, it was steadily utilized from the first for a pur-

---

[1] Mr. Sidney Lee, *Dictionary of National Biography, sub nom.*
[2] Goodman's *Court of King James*, i. 121. Ed. J. S. Brewer.
[3] *Court of King James*, p. 64.
[4] Of this affair,—the "Bye" and the "Main,"—Goodman says, "[This] I did ever think to be an old relic of the treasons in Q. Elizabeth's time, and that George Brooks was the contriver thereof, who being brother-in-law to the Secretary, and having great wit, small means, and a vast expense, did only try men's allegiance, and had an intent to betray one another, but were all taken napping and so involved in one net. This in effect appears by Brooks' confession; and certainly K. James ... had no opinion of that treason, and therefore was pleased to pardon all save only Brooks and the priests."—*Court of King James*, i. 160.

pose which it could not legitimately be made to serve. That the Catholics of England, as a body, had any connection with it there is not, nor ever appeared to be, any vestige of a proof; still less that the official superiors of the Church, including the Pope himself, were concerned in it. Yet the first act of the government was to lay it at the door of all these, thus investing it with a character which was, indeed, eminently fitted to sustain their own policy, but to which it was nowise entitled. Even in regard of Father Garnet and his fellow Jesuits, whatever judgment may now be formed concerning them, it is clear that it was determined to connect them with the conspiracy long before any evidence at all was forthcoming to sustain the charge. The actual confederates were, in fact, treated throughout as in themselves of little or no account, and as important only in so far as they might consent to incriminate those whom the authorities wished to be incriminated.

The determined manner in which this object was ever kept in view, the unscrupulous means constantly employed for its attainment, the vehemence with which matters were asserted to have been proved, any proof of which was never even seriously attempted—in a word, the elaborate system of falsification by which alone the story of the conspiracy was made to suit the purpose it so effectually served, can inspire us with no confidence that the foundation upon which such a superstructure was erected, was itself what it was said to be.

On the other hand, when we examine into the details supplied to us as to the progress of the affair, we find that much of what the conspirators are said to have done is well-nigh incredible, while it is utterly impossible that if they really acted in the manner described, the public authorities should not have had full knowledge of their proceedings. We also find not only that the same authorities, while feigning ignorance of anything of the kind, were perfectly well aware that these very conspirators had something in hand, but that long before the "discovery," in fact, at the very time when the conspiracy is said to have been hatched, their officials were working a Catholic plot, by means of secret agents, and even making arrangements as to who were to be implicated therein.

These are, in brief, some of the considerations which point to a conclusion utterly at variance with the received version of the story, the conclusion, namely, that, for purposes of State, the government of the day either found means to instigate the conspirators to undertake their enterprise, or, at least, being, from an early stage of the undertaking, fully aware of what was going on, sedulously nursed the insane scheme till the time came to make capital out of it. That the conspirators, or the greater number of them, really meant to strike a great blow is not to be denied, though it may be less easy to assure ourselves as to its precise character; and their guilt will not be palliated should it appear that, in projecting an atrocious crime, they were unwittingly playing the game of plotters more astute than themselves. At the same time, while fully endorsing the sentiment of a Catholic writer,[1] that they who suffer themselves to be drawn into a plot like fools, deserve to be hanged for it like

[1] *A plain and rational account of the Catholick Faith*, etc. Rouen, 1721, p. 200.

knaves, it is impossible not to agree with another when he writes:[1] "This account does not excuse the conspirators, but lays a heavy weight upon the devils who tempted them beyond their strength."

The view thus set forth will perhaps be considered unworthy of serious discussion, and it must be fully admitted, that there can be no excuse for making charges such as it involves, unless solid grounds can be alleged for so doing. That any such grounds are to be found historians of good repute utterly deny. Mr. Hallam roundly declares:[2] "To deny that there was such a plot, or, which is the same thing, to throw the whole on the contrivance and management of Cecil, as has sometimes been done, argues great effrontery in those who lead, and great stupidity in those who follow." Similarly, Mr. Gardiner,[3] while allowing that contemporaries accused Cecil of inventing the Plot, is content to dismiss such a charge as "absurd."

Whether it be so or not we have now to inquire.

[1] Dodd, *Church History of England*, Brussels, 1739, i. 334.
[2] *Constitutional History*, i. 406, note, Seventh Edition. In the same note the historian, discussing the case of Father Garnet, speaks of "the damning circumstance that he was taken at Hendlip in concealment along with the other conspirators." He who wrote thus can have had but a slight acquaintance with the details of the history. None of the conspirators, except Robert Winter, who was captured at Hagley Hall, were taken in concealment, and none at Hendlip, where there is no reason to suppose they ever were. Father Garnet was discovered there, nearly three months later, in company with another Jesuit, Father Oldcorne, on the very day when the conspirators were executed in London, and it was never alleged that he had ever, upon any occasion, been seen in company with "the other conspirators."
[3] *History*, i. 255, note.

CHAPTER II.

THE PERSONS CONCERNED.

AT the period with which we have to deal the chief minister of James I. was Robert Cecil, Earl of Salisbury,[1] the political heir of his father, William Cecil, Lord Burghley,[2] and of Walsingham, his predecessor in the office of secretary. It is clear that he had inherited from them ideas of statesmanship of the order then in vogue, and from nature, the kind of ability required to put these successfully in practice. Sir Robert Naunton thus describes him :[3]

"This great minister of state, and the staff of the Queen's declining age, though his little crooked person[4] could not provide any great supportation, yet

---

[1] When James came to the throne Cecil was but a knight. He was created Baron Cecil of Essendon, May 13th, 1603; Viscount Cranborne, August 20th, 1604; Earl of Salisbury, May 4th, 1605.

[2] Robert, as the second son, did not succeed to his father's title, which devolved upon Thomas, the eldest, who was created Earl of Exeter on the same day on which Robert became Earl of Salisbury.

[3] *Fragmenta Regalia*, 37. Ed. 1642.

[4] He was but little above five feet in height, and, in the phrase of the time, a " Crouchback." King James, who was not a man of much delicacy in such matters, was fond of giving him nicknames in consequence. Cecil wrote to Sir Thomas Lake, October 24th, 1605 : "I see nothing y^t I can doe, can procure me so much

it carried thereon a head and a headpiece of vast content, and therein, it seems, nature was so diligent to complete one, and the best, part about him, as that to the perfection of his memory and intellectuals, she took care also of his senses, and to put him in *Lynceos oculos*, or to pleasure him the more, borrowed of Argus, so to give him a perfective sight. And for the rest of his sensitive virtues, his predecessor had left him a receipt, to smell out what was done in the Conclave; and his good old father was so well seen in the mathematicks, as that he could tell you throughout Spain, every part, every ship, with their burthens, whither bound, what preparation, what impediments for diversion of enterprises, counsels, and resolutions." The writer then proceeds to give a striking instance to show "how docible was this little man."

Of his character, as estimated by competent judges, his contemporaries, we have very different accounts. Mr. Gardiner, who may fairly be chosen to represent his apologists, speaks thus:[1]

"Although there are circumstances in his life which tell against him, it is difficult to read the whole of the letters and documents which have come down to us from his pen, without becoming gradually convinced of his honesty of intention. It cannot be denied that he was satisfied with the ordinary morality of his

---

avor, as to be sure one whole day what title I shall have another. For from Essenden to Cranborne, from Cranborne to Salisbury, from Salisbury to Beagle, from Beagle to Thom Derry, from Thom Derry to Parret which I hate most, I have been so walked, as I think by y^t I come to Theobalds, I shall be called Tare or Sophie." (R. O. *Dom. James I.* xv. 105.)

[1] *History*, i. 92.

time, and that he thought it no shame to keep a State secret or to discover a plot by means of a falsehood. If he grasped at power as one who took pleasure in the exercise of it, he used it for what he regarded as the true interests of his king and country. Nor are we left to his own acts and words as the only means by which we are enabled to form a judgment of his character. Of all the statesmen of the day, not one has left a more blameless character than the Earl of Dorset. Dorset took the opportunity of leaving upon record in his will, which would not be read till he had no longer injury or favour to expect in this world, the very high admiration in which his colleague was held by him."

This, it must be allowed, is a somewhat facile species of argument. Though wills are not formally opened until after the testators' deaths, it is not impossible for their contents to be previously communicated to others, when there is an object for so doing.[1] But, however this may be, it can scarcely be said that the weight of evidence tends in this direction. Not to mention the fact that, while enjoying the entire confidence of Queen Elizabeth, Cecil was engaged in a secret correspondence with King James, which she would have regarded as treasonable—and which he so carefully concealed that for a century afterwards and more it was not suspected—there remains the other indubitable fact, that while similarly trusted by James, and while all affairs of State were entirely in his hands, he was in receipt of a secret pension from the King of

---

[1] In the same document James I. is spoken of as "the most judycious, learned, and rareste kinge, that ever this worlde produced." (R. O. *Dom. James I.* xxviii. 29.)

Spain,[1] the very monarch any communication with whom he treated as treason on the part of others.[2] It is certain that the Earl of Essex, when on his trial, asserted that Cecil had declared the Spanish Infanta to be the rightful heir to the crown, and though the secretary vehemently denied the imputation, he equally repudiated the notion that he favoured the King of Scots.[3] We know, moreover, that one who as Spanish Ambassador had dealings with him, pronounced him to be a venal traitor, who was ready to sell his soul for money,[4] while another intimated[5] that

[1] Digby to the King, S. P., *Spain*, Aug .8. Gardiner, *History*, ii. 216.

[2] At the trial of Essex, Cecil exclaimed, "I pray God to consume me where I stand, if I hate not the Spaniard as much as any man living." (Bruce, *Introduction to Secret Correspondence of Sir R. Cecil*, xxxiii.)

Of the Spanish pension Mr. Gardiner, after endeavouring to show that originally Cecil's acceptance of it may have been comparatively innocent, thus continues (*History of England*, i. 216): "But it is plain that, even if this is the explanation of his original intentions, such a comparatively innocent connection with Spain soon extended itself to something worse, and that he consented to furnish the ambassadors, from time to time, with information on the policy and intentions of the English Government. . . . Of the persistence with which he exacted payment there can be no doubt whatever. Five years later, when the opposition between the two governments became more decided, he asked for an increase of his payments, and demanded that they should be made in large sums as each piece of information was given."

At the same time it appears highly probable that he was similarly in the pay of France. *Ibid.*

[3] Queen Elizabeth regarded as treasonable any discussion of the question of the succession.

[4] Gardiner, i. 215.

[5] *Chamberlain to Carleton*, July 9th, 1612, R. O.

it was in his power to have charged him with "unwarrantable practices." Similarly, we hear from the French minister of the ingrained habit of falsehood which made it impossible for the English secretary to speak the truth even to friends;[1] and, from the French Ambassador, of the resolution imputed to the same statesman, to remove from his path every rival who seemed likely to jeopardize his tenure of power.[2]

What was the opinion of his own countrymen, appeared with startling emphasis when, in 1612, the Earl died. On May 22nd we find the Earl of Northampton writing to Rochester that the "little man" is dead, "for which so many rejoice, and so few even seem to be sorry."[3] Five days later, Chamberlain, writing[4] to his friend Dudley Carleton, to announce the same event, thus expresses himself: "As the case stands it was best that he gave over the world, for they say his friends fell from him apace, and some near about him, and however he had fared

---

[1] "Tout ce que vous a dit le Comte de Salisbury touchant le mariage d'Espagne est rempli de deguisements et artifices à son accoutumée. . . . Toutefois, je ne veux pas jurer qu'ils négocient plus sincerement et de meilleur foi avec lesdites Espagnols qu'avec nous. Ils corromproient par trop leur naturel, s'ils le faisoient, pour des gens qui ne leur scauroient guère de gré."—Le Fèvre de la Boderie, *Ambassade*, i. 170.

[2] (Of the Earl of Northumberland.) "On tient le Comte de Salisbury pour principal auteur de sa persécution, comme celui qui veut ne laisser personne en pied qui puisse lui faire tête." De la Boderie. *Ibid.* 178.

[3] R. O. *Dom. James I.* lxix. 56.

[4] *Ibid.*, May 27, 1612. Bishop Goodman, no enemy of Cecil, is inclined to believe that at the time of the secretary's death there was a warrant out for his arrest. *Court of King James*, i. 45.

with his health, it is verily thought he would never have been himself again in power and credit. I never knew so great a man so soon and so openly censured, for men's tongues walk very liberally and freely, but how truly I cannot judge." On June 25th he again reports: " The outrageous speeches against the deceased Lord continue still, and there be fresh libels come out every day, and I doubt his actions will be hardly censured in the next parliament, if the King be not the more gracious to repress them." Moreover, his funeral was attended by few or none of the gentry, and those only were present whose official position compelled them. His own opinion Chamberlain expresses in two epigrams and an anagram, which, although of small literary merit, contrive clearly to express the most undisguised animosity and contempt for the late minister.[1]

There is abundant proof that such sentiments were not first entertained when he had passed away, though, naturally, they were less openly expressed when he was alive and practically all powerful. Cecil seems, in fact, to have been throughout his career a lonely man, with

---

[1] The first of these epigrams, in Latin, concludes thus:

> Sero, Recurve, moreris sed serio;
> Sero, jaces (bis mortuus) sed serio:
> Sero saluti publicæ, serio tuæ.

The second is in English:

> Whiles two RR's, both crouchbacks, stood at the helm,
> The one spilt the the blood royall, the other the realm.

A marginal note explains that these were, " Richard Duke of Gloster, and Robert Earl of Salisburie;" the anagram, of which title is "A silie burs." He also styles the late minister a monkey (*cercopithecus*) and hobgoblin (*empusa*).

no real friends and many enemies, desperately fighting for his own hand, and for the retention of that power which he prized above all else, aspiring, as a contemporary satirist puts it, to be "both shepherd and dog."[1] Since the accession of James he had felt his tenure of office to be insecure. Goodman tells us[2] that "it is certain the king did not love him;" Osborne,[3] "that he had forfeited the love of the people by the hate he expressed to their darling Essex, and the desire he had to render justice and prerogative arbitrary."[4] Sir Anthony Weldon speaks of him[5] as

[1] Osborne, *Traditional Memoirs*, p. 236 (ed. 1811).
[2] *Court of King James*, i. 44.
[3] *Traditional Memoirs*, 181.
[4] This feeling was expressed in lampoons quoted by Osborne, e.g.:

"Here lies Hobinall, our pastor while here,
That once in a quarter our fleeces did sheare.
For oblation to Pan his custom was thus,
He first gave a trifle, then offer'd up us:
And through his false worship such power he did gaine,
As kept him o' th' mountain, and us on the plaine."

Again, he is described as

"Little bossive Robin that was so great,
Who seemed as sent from ugly fate,
To spoyle the prince, and rob the state,
Owning a mind of dismall endes,
As trappes for foes, and tricks for friends."

(*Ibid.* 236.)

Oldmixon (*History of Queen Elizabeth*, p. 620) says of the Earl of Essex, "'Twas not likely that Cecil, whose Soul was of a narrow Size, and had no Room for enlarged Sentiments of Ambition, Glory, and Public Spirit, should cease to undermine a Hero, in comparison with whom he was both in Body and Mind a Piece of Deformity, if there's nothing beautiful in Craft."

[5] *Court and Character of King James*, § 10.

"Sir Robert Cecil, a very wise man, but much hated in England by reason of the fresh bleeding of that universally beloved Earl of Essex, and for that clouded also in the king's favour." De la Boderie, the French Ambassador, tells us [1] that the nobility were exceedingly jealous of his dignity and power, and [2] that he in his turn was jealous of the growing influence of Prince Henry, the heir apparent, who made no secret of his dislike of him. Meanwhile there were rivals who, it seemed not improbable, might supplant him. One of these, Sir Walter Raleigh, had already been rendered harmless on account of his connection with the " Main," the mysterious conspiracy which inaugurated the reign of James. There remained the Earl of Northumberland, and it may be remarked in passing that one of the effects of the Gunpowder Plot was to dispose of him likewise.[3] Even the apologists of the

[1] *Ambassade*, i. 58.
[2] *Ibid.* 401.
[3] Against Northumberland nothing was proved (*vide* de la Boderie, *Ambassade*, i. 178), except that he had admitted Thomas Percy amongst the royal pensioners without exacting the usual oath. He in vain demanded an open trial, but was prosecuted in the Star Chamber, and there sentenced to a fine of £30,000 (equal to at least ten times that sum in our money), and to be imprisoned for life.

Mr. Gardiner considers that, in regard both of Raleigh and of Northumberland, Cecil acted with great moderation. It must, however, be remembered that in his secret correspondence with King James, before the death of the queen, he had strenuously endeavoured to poison the mind of that monarch against these his rivals. Thus he wrote, December 4th, 1601 (as usual through Lord Henry Howard) : " You must remember that I gave you notice of the diabolical triplicity, that is, Cobham, Raleigh, and Northumberland, that met every day

minister do not attempt to deny either the fact that he was accustomed to work by stratagems and disguises, nor the obloquy that followed on his death;[1] while by friends and foes alike he was compared to Ulysses of many wiles.[2]

But amongst those whom he had to dread, there can be no doubt that the members of the Catholic

---

at Durham-house, where Raleigh lies, in consultation, which awaked all the best wits of the town ... to watch what chickens they could hatch out of these cockatrice eggs that were daily and nightly sitten on." (*Secret Correspondence of Sir Robert Cecil with James VI., King of Scotland*, Edinburgh, 1766, p. 29.) Coming after this, the speedy ruin of all these men appears highly suspicious.

[1] Sir Walter Cope in his *Apology* (Gutch, *Collectanea Curiosa*, i. No. 10) says: "When living, the world observed with all admiration and applause; no sooner dead, but it seeketh finally to suppress his excellent parts, and load his memory with all imputations of corruption."

Among such charges are enumerated "His Falsehood in Friendship.—That he often made his friends fair promises, and underhand laid rubs to hinder their preferment.—The secret passage of things I know not. ... Great Counsellors have their private and their publique ends ..." etc.

[2] Lord Castlemaine after mentioning the chief features of the Gunpowder Plot, goes on: "But let it not displease you, if we ask whether Ulysses be no better known?" (*Catholique Apology*, p. 30.)

Francis Herring in his Latin poem, *Pietas Pontificia* (published 1606), speaking of Monteagle (called "Morleius," from his father's title), who took the celebrated letter to Cecil, writes thus:

> "Morleius Regis de consultoribus unum,
> (Quem norat veteri nil quicquam cedere Ulyssi,
> Juditio pollentem acri, ingenioque sagaci)
> Seligit, atque illi Rem totam ex ordine pandit."

party appeared to the secretary the most formidable. It was known on all hands, nor did he attempt to disguise the fact, that he was the irreconcilable opponent of any remission of the penal laws enacted for the purpose of stamping out the old faith.[1] The work, however, had as yet been very incompletely done. At the beginning of the reign of King James, the Catholics formed at least a half, probably a majority,[2] of the English people. There were amongst them many noblemen, fitted to hold offices of State. Moreover, the king, who before his accession had unquestionably

---

[1] This is so evident that it appears unnecessary to occupy space with proofs in detail. De la Boderie remarks (*Ambassade*, i. 71) on the extraordinary rancour of the minister against Catholics, and especially against Jesuits, and that "he wishes to destroy them everywhere." Of this a remarkable confirmation is afforded by the instructions given to Sir Thomas Parry when he was sent as ambassador, "Leiger," to Paris, in 1603, at the head of which stood these extraordinary articles:

1. "To intimate to the French king the jealousy conceived in England upon the revocation of the Jesuits, against former edicts.

2. "To inform the French king that the English were disgusted at the maintenance allowed to the French king's prelates and clergy, to priests and Jesuits that passed out of his dominions into England, Scotland, and Ireland, to do bad offices." (P.R.O. *France*, bundle 132, f. 314.)

[2] Jardine, *Gunpowder Plot*, p. 5. Strype says of the time of Elizabeth: "The faction of the Catholics in England is great, and able, if the kingdom were divided into three parts, to make two of them." (*Annals*, iii. 313, quoted by Butler, *Historical Memoirs*, ii. 177.)

At the execution of Father Oldcorne, 1606, a proof was given of their numbers which is said to have alarmed the king greatly. The Father having from the scaffold invited all Catholics to pray with him, almost all present uncovered.

assured the Catholics at least of toleration,[1] showed at his first coming a manifest disposition to relieve them from the grievous persecution under which they had groaned so long.[2] He remitted a large part of the fines which had so grievously pressed upon all recusants, declaring that he would not make merchandise of conscience, nor set a price upon faith;[3] he invited to his presence leading Catholics from various parts of the country, assuring them, and bidding them assure their co-religionists, of his gracious intentions in their regard;[4] titles of honour and lucrative employments were bestowed on some of their number;[5] one professed Catholic, Henry Howard, presently created Earl of Northampton, being enrolled in the Privy Council; and in the first speech which he addressed to his Parliament James declared that, as to the papists, he had no desire to persecute them, especially those of the laity who would be quiet.[6] The immediate effect

---

[1] Of this there can be no doubt, in spite of James's subsequent denial. Father Garnet wrote to Parsons (April 16th, 1603): "There hath happened a great alteration by the death of the Queen. Great fears were, but all are turned into greatest security, and a golden time we have of unexpected freedom abroade. . . . The Catholicks have great cause to hope for great respect, in that the nobility all almost labour for it, and have good promise thereof from his Majesty." (Stonyhurst MSS. *Anglia*, iii. 32.)

Goodman says: "And certainly they [the Catholics] had very great promises from him." (*Court of King James*, i. 86.)

[2] "The Penal Laws, a code as savage as any that can be conceived since the foundation of the world."—Lord Chief Justice Coleridge. (*To Lord Mayor Knill*, Nov. 9, 1892.)

[3] Gardiner, i. 100.

[4] Jardine, *Gunpowder Plot*, 18.   [5] *Ibid*. 20.

[6] Gardiner, i. 166.

of this milder policy was to afford evidence of the real strength of the Catholics, many now openly declaring themselves who had previously conformed to the State church. In the diocese of Chester alone the number of Catholics was increased by a thousand.[1]

It is scarcely to be wondered at that men who were familiar with the political methods of the age should see in all this a motive sufficient to explain a great stroke for the destruction of those who appeared to be so formidable, devised by such a minister as was then in power, "the statesman," writes Lord Castlemaine,[2] "who bore (as everybody knew) a particular hatred to all of our profession, and this increased to hear his Majesty speak a little in his first speech to the two Houses against persecution of papists, whereas there had been nothing within those walls but invectives and defamations for above forty years together."

This much is certain, that, whatever its origin, the Gunpowder Plot immensely increased Cecil's influence and power, and, for a time, even his popularity, assuring the success of that anti-Catholic policy with which he was identified.[3]

---

[1] Green, *History of the English People*, iii. 62. Mr. Green adds: "Rumours of Catholic conversions spread a panic which showed itself in an Act of the Parliament of 1604 confirming the statutes of Elizabeth; and to this James gave his assent. He promised, indeed, that the statute should remain inoperative." In May, 1604, the Catholics boasted that they had been joined by 10,000 converts. (Gardiner, *Hist.* i. 202.)

[2] *Catholique Apology*, 404.

[3] Salisbury, in reward of his services on this occasion, received the Garter, May 20th, 1606, and was honoured on the occasion with an almost regal triumph.

Of the proceedings subsequent to the Plot we are told: "In

THE CATHOLICS. 31

Of no less importance is it to understand the position of the Catholic body, and the character of the particular Catholics who engaged in this enterprise. We have seen with what hopes the advent of King James had been hailed by those who had suffered so much for his mother's sake, and who interpreted in a too sanguine and trustful spirit his own words and deeds. Their dream of enjoying even toleration at his hands was soon rudely dispelled. After giving them the briefest of respites, the monarch, under the influence, as all believed, of his council, and especially of his chief minister,[1] suddenly reversed his line of action and persecuted his Catholic subjects more cruelly than had his predecessor, calling up the arrears of fines which they fancied had been altogether remitted, ruining many in the process who had hitherto contrived to pay their way,[2] and adding to the sense of injury which such

---

passing these laws for the security of the Protestant Religion, the Earl of Salisbury exerted himself with distinguished zeal and vigour, which gained him great love and honour from the kingdom, as appeared in some measure, in the universal attendance on him at his installation with the Order of the Garter, on the 20th of May, 1606, at Windsor." (Birch, *Historical View*, p. 256.)

[1] This belief is so notorious that one instance must suffice as evidence for it. A paper of informations addressed to Cecil himself, April, 1604, declares that the Catholics hoped to see a good day yet, and that "his Majesty would suffer a kinde of Tolleracyon, for his inclynacyon is good, howsoever the Councell set out his speeches." (S. P. O. *Dom. James I.* vii. 86.)

[2] Mr. Gardiner (*Hist.* i. 229, note) says that arrears were never demanded in the case of the fine of £20 per lunar month for non-attendance at the parish church. Father Gerard, however, a contemporary witness, distinctly states that they were. (*Narrative of the Gunpowder Plot*, ed. Morris, p. 62.)

a course necessarily provoked by farming out wealthy recusants to needy courtiers, "to make their profit of," in particular to the Scots who had followed their royal master across the border. Soon it was announced that the king would have blood; all priests were ordered to leave the realm under pain of death, and the searches for them became more frequent and violent than ever. In no long time, as Goodman tells us,[1] "a gentlewoman was hanged only for relieving and harbouring a priest; a citizen was hanged only for being reconciled to the Church of Rome; besides the penal laws were such and so executed that they could not subsist." Father Gerard says:[2] "This being known to Catholics, it is easy to be seen how first their hopes were turned into fears, and then their fears into full knowledge that all the contrary to that they had hoped was intended and prepared for them, and, as one of the victims of these proceedings wrote, "the times of Elizabeth, although most cruel, were the mildest and happiest in comparison with those of King James."[3]

In such circumstances, the Catholic body being so numerous as it was, it is not to be wondered at that individuals should be found, who, smarting under their injuries, and indignant at the bad faith of which they considered themselves the dupes, looked to violent remedies for relief, and might without difficulty be worked upon to that effect. Their case seemed far more hopeless than ever. Queen Elizabeth's quarrel with Rome had been in a great degree personal; and moreover, as she had no direct heir, it was confidently

---

[1] *Court of King James*, i. 100.
[2] *Narrative*, p. 46.
[3] Stonyhurst MSS., *Anglia*, iii. 103.

anticipated that the demise of the crown would introduce a new era. King James's proceedings, on the other hand, seemed to indicate a deliberate policy which there was no prospect of reversing, especially as his eldest son, should he prove true to his promise, might be expected to do that zealously, and of himself, which his father was held to do under the constraint of others.[1] As Sir Everard Digby warned Cecil, in the remarkable letter which he addressed to him on the subject:[2] "If your Lordship and the State think fit to deal severely with the Catholics, within brief space there will be massacres, rebellions, and desperate attempts against the King and the State. For it is a general received reason among Catholics, that there is not that expecting and suffering course now to be run that was in the Queen's time, who was the last of her line, and last in expectance to run violent courses against Catholics; for then it was hoped that the King that now is, would have been at least free from persecuting, as his promise was before his coming into this realm, and as divers his promises have been since his coming. All these promises every man sees broken."[3]

It must likewise be remembered that if stratagems and "practices" were the recognized weapons of ministers, turbulence and arms were, at this period, the familiar, and indeed the only, resource of those in

---

[1] Of the Prince of Wales it was prophesied:
"The eighth Henry did pull down Monks and their cells,
The ninth will pull down Bishops and their bells."

[2] Concerning this letter see Appendix B, *Digby's Letter to Salisbury.*

[3] R. O. *Dom. James I.* xvii. 10.

opposition, nor did any stigma attach to their employment unless taken up on the losing side. Not a little of this kind of thing had been done on behalf of James himself. As is well known, he succeeded to the throne by a title upon which he could not have recovered at law an acre of land.[1] Elizabeth had so absolutely forbidden all discussion of the question of the succession as to leave it in a state of utter confusion.[2] There were more than a dozen possible competitors, and amongst these the claim of the King of Scots was technically not the strongest, for though nearest in blood his claims had been barred by a special Act of Parliament, excluding the Scottish line. As Professor Thorold Rogers says, " For a year after his accession James, if Acts of Parliament are to go for anything, was not legally King."[3]

Nevertheless the cause of James was vigorously taken up in all directions, and promoted by means which might well have been styled treason against the authority of Parliament. Thus, old Sir Thomas Tresham, father of Francis Tresham, the Gunpowder Conspirator, who had been an eminent sufferer for his religion, at considerable personal risk, and against much resistance on the part of the local magistrates and the populace, publicly proclaimed the new king at Northampton, while Francis Tresham himself and his brother Lewis, with Lord Monteagle, their brother-in-law, supported the Earl of Southampton in holding the Tower of London on his behalf.[4] In London in-

[1] Hallam, *Constitutional Hist.* i. 392 (3rd ed.).
[2] See Appendix C, *The Question of Succession.*
[3] *Agriculture and Prices,* v. 5.
[4] Jardine, *Gunpowder Plot,* p. 17.

deed everybody took to arms as soon as the queen's illness had been known; watch and ward were kept in the City; rich men brought their plate and treasure from the country, and placed them where they would be safest,[1] and the approaches were guarded. Cecil himself related in open court, in praise of the Londoners, how, when he himself, attended by most of the peers and privy councillors of the kingdom, wished to enter the City to proclaim the new sovereign, they found the gates closed against them till they had publicly declared that they were about to proclaim James and no one else.[2]

In times when statesmen could approve such methods of political action, it was inevitable that violent enterprises should have come to be considered the natural resource of those out of power, and it is very clear that there were numerous individuals, of whom no one party had the monopoly, who were ready at any moment to risk everything for the cause they served, and such men, although their proclivities were well known, did not suffer much in public esteem.

The Gunpowder Conspirators were eminently men of this stamp, and notoriously so. So well was their character known, that when, in 1596, eight years before the commencement of the Plot, Queen Elizabeth had been unwell, the Lords of the Council, as a precautionary measure arrested some of the principal amongst them, Catesby, the two Wrights, Tresham, and others, as being persons who would certainly give

---

[1] Gardiner, *Hist.* i. 84.
[2] Trial of Father Garnet (Cobbett's *State Trials*, ii. 243).

trouble should a chance occur.¹ Since that time they had not improved their record. All those above-named, as well as Thomas Winter, Christopher Wright, Percy, Grant, and perhaps others, had been engaged in the ill-starred rebellion of Essex, on which occasion Catesby was wounded, and both he and Tresham came remarkably near being hanged.² They had likewise been variously implicated in all the seditious attempts which had since been made—Catesby and Tresham being named by Sir Edward Coke as being engaged with Watson in the " Bye." Thomas Winter, Christopher Wright, and Faukes, had, if we may believe the same authority, been sent to Spain on treasonable embassies.³ Grant made himself very conspicuous by frequently resisting the officers of the law

---

[1] Camden, the historian, to Sir R. Cotton, March 15th, 1596. (Birch, *Original Letters*, 2nd series, iii. p. 179.) Various writers erroneously suppose this transaction to have occurred in March, 1603, on occasion of Elizabeth's last illness. The correct date, 1596, given by Sir Henry Ellis, is supplied by a statement contained in the letter, that this was her Majesty's "climacterick year," that is, her sixty-third, this number, as the multiple of the potent factors seven and nine, being held of prime importance in human life. Elizabeth was born in 1533.

From Garnet's examination of March 14th, 1605-6 (*Dom. James I.* xix. 44), we learn that Catesby was at large at the time of the queen's demise.

For Cecil's description of the men, see Winwood's *Memorials*, ii. 172.

[2] Catesby purchased his life for a fine of 4,000 marks, and Tresham of 3,000. Mr. Jessopp says that the former sum is equivalent at least to £30,000 at the present day. (*Dict. Nat. Biog.*, *Catesby*.)

[3] But see Appendix D, *The Spanish Treason*.

when they appeared to search his house.[1] John Wright and Percy had, at least till a very recent period, been notorious bravoes, who made a point of picking a quarrel with any man who was reported to be a good swordsman, they being both expert with the weapon.[2]

It is evident that men of this stamp were not unlikely to prove restive under such treatment as was meted out to the Catholics, from which moreover, as gentlemen, they themselves suffered in a special degree. Lord Castlemaine remarks that loose people may usually be drawn into a plot when statesmen lay gins, and that it was no hard thing for a Secretary of State, should he desire any such thing, to know of turbulent and ambitious spirits to be his unconscious instruments,[3] and it is obvious that no great perspicacity would have been required to fix upon those who had given such evidence of their disposition as had these men.

It must, at the same time, be confessed that the character of the plotters is one of the most perplexing features of the Plot. The crime contemplated was without parallel in its brutal and senseless atrocity. There had, it is true, been powder-plots before, notably that which had effected the destruction of the king's own father, Lord Darnley, a fact undoubtedly calcu-

---

[1] Father Gerard says of him that "he paid them [the pursuivants] so well for their labour not with crowns of gold, but with cracked crowns sometimes, and with dry blows instead of drink and other good cheer, that they durst not visit him any more unless they brought store of help with them." (*Narrative of the Gunpowder Plot*, p. 86.)

[2] *Ibid.*, p. 57.

[3] *Catholique Apology*, p. 403.

lated to make much impression upon the timorous mind of James. But what marked off our Gunpowder Plot from all others, was the wholesale and indiscriminate slaughter in which it must have resulted, and the absence of any possibility that the cause could be benefited which the conspirators had at heart. It was at once reprobated and denounced by the Catholics of England, and by the friends and near relatives of the conspirators themselves.[1] It might be supposed that those who undertook such an enterprise were criminals of the deepest dye, and ruffians of a more than usually repulsive type. In spite, however, of the turbulent element in their character of which we have seen something, such a judgment would, in the opinion of historians, be altogether erroneous. Far from their being utterly unredeemed villains, it appears, in fact, that apart from the one monstrous transgression which has made them infamous, they should be distinguished in the annals of crime as the least disreputable gang of conspirators who ever plotted a treason. On this point we have ample evidence from those who are by no means their friends. "Atrocious as their whole undertaking was," writes Mr. Gardiner,[2] "great as must have been the moral obliquity of their minds before they could have conceived such a project, there was at least nothing mean or selfish about them. They boldly risked their lives for what they honestly

---

[1] *E.g.*, by Mr. Talbot of Grafton, father-in-law of Robert Winter, who drove their envoys away with threats and reproaches (Jardine, *Gunpowder Plot*, p. 112), and by Sir Robert Digby, of Coleshill, cousin to Sir Everard, who assisted in taking prisoners. (R. O. *Gunpowder Plot Book*, 42.)

[2] *History*, i. 263.

believed to be the cause of God and of their country. Theirs was a crime which it would never have entered into the heart of any man to commit who was not raised above the low aims of the ordinary criminal." Similarly Mr. Jardine, a still less friendly witness, tells us[1] that "several at least of the conspirators were men of mild and amiable manners, averse to tumults and bloodshed, and dwelling quietly amidst the humanities of domestic life," a description which he applies especially to Rokewood and Digby; while of Guy Faukes himself he says[2] that, according to the accounts which we hear of him, he is not to be regarded as a mercenary ruffian, ready for hire to do any deed of blood; but as a zealot, misled by misguided fanaticism, who was, however, by no means destitute either of piety or of humanity. Moreover, as Mr. Jardine farther remarks, the conspirators as a body were of the class which we should least expect to find engaged in desperate enterprises, being, as Sir E. Coke described them, "gentlemen of good houses, of excellent parts, and of very competent fortunes and estates," none of them, except perhaps Catesby, being in pecuniary difficulties, while several —notably Robert Winter, Rokewood, Digby, Tresham, and Grant—were men of large possessions. It has also been observed by a recent biographer of Sir Everard Digby,[3] that, for the furtherance of their projects after the explosion, the confederates were able to provide a sum equal at least to £75,000 of our money—a sufficient proof of their worldly position.

[1] *Gunpowder Plot*, p. 151.   [2] *Ibid.*, p. 38.
[3] *Life of a Conspirator, by one of his Descendants*, p. 150.

That men of such a class should so lightly and easily have adopted a scheme so desperate and atrocious as that of "murdering a kingdom in its representatives," is undoubtedly not the least incomprehensible feature of this strange story. At the same time it must not be forgotten that there is another, and a very different account of these men, which comes to us on the authority of a Catholic priest living in England at the time,[1] who speaks of the conspirators as follows:

"They were a few wicked and desperate wretches, whom many Protestants termed Papists, although the priests and the true Catholics knew them not to be such. . . . They were never frequenters of Catholic Sacraments with any priest, as I could ever learn; and, as all the Protestant Courts will witness, not one of them was a convicted or known Catholic or Recusant."[2]

Similarly Cornwallis, writing from Madrid,[3] reported that the king and Estate of Spain were "much grieved that they being atheists and devils in their inward parts, should paint their outside with Catholicism."

In view of evidence so contradictory, it is difficult, if not impossible, to form a confident judgment as to the real character of those whose history we are attempting to trace; but, leaving aside what is matter

---

[1] *English Protestants' Plea and Petition for English Priests and Papists.* The author of this book (published 1621) describes himself as a priest who has been for many years on the English mission. His title indicates that he draws his arguments from Protestant sources.

[2] P. 56.

[3] November 25th, 1605, *Stowe MSS.* 168, 61.

of doubt, the undisputed facts of their previous career appear to show unmistakably that they were just the men who would be ready to look to violence for a remedy of existing evils, and to whom it would not be difficult to suggest its adoption.

CHAPTER III.

THE OPINION OF CONTEMPORARIES AND HISTORIANS.

WE have now for so long a period been accustomed to accept the official story regarding the Gunpowder Plot, that most readers will be surprised to hear that at the time of its occurrence, and for more than a century afterwards, there were, to say the least, many intelligent men who took for granted that in some way or other the actual conspirators were but the dupes and instruments of more crafty men than themselves, and in their mad enterprise unwittingly played the game of ministers of State.

From the beginning the government itself anticipated this, as is evidenced by the careful and elaborate account of the whole affair drawn up on the 7th of November, 1605—two days after the "discovery"—seemingly for the benefit of the Privy Council.[1] This important document, which is in the handwriting of Levinus Munck, Cecil's secretary, with numerous and significant emendations from the hand of Cecil himself, speaks, amongst other things, of the need of circumspection, "considering how apt the world is nowadays to think all providence and intelligences to

[1] *Gunpowder Plot Book*, 129. Printed in *Archæologia*, xii. 202*.

be but practices." The result did not falsify the expectation. Within five weeks we find a letter written from London to a correspondent abroad,[1] wherein it is said: "Those that have practical experience of the way in which things are done, hold it as certain that there has been foul play, and that some of the Council secretly spun the web to entangle these poor gentlemen, as did Secretary Walsingham in other cases," and it is clear that the writer has but recorded an opinion widely prevalent. To this the government again bear witness, for they found it advisable to issue an official version of the history, in the *True and Perfect Relation*, and the *Discourse of the Manner of the Discovery of the Gunpowder Plot*, the appearance of which was justified expressly on the ground that "there do pass from hand to hand divers uncertain, untrue, and incoherent reports and relations," and that it is very important "for men to understand the birth and growth of the said abominable and detestable conspiracy." The accounts published with this object are, by the common consent of historians, flagrantly untruthful and untrustworthy.[2]

[1] R. O. *Roman Transcripts* (Bliss), No. 86, December 10th, 1605 (Italian).

[2] Mr. Jardine writes (*Criminal Trials*, ii. p. 235), "*The True and Perfect Relation* . . . is certainly not deserving of the character which its title imports. It is not *true*, because many occurrences on the trial are wilfully misrepresented; and it is not *perfect*, because the whole evidence, and many facts and circumstances which must have happened, are omitted, and incidents are inserted which could not by possibility have taken place on the occasion. It is obviously a false and imperfect relation of the proceedings; a tale artfully garbled and misrepresented, like many others of the same age, to serve a State

We likewise find Secretary Cecil writing to instruct Sir E. Coke, the Attorney-General, as to his conduct of the case against the conspirators, in view of the "lewd" reports current in regard of the manner in which it had been discovered.[1] The same minister, in the curious political manifesto which he issued in connection with the affair,[2] again bears witness to the same effect, when he declares that the papists, after the manner of Nero, were throwing the blame of their crime upon others.

Clearly, however, it was not to the papists alone that such an explanation commended itself. The Puritan Osborne[3] speaks of the manner in which the "discovery" was managed as "a neat device of the Treasurer's, he being very plentiful in such plots." Goodman, Anglican Bishop of Gloucester, another contemporary, is even more explicit. After describing the indignation of the Catholics when they found themselves deceived in their hopes at the hands of James, he goes on: " The great statesman had intelligence of all this, and because he would show his service to the State, he would first contrive and then discover a

purpose, and intended and calculated to mislead the judgment of the world upon the facts of the case." Of the *Discourse* he speaks in similar terms. (*Ibid.*, p. 4.)

[1] R. O. *Dom. James I.* xix. 94. Printed by Jardine, *Criminal Trials*, ii. 120 (note).

[2] *Answere to certaine Scandalous Papers, scattered abroad under colour of a Catholic Admonition.* (Published in January, 1605-6.)

[3] *Traditional Memoirs*, 36. Of this writer Lord Castlemaine says, " He was born before this plot, and was also an inquisitive man, a frequenter of company, of a noted wit, of an excellent family, and as Protestant a one as any in the whole nation."

treason, and the more odious and hateful the treason were, his service would be the greater and the more acceptable."[1] Another notable witness is quoted by the Jesuit Father Martin Grene, in a letter to his brother Christopher, January 1st, 1665-6:[2] "I have heard strange things, which, if ever I can make out, will be very pertinent: for certain, the late Bishop of Armagh, Usher, was divers times heard to say, that if papists knew what he knew, the blame of the Gunpowder Treason would not lie on them." In like manner we find it frequently asserted on the authority of Lord Cobham and others,[3] that King James himself, when he had time to realize the truth of the matter, was in the habit of speaking of the Fifth of November as "Cecil's holiday."

Such a belief must have been widely entertained, otherwise it could not have been handed on, as it was, for generations. It is not too much to say that historians for almost a century and a half, if they did not themselves favour the theory of the government's complicity, at least bore witness how widely that idea prevailed. Thus, to confine ourselves at present to Protestant writers, Sanderson,[4] acknowledging that the secretary was accused of having manipulated the

[1] *Court of King James* (1839), i. 102.
[2] Stonyhurst MSS., *Anglia*, v. 67.
[3] *E.g.*, in the *Advocate of Conscience Liberty* (1673), p. 225.
[4] *History of Mary Queen of Scots and James I.*, p. 334. Bishop Kennet, in his Fifth of November Sermon, 1715, boldly declares that Sanderson speaks not of Cecil the statesman, but of Cecil "a busy Romish priest" (and, he might have added, a paid government spy). The assertion is utterly and obviously false.

transaction, says no word to indicate that he repudiates such a charge. Welwood[1] is of opinion that Cecil was aware of the Plot long before the "discovery," and that the famous letter to Monteagle was "a contrivance of his own." Oldmixon writes[2] "notwithstanding the general joy, . . . there were some who insinuated that the Plot was of the King's own making, or that he was privy to it from first to last." Carte[3] does not believe that James knew anything of it, but considers it "not improbable" that Cecil was better informed. Burnet[4] complains of the impudence of the papists of his day, who denied the conspiracy, and pretended it was an artifice of the minister's "to engage some desperate men into a plot, which he managed so that he could discover it when he pleased." Fuller[5] bears witness to the general belief, but considers it inconsistent with the well-known piety of King James. Bishop Kennet, in his Fifth of November sermon at St. Paul's, in 1715, talks in a similar strain. So extreme, indeed, does the incredulity and uncertainty appear to have been, that the Puritan Prynne[6] is inclined to suspect Bancroft, the Archbishop of Canterbury, of having been engaged in the conspiracy; while one of the furious zealots who followed the lead of Titus Oates, mournfully testified that there were those in his day who looked upon the Powder Treason "as upon a romantic

---

[1] *Memoirs*, p. 22.
[2] *History of England, Royal House of Stuart*, p. 27.
[3] *General History of England*, iii. 757.
[4] *History of His Own Times*, i. 11.
[5] *Church History*, Book X. § 39.
[6] *Antipathie of the English Lordly Prelacie, to the regall Monarchie and Civill Unity*, p. 151.

story, or a politic invention, or a State trick," giving no more credence to it than to the histories of the "Grand Cyrus, or Guy of Warwick, or Amadis de Gaul,"—or, as we should now say, Jack the Giant Killer.

The general scope and drift of such suspicions are well indicated by Bevil Higgons, "This impious design," he writes [1] of the Plot, "gave the greatest blow to the Catholic interest in England, by rendering that religion so odious to the people. The common opinion concerning the discovery of the Plot, by a letter to the Lord Mounteagle, has not been universally allowed to be the real truth of the matter, for some have affirmed that this design was first hammered in the forge of Cecil, who intended to have produced this plot in the time of Queen Elizabeth, but prevented by her death he resumed his project in this reign, with a design to have so enraged the nation as to have expelled all Roman Catholics, and confiscated their estates. To this end, by his secret emissaries, he enticed some hot-headed men of that persuasion, who, ignorant whence the design first came, heartily engaged in this execrable Powder Treason. . . . Though this account should not be true," he continues, "it is certain that the Court of England had notice of this Plot from France and Italy long before the pretended discovery; upon which Cecil . . . framed that letter to the Lord Mounteagle, with a design to make the discovery seem the more miraculous, and at the same time magnify the judgment of the king, who by his deep penetration was to have the honour of unravelling so ambiguous and dark a riddle."

[1] *A Short View of the English History*, p. 296.

It may be added that amongst modern historians who have given special attention to this period, several, though repudiating the notion that Cecil originated the Plot, are strongly of opinion that as to the important episode of the "discovery," the traditional story is a fabrication. Thus, Mr. Brewer [1] declares it to be quite certain that Cecil had previous knowledge of the design, and that the "discovery" was a fraud. Lodge [2] is of the same opinion, and so is the author of the *Annals of England*.[3] Jardine [4] inclines to the belief that the government contrived the letter to Monteagle in order to conceal the means by which their information had in reality been obtained. Mr. Gardiner, though dismissing the idea as "absurd," acknowledges that his contemporaries accused Cecil of inventing the whole Plot.[5]

So much for the testimony of Protestants. As for those who had to suffer in consequence of the affair, there is no need to multiply testimonies. Lord Castlemaine tells us [6] that "the Catholics of England, who knew Cecil's ways of acting and their own innocence,

---

[1] Note to *Fuller's Church History*, x. § 39, and to *Student's Hume*.

[2] *Illustrations*, iii. 172.

[3] Parker and Co. This author says of Cecil and his rival Raleigh, "Both were unprincipled men, but Cecil was probably the worst. He is suspected not only of having contrived the strange plot in which Raleigh was involved, but of being privy to the proceedings of Catesby and his associates, though he suffered them to remain unmolested, in order to secure the forfeiture of their estates" (p. 338).

[4] *Criminal Trials*, ii. 68.

[5] *History of England*, i. 254, note.

[6] *Catholique Apology*, p. 412.

suspected him from the beginning, as hundreds still alive can testify." Father Henry More, S.J., a contemporary, speaks to the same effect.[1] Father John Gerard, who was not only a contemporary, but one of those accused of complicity, intimates[2] his utter disbelief of the official narrative concerning the discovery, and his conviction that those who had the scanning of the redoubtable letter were "well able in shorter time and with fewer doubts to decipher a darker riddle and find out a greater secret than that matter was." One Floyde, a spy, testified in 1615[3] to having frequently heard various Jesuits say, that the government were aware of the Plot several months before they thought fit to " discover " it.

The Catholic view is expressed with much point and force by an anonymous writer of the eighteenth century:[4] " I shall touch briefly upon a few particulars relating to this Plot, for the happy discovery whereof an anniversary holiday has now been kept for above a hundred years. Is it out of pure gratitude to God the nation is so particularly devout on this occasion? If so, it is highly commendable: for we ought to thank God for all things, and therefore I cannot deny but there is all the reason in the world to give him solemn thanks, for that the king and Parliament never were in any danger of being hurt by the Powder Plot. . . . I am far from denying the Gunpowder Plot. Nay, I believe as firmly that Catesby, with twelve more popish associates, had

---

[1] *Hist. Prov. Angl. S. J.*, p. 310.
[2] *Condition of Catholics under James I.*, p. 100.
[3] R. O. *Dom. James I.* lxxxi. 70, August 29th, 1615.
[4] *A Plain and Rational Account of the Catholick Faith*, Rouen, 1721, p. 197.

a design to blow up K. James, as I believe that the father of that same king was effectually blown up by the Earls of Murray, Morton, Bothwell, and others of the Reformed Church of Scotland. However.... I humbly conceive I may say the king and Parliament were in no danger of being hurt by it, and my reason is because they had not less a man than the prime minister of state for their tutelar angel; a person deeply read in politics; who had inherited the double spirit of his predecessor Walsingham, knew all his tricks of legerdemain, and could as seasonably discover plots as contrive them. ... This much at least is certain, that the letter written to my Lord Mounteagle, by which the Plot was discovered, had not a fool, but a very wise sophister for its author: for it was so craftily worded, that though it was mysterious enough on the one hand to prevent a full evidence that it was written on purpose to discover the Plot, yet it was clear enough on the other to be understood with the help of a little consideration, as the event soon showed. Indeed, when it was brought to Secretary Cecil, he, poor gentleman, had not penetration enough to understand the meaning of it, and said it was certainly written by a madman. But there, I fear, he wronged himself. For the secretary was no madman. On the contrary, he had too much wit to explain it himself, and was too refined a politician to let slip so favourable an occasion of making his court to the king, who was to have the compliment made him of being the only Solomon wise enough to unfold this dark mystery. Which while his Majesty was doing with a great deal of ease, the secretary was all the while at his elbow admiring and applauding his wonderful sagacity. . . . So that, in all probability, the same man was the chief underhand contriver and discoverer of the Plot ; and the greatest part of the bubbles concerned in it were trapanned into it by one who took sure care that none but themselves should be hurt by it. . . . But be that as it will, there is no doubt but that they who suffer themselves to be drawn into a plot like fools, deserve to be hanged for it like knaves."

The opinion of Dodd, the historian, has already been indicated, which in another place he thus emphasizes and explains :[1] " Some persons in chief power suspecting the king would be very indulgent to Catholics, several stratagems were made use of to exasperate him against them, and cherishing the Gunpowder Plot is thought to be a masterpiece in this way."[2]

It would not be difficult to continue similar citations, but enough has now been said to show that it is nothing new to charge the chief minister of James I. with having fostered the conspiracy for his own purposes, or even to have actually set it a-going. It appears perfectly clear that from the first there were

---

[1] *Certamen utriusque Ecclesiæ*, James I.

[2] The author of the *English Protestants' Plea* (1621) says : " Old stratagems and tragedies of Queene Elizabeth's time must needs be renewed and playde againe, to bring not only the Catholikes of England, but their holy religion into obloquy " (p. 56).

Peter Talbot, Bishop of Dublin, in the *Polititian's Catechisme* (1658) writes : " That Cecil was the contriver, or at least the fomenter of [the Plot,] was testified by one of his own domestick Gentlemen, who advertised a certain Catholike, by name Master Buck, two months before, of a wicked designe his Master had against Catholikes" (p. 94).

not a few, and those not Catholics only, who entertained such a belief, and that the facts of the case are inadequately represented by historians, who imply, like Mr. Jardine, that such a theory was first broached long afterwards, and adopted by Catholics alone.[1]

It is moreover apparent that if in recent times historians have forgotten that such a view was ever held, or consider it too preposterous for serious discussion, this is not because fuller knowledge of the details of the conspiracy have discredited it. The official version of the story has remained in possession of the field, and it has gradually been assumed that this must substantially be true. In consequence, as it seems, writers of history, approaching the subject with this conviction, have failed to remark many points suggested even by the documentary evidence at our disposal, and still more emphatically by the recorded facts, which cannot but throw grave doubt upon almost every particular of the traditional account, while making it impossible to believe that, as to what is most essential, the Plot was in reality what has for so long been supposed. That long before the "discovery" the Plot must have been, and in fact was, known to the government; that this knowledge was artfully dissimulated, in order to make political capital

---

[1] A writer, signing himself "Architect," in an article describing the old palace of Westminster (*Gentleman's Magazine*, July, 1800, p. 627), having occasion to mention the Gunpowder Plot, observes: "This Plot is now pretty well understood not to have been hatched by the Papists, but by an inveterate foe of the Catholicks of that day, the famous minister of James . . . . All well-informed persons at present laugh at the whole of this business."

out of it; that for the same purpose the sensational circumstances of its discovery were deliberately arranged; and that there are grave reasons for suspecting the beginnings of the desperate enterprise, as well as its catastrophe, to have been dexterously manipulated for State purposes;—such are the conclusions, the evidence for which will now be considered.

CHAPTER IV.

THE TRADITIONAL STORY.

THE history of the Gunpowder Plot prior to its discovery, as related with much circumstantiality by the government of the day, has, in all essential particulars, been accepted without demur by the great majority of modern writers. We have already seen that those who lived nearer to the period in question were less easily convinced; it remains to show that the internal evidence of the story itself is incompatible with its truthfulness.

The point upon which everything turns is the secret, and therefore dangerous, character of the conspiracy, which, as we are told, completely eluded the vigilance of the authorities, and was on the very verge of success before even a breath of suspicion was aroused, being balked only by a lucky accident occurring at the eleventh hour, in a manner fitly described as miraculous.

On the other hand, however, many plain and obvious considerations combine to show that such an account cannot be true. It is not easy to believe that much which is said to have been done by the conspirators ever occurred at all. It is clear that, if such things did occur, they can by no possibility have escaped observation. There is evidence that the government knew of the Plot long before they suddenly "discovered" it. Finally, the story of the said "discovery," and the manner in which it took place, is plainly not only untrue, but devised to conceal the truth; while the elaborate care expended upon it sufficiently indicates how important it was held that the truth should be concealed.

There are, moreover, arguments, which appear to deserve consideration, suggesting the conclusion that the Plot was actually set on foot by the secret instigation of those who designed to make it serve their ends, as in fact it did. For our purpose, however, it is not necessary to insist greatly upon these. It will be enough to show that, whatever its origin, the conspiracy was, and must have been, known to those in power, who, playing with their infatuated dupes, allowed them to go on with their mad scheme, till the moment came to strike with full effect; thus impressing the nation with a profound sense of its marvellous deliverance, and winning its confidence for those to whose vigilance and sagacity alone that deliverance appeared due.

That we may rightly follow the details of the story told to us, we must in the first place understand the topography of the scene of operations, which, with the aid of the illustrations given, will not be difficult.

The old House of Lords [1] was a chamber occupying

---

[1] The name "old House of Lords" is somewhat ambiguous, being variously applicable to three different buildings:

(i.) That here described, which continued to be used till the Irish Union, A.D. 1800.

(ii.) The "Court of Requests," or "White Hall," used from 1800 till the fire of 1834.

(iii.) The "Painted Chamber," which, having been repaired

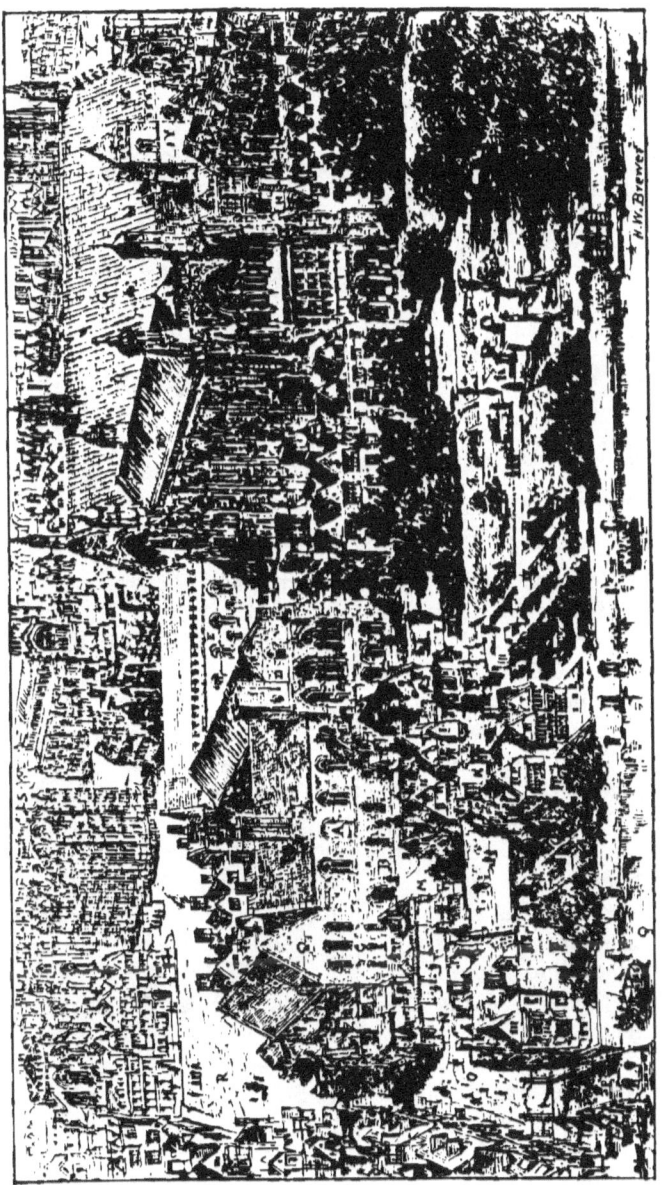

HOUSES OF PARLIAMENT IN THE TIME OF JAMES I.

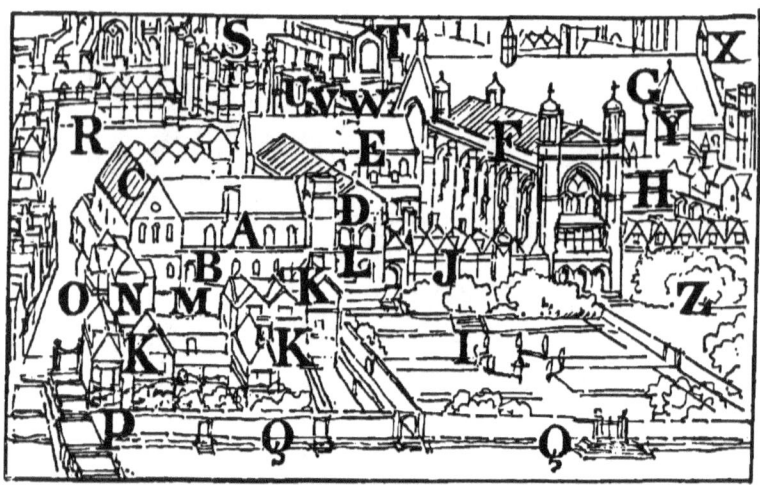

INDEX. PARLIAMENT HOUSES IN THE TIME OF JAMES I.

A. The House of Lords.
B. Chamber under the House of Lords, called "Guy Faukes' Cellar."
C. The Prince's Chamber.
D. The Painted Chamber.
E. The "White Hall" or Court of Requests.
F. The House of Commons (formerly St. Stephen's Chapel).
G. Westminster Hall.
H. St. Stephen's Cloisters, converted into houses for the Tellers of the Exchequer.
I. Garden of the Old Palace (afterwards called "Cotton Garden").
J. House built on the site of the Chapel of "Our Lady of the Pew" (called later "Cotton House").
K K K. Houses built upon ruins of the walls of the Old Palace.
L. Vault under the Painted Chamber.
M. Yard or Court into which a doorway opened from Guy Faukes' Cellar.
N. Passage leading from the same Yard or Court into Parliament Place.
O. Parliament Place.
P. Parliament Stairs (formerly called "The Queen's Bridge").
Q Q. The River Thames.
R. Old Palace Yard.
S. Westminster Abbey.
T. St. Margaret's Church.
U V W. Buildings of the Old Palace, called "Heaven" (or "Paradise"), "Hell," and "Purgatory."
X. New Palace Yard.
Y. Bell Tower of St. Stephen's.
Z. The Speaker's Garden.

the first floor of a building which stood about fifty yards from the left bank of the Thames, to which it was parallel, the stream at this point running almost due north. Beneath the Peers' Chamber, on the ground floor, was a large room, which plays an important part in our history. This had originally served as the palace kitchen,[1] and though commonly described as a "cellar" or a "vault" was in reality neither, for it stood on the level of the ground outside, and had a flat ceiling, formed by the beams which supported the flooring of the Lords' apartment above.[2] It ran beneath the said Peers' Chamber from end to end, and measured 77 feet in length, by 24 feet 4 inches in width.

At either end, the building abutted upon another running transversely to it; that on the north being the "Painted Chamber," probably erected by Edward the Confessor, and that on the south the "Prince's

after the said fire, became the place of assembly for the Lords, as did the Court of Requests for the Commons.

The original House of Lords was demolished in 1823 by Sir John Soane, who on its site erected his Royal Gallery. (See Brayley and Britton, *History of the Palace of Westminster*.)

[1] The authority for this is the Earl of Northampton, who at Father Garnet's trial mentioned that it was so stated in ancient records. Remains of a buttery hatch in the south wall confirmed his assertion.

The foundations of the building were believed to date from the time of Edward the Confessor, and the style of architecture of the superstructure assigned it to the early part of the thirteenth century, as likewise the "Prince's Chamber."

[2] Brayley and Britton, *History of the Palace of Westminster*, p. 421; J. T. Smith, *Antiquities of Westminster*, p. 39 (where illustrations will be found); *Gentleman's Magazine*, July, 1800, p. 626.

Chamber," assigned by its architectural features to the reign of Henry III. The former served as a place of conference for Lords and Commons,[1] the latter as the robing-room of the Lords. The royal throne stood at

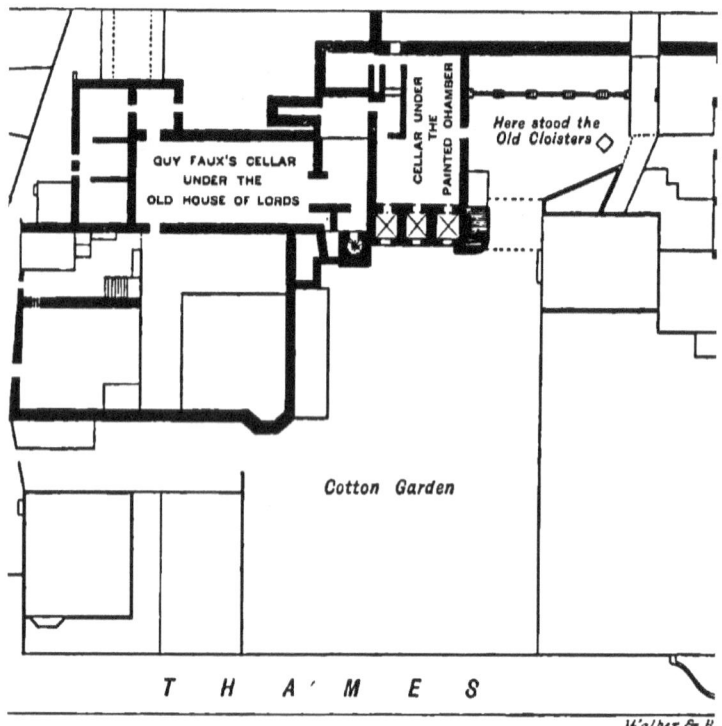

GROUND PLAN OF THE SCENE OF ACTION.

the south end of the House, near the Prince's Chamber.

Originally the Parliament Chamber and the "cellar" beneath it were lighted by large windows on both sides; subsequently, houses raised against it

[1] It was here that the death warrant of Charles I. was signed,

blocked these up, and the Lords were supplied with light by dormers constructed in the roof. The walls of their apartment were then hung with tapestry, representing the defeat of the Spanish Armada. Although precise information on the point is not easy to obtain, it would appear that this did not occur till a period later than that with which we are concerned.[1]

Such was the position to be attacked. As a first step, the conspirators resolved to hire a house in the immediate neighbourhood, to serve them as a base of operations. Thomas Percy was selected to appear as the principal in this part of the business, for, being one of the king's pensioners, he had frequently to be in attendance at Court, and might naturally wish to have a lodging close at hand. The house chosen was one, or rather a part of one,[2] standing near the Prince's Chamber, and on the side towards the river.[3]

In treating for the lease of this tenement Percy seems to have conducted himself in a manner altogether different from what we might have expected of one whose object required him, above all, to avoid

---

[1] An old print (which states that it is taken from "a painted print in the Cottonian library,") representing the two Houses assembled in presence of Queen Elizabeth, has windows on both sides. The same plate, with the figure of the sovereign alone changed, was made to do duty likewise for a Parliament of James I. By Hollar's time (1640-77) the windows had been blocked up and the tapestry hung.

[2] Cecil wrote to Cornwallis, Edmondes, and others, November 9th, 1605, "This Piercey had about a year and a half a goe hyred a parte of Vyniards house in the old Palace," which appears to be Mr. Hepworth Dixon's sole authority for styling the tenement "Vinegar House."

[3] See Appendix E, *Site of Percy's house.*

attracting notice. He appears, in fact, to have made the greatest possible ado about the business. The apartments were already let to one Ferrers, who was unwilling to give them up, and Percy eventually succeeded in his purpose, after not only "long suit by himself," but also "great intreaty of Mr. Carleton, Mr.

THE OLD HOUSE OF LORDS, FROM THE EAST OR RIVER SIDE, SHOWING THE GARDEN.

Epsley, and other gentlemen belonging to the Earl of Northumberland."[1] These gentlemen were never said to have been privy to the Conspiracy, and one of them, the well-known Dudley Carleton, afterwards Viscount Dorchester, was not only at this time secretary to Sir

[1] Evidence of Mrs. Whynniard, November 7th, 1605. Epsley is evidently the same person as Hoppisley, who was examined on the 23rd of the same month.

Thomas Parry, the Ambassador in France, but was "patronised" by Cecil himself.[1]

Neither does the house appear to have been well suited to serve the purposes for which it was taken. Speed tells us,[2] and he is confirmed by Bishop Barlow of Lincoln,[3] that it was let out to tenants only when Parliament was not assembled, and during a session formed part of the premises at the disposal of the Lords, whom it served as a withdrawing room. As the Plot was, of necessity, to take effect during a session,[4] when the place would thus be in other hands, it is very hard to understand how it was intended that the final and all important operation should be conducted.

The bargain for the house was concluded May 24th, 1604,[5] but the proposed operations were delayed till a much later date, by a circumstance which clearly shows the public nature of the premises, and that the lease obtained conferred no exclusive right of occupation. The question of a union with Scotland, for which King James was very anxious, was at the time being agitated, and commissioners having been appointed to discuss it, this very house was placed at their disposal for their meetings. Consequently the

---

[1] Birch, *Historical View*, p. 227.
[2] *Historie*, p. 1231.
[3] *Gunpowder Treason, Harleian Miscellany*, iii. 121.
[4] At his first examination, November 5th 1605, Faukes declared that he had not been sure the king would come to the Parliament House on that day, and that his purpose was to have blown it up whenever his Majesty was there.
[5] The agreement between Percy and Ferrers is in the Record Office (*Gunpowder Plot Book*, 1.) and is endorsed by Cecil, "The bargaine ... for the bloody sellar." Upon this there will be more to remark later.

summer and autumn passed without any farther steps being taken by the conspirators.

At last, in December, they were free to take in hand the extraordinary scheme they had matured. This was, starting from a cellar of Percy's house,[1] to dig thence an underground mine to the foundations of the Parliament House, and through them; and then to construct within, beneath the Peers' Chamber itself, a "concavity" large enough to contain the amount of powder requisite for their purpose. On December 11th, 1604, they commenced operations,[2] and in a fortnight, that is by Christmas, they had tunnelled from their starting-point to the wall they had to breach; and that this first operation was of no small magnitude, especially for men who had never before handled pick or shovel,[3] is shown by the fact that what they contrived to do in so short a time was quoted as evidence of the extraordinary zeal they displayed in their nefarious enterprise.[4] Having rested a little, for

[1] Jardine, *Gunpowder Plot*, p. 42.

[2] The 11th of December, O. S., was at that period the shortest day, which circumstance suggested to Sir E. Coke, on the trial of the conspirators, one of his characteristic facetiæ; he bade his hearers note "That it was in the entring of the Sun into the Tropick of Capricorn, when they began their Mine; noting that by Mining they should descend, and by Hanging, ascend."

[3] "Gentlemen not accustomed to labour or to be pioneers." —Goodman, *Court of King James*, p. 103.

[4] "The Moles that first underwent these underminings were all grounded Schollers of the Romish Schoole, and such earnest Labourers in their Vault of Villany, that by Christmas Eve they had brought the worke under an entry, unto the Wall of the Parliament House, underpropping still as they went the Earth with their framed Timber."—Speed, *Historie*, p. 1232 (pub. 1611).

the Christmas holidays, they began upon the wall, which presented an unexpected obstacle. They found that it was not only "very hard to beat through," but, moreover, nine feet thick, though since, as we shall see, they never penetrated to the other side, it is not clear how they were able to measure it.[1] Up to this point but five persons had engaged in the work, Catesby, Percy, Thomas Winter, John Wright, and Faukes. In consequence however of the difficulties now experienced, Keyes was called in to their aid. He had already been initiated in the Plot, and appointed to take charge of the powder, which was being accumulated and stored in a house hired for the purpose across the Thames, at Lambeth. It was therefore necessary to bring over the powder with him, which amounted at this time to twenty barrels, and was placed either in Percy's lodging itself, or in an outhouse belonging to it. About the same time Christopher Wright was also initiated and took his share of the labour.[2]

The gang thus composed laboured upon the wall from the beginning of January, 1604-5, to the middle of March,[3] by which time they had succeeded in get-

[1] In Barlow's *Gunpowder Treason* these foundations are stated to have been three ells thick, *i.e.*, eleven and a quarter feet. *Harleian Miscellany*, iii. 122.

[2] See Appendix F, *The enrolment of the Conspirators*, for the discrepancies as to dates. T. Winter (November 23rd, 1605) says that the powder was laid "in Mr. Percy's house;" Faukes, " in a low Room new builded."

[3] There is, as usual, hopeless contradiction between the two witnesses upon whom, as will be seen, we wholly depend for this portion of the story. Faukes (November 17th, 1605) makes the mining operations terminate at Candlemas. T. Winter

ting only half way through. While the others worked, Faukes stood on sentry to warn them of any danger.

Meanwhile, it must be asked how proceedings so remarkable could have escaped the notice, not only of the government, but of the entire neighbourhood. This, it must be remembered, was most populous. There were people living in the very building, a part of which sheltered the conspirators. Around, were thickly clustered the dwellings of the keeper of the Wardrobe, auditors and tellers of the Exchequer, and other such officials.[1] There were tradespeople and workmen constantly employed close to the spot where the work was going on; while the public character of the place makes it impossible to suppose that tenants such as Percy and his friends, who were little better than lodgers, could claim the exclusive use of anything beyond the rooms they rented—even when allowed the use of these—or could shut against the neighbours and visitors in general the precincts of so much frequented a spot.

How, then, did they dispose of the mass of soil dug out in making a tunnel through which barrels and hogsheads were to be conveyed? No man who has had practical experience of the unexpected quantity of earth which comes out of the most

(November 23rd) says that they went on to "near Easter" (March 31st). The date of hiring the "cellar," was about Lady Day (March 25th).

[1] The buildings of the dissolved College of St. Stephen, comprising those around the House of Lords, were granted by Edward VI. to Sir Ralph Lane. They reverted to the crown under Elizabeth, and were appropriated as residences for the auditors and tellers of the Exchequer. The locality became so populous that in 1606 it was forbidden to erect more houses.

insignificant excavation, will be likely to rest satisfied with the explanation officially given, that it was sufficiently concealed by being hidden beneath the turf in the little garden adjoining.[1] What, moreover, was done with the great stones that came out of the foundations? Of these there must have been on hand at least some sixty cubic feet, probably much more, and they, at any rate, can scarcely have been stowed away beneath the turf.

What, above all, of the noise made during the space of a couple of months, in assaulting a wall "very hard to beat through"? It is a matter of common observation how sound travels in the ground, and every stroke of the pick upon the stone must have been distinctly heard for more than a hundred yards all around, constituting a public nuisance. Meanwhile, not only were there people living close by on every side, but men were constantly at work right over the heads of the diggers, and only a few feet from them: yet we are required to believe that neither these nor any others had any notion that anything unusual was going on.

Neither is it easy to understand how these amateurs contrived to do so much without a catastrophe. To make a tunnel through soft earth is a very delicate operation, replete with unlooked-for difficulties. To shore up the roof and sides there must, moreover, have been required a large quantity of the "framed timber" of which Speed tells us, and the provision and importation of this must have been almost as hard to keep dark as the exportation of the earth and stones. A

---

[1] Jardine, *Gunpowder Plot*, p. 48.

still more critical operation is that of meddling with the foundations of a house—especially of an old and heavy structure—which a professional craftsman would not venture upon except with extreme care, and the employment of many precautions of which these light-hearted adventurers knew nothing. Yet, recklessly breaking their way out of one building, and to a large extent into another, they appear to have occasioned neither crack nor settlement in either.

We are by no means at the end of our difficulties. According to the tale told by Faukes,[1] all the seven miners "lay in Percy's house," never showing themselves while the work was in progress. This circumstance, to say nothing of the storage of powder barrels and timber, seems to imply that the premises were spacious and commodious. We learn, however, on the unimpeachable evidence of Mrs. Whynniard's servant,[2] that the house afforded accommodation only for one person at a time, so that when Percy came there to spend the night, Faukes, who passed for his man, had to lodge out. This suggests another question. Percy's pretext for laying in so much fuel was that he meant to bring up his wife to live there. But how could this be under such conditions?

Still more serious is another problem. When the mining operations were commenced, in December, 1604, Parliament was appointed to meet on the 7th of February following, by which time, as is evident, the preparations of the conspirators could not have been completed. While they were working, however, news came that the session was to be postponed till October.

---

[1] November 17th, 1605.   [2] November 7th, 1605.

This information the conspirators appear to have received quite casually before Christmas, for it is said that on the strength of it, they thought they could afford to take a holiday.[1] Early in January they were again at work,[2] and they continued their operations thenceforth, without any circumstance intervening to interrupt or alarm them, of which we hear anything either from themselves or from subsequent writers. Nevertheless, it is quite certain that the Lords actually met on February 7th—that is while the mining operations were going on—and not only went through the ceremony of prorogation, but transacted some little business besides, Lord Denny being introduced and his writ of summons read.[3] It is equally incompre-

---

[1] Winter says: ". . . We heard that the Parliament should be anew adjourned until after Michaelmas; upon which tidings we broke off both discourse and working until after Christmas" (November 23rd, 1605).

Lingard writes, "When a fortnight had thus been devoted to uninterrupted labour, Faukes informed his associates that the Parliament was prorogued from the 7th of February to the 3rd of October. They immediately separated to spend the Christmas holidays at their respective homes."—*History*, vii. 47 (ed. 1883).

[2] Faukes, as has been said, makes the work upon the wall terminate at Candlemas. Winter (*ut sup.*) says that they brought over the powder at Candlemas, that is, after they had been some time engaged upon the wall, and found the need of the assistance of Keyes.

[3] *Lord's Journals* "A° 1604(5) 2 Jac.—Memorandum quod hodierno die, septimo die Februarii, A° Regis ñri Jacobi, *viz.* Angliae (etc.) 2^{ndo}, & Scotiae 38°, in quem diem prorogatum fuerat hoc praesens parliamentum, convenere Proceres tam Spirituales quam Temporales, quorum nomina subscribuntur."

Then follow twenty-nine names, including the Archbishop of Canterbury, Lords Ellesmere (*Chancellor*), Dorset (*Treasurer*),

hensible that the miners should have known nothing of so startling an occurrence, or that knowing of it they should never have made the slightest mention thereof. It is even more difficult to explain how the Peers thus assembled, and their attendants, could have failed to remark the mine, then actually open, in premises belonging to themselves, or any suspicious features of earth, stones, timber, or barrels.

The difficulties presented by the stubborn nature of the foundation-wall proved well-nigh insuperable, but, as is observed by Father Greenway,[1] one still more grave awaited the diggers had they succeeded in making their way through. The "concavity" to be excavated within, to contain the large number of powder barrels required for their purpose, would have involved engineering work of the most hazardous kind, and heavily laden as the floor above proved to be, it must, according to all rules of calculation, have collapsed, when thus undermined. But at this juncture, when the wall had been half pierced, a circumstance occurred, not less extraordinary than others we have considered, to change the whole plan of operations.

All this time, ridiculous as is the supposition, the conspirators appear to have been ignorant of the existence of the "cellar," and to have fancied that they were working their way immediately beneath the Chamber of the Peers.[2] If such a circumstance be

---

Nottingham (*Admiral*), Suffolk (*Chamberlain*), Northumberland, Cranborne (Cecil), Northampton, etc. It is noted "Lords Montagu, Petre, and Gerard [all three Catholics] were present, though they were none of the Commissioners."

[1] *Narrative* (Stonyhurst MSS.), fol. 44 b.
[2] This absurd supposition is obviously implied by Faukes

incredible, the consequences must be borne by the narrative of which it forms an essential feature. That it is incredible can hardly be questioned. The so-called "cellar," as we have seen, was a large and conspicuous room above ground. There are reasons for believing that it served habitually as a passage between the different parts of the palace. It appears certain that some of the conspirators, Percy in particular, as being one of his Majesty's pensioners, must have frequently been in the House of Lords itself, and therefore have known where it was; and clearly men of their position were able to attend there when they chose.[1]

The manner in which they came at last to discover the "cellar" is thus related by Mr. Jardine:[2] "One morning, while working upon the wall, they suddenly heard a rushing noise in a cellar, nearly above their heads. At first they imagined that they had been discovered; but Fawkes being despatched to reconnoitre, found that one Bright, to whom the cellar

(November 17th, 1605), and T. Winter (November 23rd), in the only two accounts furnished by any of the conspirators wherein the episode of the mine is mentioned. In Barlow's *Gunpowder Treason* (*Harleian Miscellany*, iii. 123) it is expressly stated that the confederates "came to the knowledge of the vault" only on the occasion now detailed. Tierney says (Dodd's *Church History*, iv. 45, note): "At this moment an accidental noise . . . first acquainted them with the existence of the cellar."

[1] On the 3rd of October following, Thomas Winter was sent to be present at the ceremony of prorogation, and to watch the demeanour of the assembled peers.

[2] *Gunpowder Plot*, p. 55. This account is based almost entirely on that of Faukes, November 17th, 1605.

belonged, was selling off his coals[1] in order to remove, and that the noise proceeded from this cause. Fawkes

N.W. Corner.

S.E. Corner.

CELLAR UNDER HOUSE OF LORDS.

[1] In his Italian version of Father Gerard's history, Father Greenway interpolates the following note: "Questi non erano carboni di legno, ma una sorte di pietra negra, la quale come carbone abrugia et fa un fuogo bellissimo et ottimo" (fol. 44 b).

carefully surveyed the place, which proved to be a large vault, situated immediately below the House of Lords, and extremely convenient for the purpose they had in view. . . . Finding that the cellar would shortly become vacant, the conspirators agreed that it should be hired in Percy's name, under the pretext that he wanted it for his own coals and wood. This was accordingly done, and immediate possession was obtained."[1]

It is obvious that Mr. Bright's men must on this, as presumably upon many previous occasions, have been at work among the coals, while the miners were hammering at the foundations beneath them, and yet have been as little aware of what was going on as were the others of the existence of the "cellar." It must, farther, be noted that the hiring of this receptacle was, in fact, by no means so easy a matter as the accounts ordinarily given would lead us to suppose.

[1] " These Pioneers through Piercies chamber brought
Th' exhausted earth, great baskets full of clay ;
Thereby t' have made a mighty concave vau't,
And of the house the ground worke tooke away :
　But then at last an obstacle they finde,
　Which to remove proud Piercy casts in 's mind.
A thick stone wall their passage then did let ;
Whereby they cou'd not finish their intent.
Then forthwith Piercy did a sellar get,
Under that sacred house for yearly rent :
　Feigning to fill 't with Char coal, Wood, & Beere,
　From all suspect themselves to cloake & cleere."
　　　　　　　JOHN VICARS, *Mischeefes Mysterie.*

This remarkable poem, published 1617, is a much expanded translation of *Pietas Pontificia* (in Latin hexameter verse) by Francis Herring, which appeared in 1606.

THE "CELLAR." 73

Faukes, in the narrative on which the whole history of this episode has been based, is made to say that he found that the coals were a-selling, and the cellar was to be let, whereupon Percy went and hired it. Mrs. Whynniard, however, tells us that the cellar was not to let, and that Bright had not the disposal of the

VAULT, EAST END OF PAINTED CHAMBER, ERRONEOUSLY STYLED "GUY FAUKES' CELLAR."

lease, but one Skinner, and that Percy "laboured very earnestly" before he succeeded in obtaining it.

But, whatever the circumstances and manner of the transaction, it appears that at Lady-day, 1605, this chamber came into the hands of those who were to make it so famous; whereupon, we are told, they resolved to abandon the mine, and use this ready-made cavity for their purposes. To it, accordingly, they transferred their powder, the barrels, by subsequent additions, being increased to thirty-six, and the amount to nine or ten thousand pounds.[1] The casks were covered with firewood, 500 faggots and 3,000 billets being brought in by hired porters and piled up by Faukes, to whose charge, in his assumed character of Percy's servant, the cellar was committed. It is stated in Winter's long declaration on this subject,[2] that the barrels were thus completely hidden, "because we might have the house free, to suffer anyone to enter that would," and we find it mentioned by various writers subsequently, that free ingress was actually allowed to the public. Thus we read[3] of "the deep

[1] On this point we are furnished with more than the usual amount of variety as to details. Cecil, writing to the ambassadors (Cornwallis, Edmondes, etc.), says there were "two hodgsheads and some 30 small barrels." The King's *Discourse* mentions 36 barrels. Barclay (*Conspiratio Anglicana*) says there were over 9,000 lb. of powder, in 32 barrels, and that one of extra size had been placed under the throne, for treason could not without dread assail Majesty even when unarmed. The indictment of the conspirators named 30 barrels and 4 hogsheads. Sir E. Coke always said 36 barrels. Barlow's *Gunpowder Treason* makes the extraordinary statement, frequently reproduced, that "to the 20 Barrels of Powder laid in at first, they added in July 20 more, and at last made up the number Thirty-six." Faukes (November 5th) said that of the powder "some was put in hoggesheads, some in Barrels, and some in firkins." Faukes also says that the powder was conveyed to the place in hampers. John Chamberlain, writing to Dudley Carleton, November 7th, 1605, says it was carried in satchels. Barlow (*ut sup.*) quotes the amount as 9,000 or 10,000 lb.

[2] November 23rd, 1605.

[3] *The Gunpowder Plot*, by L., 1805. It seems highly probable that the "cellar" was used as a public passage.

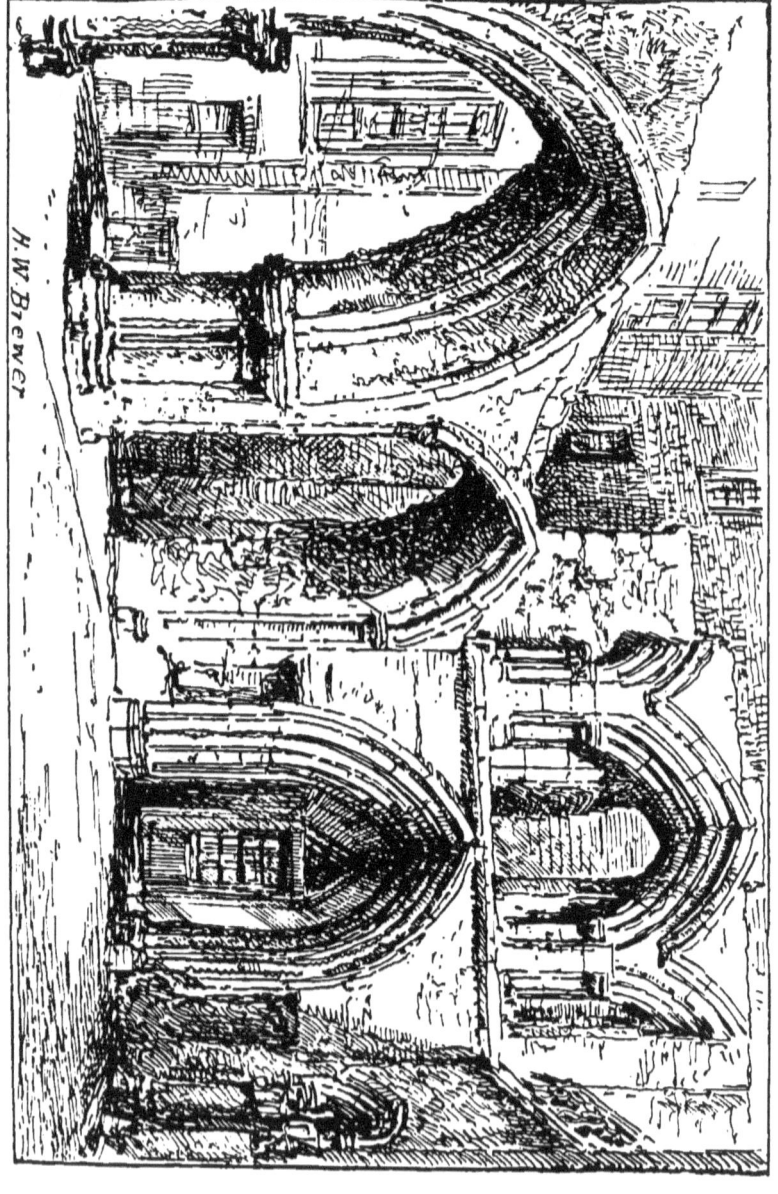

ARCHES FROM THE "CELLAR" UNDER THE HOUSE OF LORDS.

cunning [of the conspirators] in throwing open the vault, as if there had been nothing to conceal;" while another writer[1] tells us, "The place was hired by Percy; 36 barrels of gunpowder were lodged in it; the whole covered up with billets and faggots; the doors of the cellar boldly flung open, and everybody admitted, as though it contained nothing dangerous." On the top of the barrels were likewise placed "great bars of iron and massy stones," in order "to make the breach the greater."

We may here pause to review the extraordinary story to which we have been listening. A group of men, known for as dangerous characters as any in England, men, in Cecil's own words,[2] "spent in their fortunes," "hunger-starved for innovations," "turbulent spirits," and "fit for all alterations," take a house within the precincts of a royal palace, and close to the Upper House of Parliament, dig a mine, hammer away for over two months at the wall, acquire and bring in four tons of gunpowder, storing it in a large and conspicuous chamber immediately beneath that of the Peers, and covering it with an amount of fuel sufficient for a royal establishment—and meanwhile those responsible for the government of the country have not even the faintest suspicion of any possible danger. "Never," it is said,[3] "was treason more secret, or ruin more apparently inevitable," while the

[1] Hugh F. Martyndale, *A Familiar Analysis of the Calendar of the Church of England* (November 5th). London, Effingham Wilson.

[2] *Letter to Cornwallis and Edmondes*, November 9th, 1605.

[3] H. F. Martyndale, *ut sup.*

Secretary of State himself declared[1] that such ruin was averted only by the direct interposition of Heaven, in a manner nothing short of miraculous.

It must be remembered that the government thus credited with childlike and culpable simplicity, was probably the most suspicious and inquisitive that ever held power in this country, for its tenure whereof it trusted mainly to the elaborate efficiency of its intelligence department. Of a former secretary, Walsingham, Parsons wrote that he "spent infinite upon spyery,"[2] and there can be no doubt that his successor, now in office, had studied his methods to good purpose. "He," according to a panegyrist,[3] "was his craft's master in foreign intelligence and for domestic affairs," who could tell at any moment what ships there were in every port of Spain, their burdens, their equipment, and their destination. We are told[4] that he could discover the most secret business transacted in the Papal Court before it was known to the Catholics in England. He could intercept letters written from Paris to Brussels, or from Rome to Naples.[5] What was his activity at home is sufficiently evidenced by the reports furnished by his numerous agents concerning everything done throughout the country, in particular by Recusants; whereof we shall see more, in connection with this particular

---

[1] Letter to the Ambassadors, *ut sup.*
[2] *An Advertisement written to a Secretarie*, etc. (1592), p. 13.
[3] Sir R. Naunton, *Fragmenta Regalia* (*Harleian Miscellany*, ii. 106).
[4] Blount to Parsons (Stonyhurst MSS.), *Anglia*, vi. 64.
[5] Such letters are found amongst the State Papers.

affair. That those so remarkably wide-awake in regard of all else should have been blind and deaf to what was passing at their own doors appears altogether incredible.

More especially do difficulties connect themselves with the gunpowder itself. Of this, according to the lowest figure given us, there were over four tons.[1] How, we may ask, could half a dozen men, "notorious Recusants," and bearing, moreover, such a character as we have heard, without attracting any notice, and no question being asked, possess themselves of such a quantity of so dangerous a material?[2] How large was the amount may be estimated from the fact that

---

[1] The amount, it would seem, cannot have been less than this. A barrel of gunpowder, containing four firkins, weighed 400 lb., and had the casks in the cellar all been barrels, in the strict sense of the word, the amount would therefore have exceeded six tons. Some of these casks, we are told, were small, but some were hogsheads. The twenty barrels first laid in are described as "whole barrels." (Faukes, January 20th, 1605-6.)

[2] An interesting illustration of this point is furnished by a strange piece of evidence furnished by W. Andrew, servant to Sir E. Digby. Sir Everard's office was to organize the rising in the Midlands, after the catastrophe, but he apparently forgot to supply himself with powder till the very eve of the appointed day. Andrew averred that on the night of November 4th, his master secretly asked him to procure some powder in the neighbouring town, whereupon he asked, "How much? A pound, or half a pound?" Sir Everard said 200 or 300 lb. Deponent purchased one pound. (Tanner MSS. lxxv. f. 205 b.)

One Matthew Batty mentioned Lord Monteagle as having bought gunpowder. (*Ibid.* v. 40.)

In the same collection is a copy of some notes by Sir E. Coke (f. 185 b), in which the price of the powder discovered is put down as £200, *i.e.* some £2,000 of our money.

it was more than a quarter of what, in 1607, was delivered from the royal store, for all purposes, and was equal to what was thought sufficient for Dover Castle, while there was no more in the four fortresses of Arcliffe, Walmer, Deal, and Camber together.[1]

The twenty barrels first procured were first, as we have seen, stored beyond the Thames, at Lambeth, whence they had to be ferried across the river, hauled up the much frequented Parliament Stairs, carried down Parliament Place, as busy a quarter as any in the city of Westminster, and into the building adjoining the Parliament House, or the "cellar" beneath the same. All this, we are to suppose, without attracting attention or remark.[2]

[1] Gunpowder was measured by the *last* = 2,400 lb. (Tomline's *Law Dictionary*.) In 1607 there were delivered out of the store 14 lasts and some cwts. In 1608 the amount in various strong places is entered as: "*Dover Castle*, 4 lasts; *Arcliffe Bullwark*, 1 last; *Walmer*, 1 last, 8 cwt.; *Deal Castle*, 1 last; *Sandown Castle*, 2 lasts, etc.; *Sandgate*, 1 last; *Camber*, 1 last."

[2] The position and character of the "cellar" admit of no doubt, as appears from the testimony of Smith's *Antiquities of Westminster*, Brayley and Britton's *Ancient Palace of Westminster*, and Capon's notes on the same, *Vetusta Monumenta*, v. They are, however, inconsistent with some circumstances alleged by the government. Thus, Sir Everard Digby's complicity with "the worst part" of the treason, which on several occasions he denied, is held to be established by a confession of Faukes, which cannot now be found among the State Papers, but which is mentioned in Sir E. Coke's speech upon Digby's arraignment, and is printed in Barlow's *Gunpowder Treason*, p. 68. In Sir E. Coke's version it runs thus: "Fawkes, then present at the bar, had confessed, that some time before that session, the said Fawkes being with Digby at

The conspirators, while making these material preparations, were likewise busy in settling their plan of action when the intended blow should have been struck. It was by no means their intention to attempt a revolution. Their quarrel was purely personal with King James, his Council, and his Parliament, and, these being removed, they desired to continue the succession in its legitimate course, and to seat on the throne the nearest heir who might be available for the purpose; placing the new sovereign, however, under such tutelage as should insure the inauguration of a right course of policy. The details of the scheme were of as lunatic a character as the rest of the business. The confederates would have wished to possess themselves of Prince Henry, the king's eldest son;

---

his house in the country, about which time there had fallen much wet, Digby taking Fawkes aside after supper, told him he was much afraid that the powder in the cellar was grown damp, and that some new must be provided, lest that should not take fire."

Seeing, however, that the powder stood above ground, within a most substantial building, and could be reached by the rain only if this should first flood the Chamber of the Peers, it does not seem as if the idea of such a danger should have suggested itself.

Another interesting point in connection with the "cellar" is that the House of Lords having subsequently been removed to the Court of Requests, and afterwards to the Painted Chamber, "Guy Faukes' Cellar" on each occasion accompanied the migration. From Leigh's *New Picture of London* we find that in 1824-5, when the Court of Requests was in use, and the old cellar had completely disappeared, Guy's Cellar was still shown; while a plate given in Knight's *Old England*, and elsewhere, represents a vault under the Painted Chamber, not used as the House of Lords till after 1832. Such a cellar seems to have been considered a necessary appurtenance of the House.

but as he would probably accompany his father to the opening of Parliament, and so perish, their desire was to get hold of his brother, the Duke of York, afterwards Charles I., then but five years old. It was, however, possible that he too might go to Parliament, and otherwise it might not improbably be impossible to get possession of him: in which case they were prepared to be satisfied with the Princess Elizabeth,[1] or even with her infant sister Mary, for whom, as being English born, a special claim might be urged.

Such was the project in general. When we come to details, we are confronted, as might be anticipated, with statements impossible to reconcile. We are told,[2] that Percy undertook to seize and carry off Duke Charles; and again,[3] that, despairing of being able to lay hands upon him, they resolved "to serve themselves with the Lady Elizabeth," and that Percy was one of those who made arrangements for seizing her;[4] and again, that having learnt that Prince Henry was not to go to the House, they determined to surprise him, "and leave the young Duke alone;"[5] and once more, that they never entered into any consultation or formed any project whatever as to the succession.[6]

[1] Afterwards the Electress Palatine.
[2] Gardiner, *Hist.* i. 245; Lingard, vii. 59; T. Winter, November 23rd, 1605.
[3] Faukes, November 17th, 1605.
[4] Harry Morgan, *Examination* (R. O.), November 12th, 1605.
[5] T. Winter, November 23rd and 25th, 1605. As the information about Prince Henry was alleged to have been communicated by Lord Monteagle, the passage has been mutilated in the published version to conceal this circumstance.
[6] Faukes, November 5th, 1605.

Still more serious are the contradictions on another point. We are told, on the one hand, that a proclamation was drawn up for the inauguration of the new sovereign—whoever this was [1]—and, on the other, that the associates were resolved not to avow the explosion to be their work until they should see how the country took it, or till they had gathered a sufficient force,[2] and accordingly that they had no more than a project of a proclamation to be issued in due season. But, again, it is said [3] that Catesby on his way out of town, after the event, was to proclaim the new monarch at Charing Cross, though it is equally hard to understand, either how he was to know which of the plans had succeeded, and who that monarch was to be,—whether a king or a queen,—or what effect such proclamation by an obscure individual like himself was expected to produce; or how this, or indeed any item in the programme was compatible with the incognito of the actors in the great tragedy.

Amid this hopeless tangle one point alone is perfectly clear. Whatever was the scheme, it was absolutely insane, and could by no possibility have succeeded. As Mr. Gardiner says:[4] "With the advantage of having an infant sovereign in their hands, with a little money and a few horses, these sanguine dreamers fancied that they would have the whole of England at their feet."

Such is in outline the authorized version of the history concerning what Father John Gerard styles

[1] Sir E. Digby, Barlow's *Gunpowder Treason*, App. 249.
[2] Faukes, November 17th, 1605.
[3] Digby, *ut sup.*
[4] *History*, i. 239.

CELL IN STAIRCASE TURRET, S. E. CORNER, PAINTED CHAMBER, OFTEN CALLED "GUY FAUKES' CELL."

"this preposterous Plot of Powder;" and preposterous it undoubtedly appears to be in more senses than he intended. It is, in the first place, almost impossible to believe that the important and dramatic episode of the mine ever, in fact, occurred. We have seen something of the difficulties against accepting this part of the story, which the circumstantial evidence suggests. When, on the other hand, we ask upon what testimony it rests, it is a surprise to find that for so prominent and striking an incident we are wholly dependent upon two documents, published by the government, a confession of Thomas Winter and another of Faukes, both of which present features rendering them in the highest degree suspicious. Amongst the many confessions and declarations made by the conspirators in general, and these individuals in particular, these two alone describe the mining operations.[1]

On the other hand, it is somewhat startling to find no less a person than the Earl of Salisbury himself ignorant or oblivious of so remarkable a circumstance. In Thomas Winter's lodging was found the agreement between Percy and Ferrers for the lease of the house,

---

[1] There is also an allusion to the same in the confession of Keyes, November 30th, 1605; but this document also is of a highly suspicious character. Of the seven miners, none but these three were taken alive; Catesby, Percy, and the two Wrights being killed in the field. Strangely enough, though Keyes may be cited as a witness on this subject, on which his evidence is of such singular importance, the government, for some purpose of its own, tampered with the confession of Faukes wherein he is mentioned as one of the excavators, substituting Robert Winter's name for his, and placing Keyes amongst those "that wrought not in the myne." See Jardine's remarks on this point, *Criminal Trials*, ii. 6.

which was taken, as has been said, in May, 1604. This is still preserved, and has been endorsed by Cecil, "The bargaine between Percy and Ferrers for the bloody sellar. . . ." But this contract had nothing to do with the "bloody sellar," which was not rented till ten months later. Again, writing November 9th, 1605, to Cornwallis and Edmondes, Cecil says: "This Percy had about a year and a half ago hired a part of Vyniard's house in the old Palace, from whence he had access into this vault to lay his wood and coal, and as it seemeth now [had] taken this place of purpose to work some mischief in a fit time." When this was written the premises had been for four days in the hands of the government. It is clearly impossible that the remains of the mine, had they existed, should not have been found, and equally so that Cecil should not have alluded to the overwhelming evidence they afforded as to the intention of Percy and his associates to "work some mischief," but should, again, have connected the tenancy of the house only with the "cellar."

It will, moreover, be found by investigators that when exceptional stress is laid on any point by Sir E. Coke, the Attorney General, a *prima facie* case against the genuine nature of the evidence in regard of that point is thereby established. In his speech on the trial of the conspirators we find him declaring that, "If the cellar had not been hired, the mine work could hardly, or not at all, have been discovered, for the mine was neither found nor suspected until the danger was past, and the capital offenders apprehended, and by themselves, upon examination, confessed." That is to say, the government could not, though provided with information that there was a powder-mine under the Parliament House, have discovered this extraordinary piece of engineering; and moreover, after its abandonment, the traces of the excavation were so artfully hidden as to elude observation till the prisoners drew attention to them. Such assertions cannot possibly be true; but they might serve to meet the objection that no one had seen the mine.

We likewise find that in his examination of November 5th, Faukes is made to say: "He confesseth that about Christmas last [1604], he brought in the night-time Gunpowder *to the cellar under the upper house of Parliament,*" that is some three months before the cellar was hired. Moreover, the words italicised have been added as an interlineation, apparently by Cecil himself. Evidently when this was done the mine was still undiscovered.

Yet more remarkable is the fact that it would appear to have remained undiscovered ever afterwards, and that no marks seem to have been left upon the wall which had been so roughly handled. It is certainly impossible to find any record that such traces were observed when the building was demolished, though they could scarcely have failed to attract attention and interest. On this subject we have the important evidence of Mr. William Capon, who carefully examined every detail connected with the old palace, and evidently had the opportunity of studying the foundations of the House of Lords when, in 1823, that building was removed.[1] He does, in-

[1] His detailed notes and plans are given in *Vetusta Monumenta*, vol. v.

deed, mention what he conceives to be the traces of the conspirators' work, of which he gives the following description :

"Adjoining the south end of the Cellar, or more properly the ancient Kitchen, to the west, was a small room separated only by a stone doorway, with a pointed head, and with very substantial masonry joined to the older walls. . . . At the North side [of this] there had been an opening, a doorway of very solid thick stonemasonry, through which was a way seemingly forced through by great violence. . . . In 1799 it was asserted that this was always understood to have been the place where the conspirators broke into the vault which adjoined that called Guy Vaux's cellar."[1]

But against such a supposition there are three fatal objections. (1) This places the conspirators on the wrong side of the house, for they most certainly worked from the east, or river side, not from the west.[2] (2) It makes the mine above ground instead of below. (3) The conspirators never broke into the cellar at all, but hired it in the ordinary way of business.

Such considerations as the above may well make us sceptical in regard to the mine, and if this element of the story, upon which so much stress has always been laid, prove to be untrustworthy, it must needs follow that grave suspicion will be cast upon the rest.

There are, likewise, various problems in connection with the "cellar," especially as concerns the means of ingress to it, and its consequent privacy or publicity.

---

[1] Page 4.   [2] See Appendix E, *Site of Percy's house.*

(*a*) Faukes says (November 6th, 1605) that about the middle of Lent of that year Percy caused "a new dore" to be made into it, "that he might have a neerer way out of his own house into the cellar."

This seems to imply that Percy took the cellar for his firewood when there was no convenient communication between it and his house. Moreover it is not very easy to understand how a tenant under such conditions as his was allowed at discretion to knock doors through the walls of a royal palace. Neither did the landlady say anything of this door-making, when detailing what she knew about Percy's proceedings.

(*b*) In some notes by Sir E. Coke,[1] it is said: "The powder was first brought into Percy's house, and lay there in a low room new built, and could not have been conveyed into the cellar by the old door but that all the street must have seen it; and therefore he caused a new door out of his house into the cellar to be made, where before there had been a grate of iron."

This, it must be confessed, looks very like an afterthought to explain away a difficulty, but failing to do so. When the door is said to have been made, the powder was already on the premises, having been brought there in sight of the whole street and the river. It could hardly, in so small a tenement, escape the observation of the workmen,[2] while the operations of these latter in breaking through the wall

[1] Tanner MSS. lxxv. § 185, b.
[2] Faukes, November 6th, uses the same expression, "a low room new builded," which seems to imply that this receptacle had been constructed since Percy came into possession of the house.

would have served yet farther to attract the attention of the neighbourhood.

(c) We are told by Faukes and others, that either he or Percy always kept the key, and that marks were made to indicate whether anyone had entered the place in their absence.

(d) On the other hand, to say nothing of Winter's declaration that the confederates so arranged as to leave the cellar free for all to enter who would, Lord Salisbury informed Sir Thomas Parry [1] that the captors of Faukes entered through "another door," which clearly did not require to be opened by him; while as to the ordinary door, whichever this was, the "King's Book" itself plainly intimates, in the account of the chamberlain's visit, that Whynniard, the landlord, was able to open it when he chose.

The "other door" spoken of by Cecil, a most important feature of the chamber, is nowhere else mentioned.[2]

It appears certain that the conspirators really had a plot in hand, that they fancied themselves to be about to strike a great blow, and that by means of gunpowder; but what was the precise nature of their plans and preparations it is not so easy to determine. Farther discussion of these particulars must be deferred to a later chapter. Meanwhile, according to the accepted history, when they had stored their powder there was nothing more to do but to await the assem-

---

[1] November 6th, 1605. More will be seen of the important document containing this information.

[2] According to Smith's plan (*sup.* p. 59) there were four entrances to the cellar, none of which can have been Percy's "new dore."

THE POWDER PLOT. II.

bling of the intended victims. Parliament stood prorogued till October 3rd, and was afterwards further adjourned till the fateful 5th of November. That they might not excite suspicion, the confederates separated, most of them retiring to their country seats, and Faukes going over to Flanders.[1] In his absence Percy kept the key of the cellar, and, according to Faukes,[2] laid in more powder and wood while he himself was absent.

It is not easy to understand what became of the cellar during this long interval, and apparently it was left in great measure, with its compromising contents, to take care of itself, for Percy, amongst other places, went with Catesby to Bath to take the waters.[3] If the premises were of so public a nature as the testimony of Winter and others would imply, it appears impossible that they should have remained all this time sealed up, or that these astute and crafty plotters should with a light heart have ignored the probability that they would be visited and inspected. As Father Greenway observes,[4] it can hardly be supposed that the landlord[5]

---

[1] We are told that Faukes was selected to take charge of the house, and perform other duties which would bring him into notice, because being unknown in London he was not likely to excite remark. In his declaration, November 8th, however, he gives as his reason for going abroad, "lest, being a dangerous man, he should be known and suspected." It is obvious that in the meantime the cellar must either have been left in charge of others better known, and therefore more likely to excite suspicion, or have been left unprotected.

[2] November 17th, 1605.

[3] Thomas Winter, November 23rd, 1605.

[4] F. 66.

[5] This, as we have heard, was Mr. Whynniard, who unfor-

had not a duplicate key, while Cecil himself, in his letter to Sir Thomas Parry, plainly indicates that access to the cellar could freely be procured independently of the conspirators. We can only say that the conduct of the confederates in this particular appears to have been quite in keeping with their method of conspiring secretly as we have already seen it, and undoubtedly one more difficulty is thus opposed to the supposition that their enterprise was chiefly dangerous on account of the clandestine and dexterous manner in which it was conducted.

tunately died very suddenly on the morning of November 5th, on hearing of the "discovery," evidence of great importance as to the hiring of the house and "cellar" being thus lost. "As for the keeper of the parliament house," says Goodman, "who let out the lodgings to Percy, it is said that as soon as ever he heard of the news what Percy intended, he instantly fell into a fright and died; so that it could not be certainly known who procured him the house, or by whose means."—*Court o King James*, i. 107.

CHAPTER V.

THE GOVERNMENT INTELLIGENCE DEPARTMENT.

HAVING followed the history of the plotters and their doings, to the point when everything was ready for action, we have now to inquire what, in the meantime, those were about for whose destruction such notable preparations were making, and whether in truth they were, as we are assured, wrapped in a sense of false security, and altogether unconscious of the signs and tokens that should have awakened their suspicion and alarm.

When, by the aid of such evidence as remains to us, we turn to examine the facts of the case, we discover in them, it must be confessed, no symptoms whatever of supineness or lethargy. It appears, on the contrary, that throughout the period when the government are supposed to have been living in a fool's paradise, and tranquilly assuming that all was well, they were in reality busily at work through their emissaries and informers, prying into all the doings of the recusant Catholics, receiving frequent intimation of all that was undertaken, or even projected, and, apparently, regulating the main features of a treasonable conspiracy, which can have been no other than the Powder Plot itself, determining, in particular, what individuals should be implicated therein.

In April, 1604, at the very time when we hear of the Plot as being hatched, a letter was addressed to Sir Thomas Challoner, an official frequently mixed up with business of this kind, by one Henry Wright,[1] reporting the proceedings of a subordinate agent, by name Davies, whom he styles a "discoverer,"[2] then engaged in working a Catholic treason, with the special object of incriminating priests. Davies has offered to "set," or mark down,[3] over threescore of these, but Wright has told him that so many are not required, and that he will satisfy his employers if he implicate twenty, provided they be "most principal Jesuits and seminary priests," and therewithal has given him thirteen or fourteen names that will serve the required purpose. Davies replies, "that by God's grace he will absolutely do it ere long."[4]

That the treason in question was none other than the Gunpowder Plot there can be no question, unless indeed we are to say that the authorities were engaged in fabricating a bogus conspiracy for which there was no foundation whatever in fact. It was not the way of statesmen of the period, when on the track of sedition, to relinquish the pursuit till they had sifted it to the bottom, and at this juncture, especially, every shred of evidence regarding Catholics and their conduct was threshed out to the uttermost. In consequence, we are able to say with certainty, that

---

[1] He appears to have been no relation of John and Christopher Wright, the conspirators.

[2] Davies was employed in other affairs of a similar nature. See *Dom. James I.*, xix. 83, 1 (P. R. O.).

[3] Cf. a "setter dog."

[4] See the full text of Wright's letter, Appendix G.

besides the enterprise of Catesby and his associates, there was no other conspiracy of any kind on foot. We have, moreover, already seen that the very same point thus by anticipation represented as all important, is that which after the "discovery" every nerve was strained to establish, namely, the complicity of the Catholic clergy. If we had no more than this internal evidence, it would abundantly suffice to assure us that the conspiracy thus sedulously watched was the same as that miraculously "discovered" a year and a half later.

But we are not left to such inferences alone. In March, 1606, we find Wright applying to the minister for a reward on account of his services "in discovering villainous practices," thus indicating that by this time those which he had been tracking had been brought to light. More explicit still is a memorial presented to the king, at a later date, on his behalf. This is entitled—"Touching Wright and his services performed *in the damnable plot of the Powder treason.*" King James is reminded that Chief Justice Popham and Sir Thomas Challoner had a hand in the discovery of the Powder, and this by means of information supplied by Wright, "for two years space almost" before his Majesty interpreted the famous letter to Lord Monteagle, "like an angel of God." This information Popham and Challoner had from time to time communicated to his Majesty, "whose hand Wright hath in testimony of his services in the matter."[1]

In the same month of April, 1604, was supplied

---

[1] See the text of the memorial, Appendix G.

another piece of information, singularly interesting and important,[1] in which were detailed the particulars of a design amongst the Catholics at home and abroad. Much, in fact the bulk, of the information given, is seen, in the light of our present knowledge, to be purely fictitious, affording a good example of the "sophistications" which, as Cecil himself complained, his agents were wont to mingle with their intelligence. The design in question was represented as being of the most serious and secret nature, the papists thinking that it "must now be so handled and carried as the great cause may lose no reputation, or if any suspicion should grow in the state, or any come in question therefore, the main point might never come to light;" the said "main point" being of course the complicity of the Catholic clergy.

What invests this document with singular importance is the fact that we hear of it again. In April, 1606, it was quoted for the benefit of Parliament by the Attorney General, Sir E. Coke, and explicitly as having reference to the Gunpowder Plot, forming part of the evidence adduced by him to secure the attainder of persons accused of being partakers in that treason.[2] It thus affords a proof, on the authority of the government itself, that eighteen months before the conspiracy was "discovered," intelligence regarding it had been received and was being attended to.

---

[1] Copy in the P. R. O. *Dom. James I.* vii. 86, and xx. 52. The informer's name is given in the latter, viz., Ralph Ratcliffe.

[2] It was likewise cited in the interrogatories prepared for the Jesuit Thomas Strange (Brit. Mus. *MSS. Add.* 6178, 74) in November, 1605, and in this case also as treating of the Gunpowder Plot and no other.

A VIEW OF THE HOUSE OF PEERS, 1755.

This is, however, by no means the only information of which we find traces. Amongst the Cecil papers at Hatfield is a letter dated December 20th, 1605, addressed to the Earl of Salisbury by one Thomas Coe, who claims to have previously forwarded to his Majesty "the primary intelligence of these late dangerous treasons," upon which communication the historian Lodge observes,[1] "It should seem then that the famous letter transmitted to James by Lord Monteagle, for the right construction of which that Prince's penetration hath been so highly extolled by some historians, was not the only previous intelligence communicated to him of the Gunpowder Treason."

Meanwhile the officers of the government, in all parts, appear to have been no less alert than was their wont. On the 9th of January, 1604-5, for instance, Sir Thomas Parry writes from Paris,[2] inclosing a note from an informer at Dieppe, concerning an English Catholic returning from Italy and Spain with letters for Fathers Garnet and Oldcorne, and a cipher of three lines for a lawyer at Douay, and although the messenger has contrived to give him the slip, he is able to send particulars concerning his personal appearance, and the locality in London where he is likely to be found. On the 25th of the same month, Cecil replies to Parry[3] concerning priests and their doings, and makes the valuable admission that their proceedings are always known to him by means of false brethren, though, he adds, these informers always add to their intelligence "sophistications" of their own, a fact which must not be lost sight of in studying the

---

[1] *Illustrations*, iii. 301.
[2] P. R. O. *France*, b. 132.   [3] *Ibid.*

reports of such folk. We hear particularly of informations supplied by the priests Bagshawe and Cecil, by Captain Turner, Charles Paget, and sundry others.

At the beginning of October, 1605, we make the acquaintance of another notable informer. On the first of the month, William Willaston, then engaged on a commission in France in connection with a proposed commercial treaty, writes to Cecil from Paris[1] concerning a Catholic design attributed chiefly to priests and Jesuits, who have assurance that their friends in England, who are many and of good sort, intend "to kindle a fire in many corners of our land, and a rebellion in Ireland," and that these matters be almost grown to a head, " some of their fingers itching to be set to work." Willaston adds, "there is a particular irreconcilable desperate malice against your Honour's person, which is principally the cause I make bold to write unto your Lordship. You have yet the papists in your hands, and are masters; if you let them increase and grow so insolent, assuredly it will come to pass as to the King of Israel, who having overthrown Benhadab..." and so on.

On October 14th, Willaston again writes from Rouen[2] "about some matters pretended by our Romish Catholics." The party, he says, "who" has given light into this business "is one George Southwaick, well-known to many of your Lordship's followers." This Southwaick, he holds to be "very honest;" he is going to England with sundry priests and others, and upon landing will at once communicate with the authorities and have his comrades arrested. "South-

---

[1] P. R. O. *France*, bundle 132. [2] *Ibid.* f. 273 b.

waick himself," adds Willaston, "must be taken as well as the others, for he desireth not to be known to have given any information against the rest. If it please your Lordship to take order for his imprisonment apart, that conference privately may be had with him, until such time as shall be thought fit to deliver him, he can give you good directions for many matters, and may stand your honour in stead for such purposes."

There follows a notable suggestion: "If your Lordship would be pleased to set some man to win the Nuncio of the Pope his secretary in Paris, you should receive very direct and sound instructions from him." The writer goes on to speak of an intended rebellion in England, and the kindling of a fire there, and dutifully concludes, "God grant they touch not the person of the King nor of his children."

On the 27th of October, nine days before the "discovery," Southwaick himself, now in England, writes to Cecil,[1] urging that the impending arrest of priests and others should be deferred, and that for better management of "the business, and for the better and more substantial manifestation thereof," he ventures to suggest that "more scope of time would make the service of more worth." Moreover, he gives warning of preparations for trouble in the shires, in connection with "their plot," and finally promises, "your Honour shall not only have knowledge of all such as are any way intercepted in the same, but also knowledge of the end of their whole purpose, and withal be certain of their meeting here in London, where I do not doubt to apprehend forty priests, with many great of name, at mass, in good speed of their great intent."

[1] Hatfield MSS. 112, n. 141.

On the morning of the 5th of November itself, evidently before receiving news that the final blow had been struck, Southwaick writes to Levinus Munck, Cecil's private secretary.[1] He excuses himself for recent silence on the ground that he could not without prejudice to "the business" have communicated with his employers. "The parties," he declares, "have had, ever since I saw you, such obscure meetings, such mutable purposes, such uncertain resolutions, as hath made me ride both day and night, as well in foul weather as fair, omitting no opportunities, lest I should not effect what I have by the weight of my credit and the engagement of my duty and reputation propounded to my honourable Lord." He farther begs that nothing may be done that might disclose his true character to his intended victims, and concludes by declaring that, if he be not much mistaken, he is about "a singular service."

If such letters proved nothing more, they would abundantly serve to discredit the idea that a government which conducted its operations in such a fashion could be hoodwinked by such clumsy contrivances as those of the cellar and the mine.

Five days later,[2] Southwaick again writes to Munck, inclosing a note of the priests who have had meetings in Paris, or have been written to in England. The Ambassador (in Paris) will, he says, bear witness that, although unable to particularize, he had given notice two months since that there was a plot brewing. He adds a significant hint, the like of which we have

---

[1] P. R. O. *Gunpowder Plot Book*, 16.
[2] November 10th, 1605, *Dom. James I.* xvi. 44.

already seen: "Should I chance to be apprehended, I will rest myself upon my honourable Lord."[1]

Meanwhile the English ambassadors abroad were no less active and vigilant than the informers at home, and while clearly aware that there was some danger on foot, never doubted that the king's government would not be caught napping.

On the 9th of October, Sir Thomas Edmondes wrote to Cecil from Brussels[2] to warn him of suspicious symptoms in the Low Countries; and on the following day Cecil wrote to Edmondes[3] expressing apprehensions of trouble from the Jesuits abroad. On the same day, October 10th, Sir Thomas Parry wrote from Paris to the secretary,[4] of a petition which the Catholics were preparing against the meeting of Parliament, "and some further designs upon refusal;" and in another letter informed Edmondes:[5] "somewhat is at present in hand amongst these desperate hypocrites, which I trust God shall divert, by the vigilant care of his Majesty's faithful servants and friends abroad, and prudence of his council at home."

That such confidence was not misplaced is shown by Cecil's assurance to Sir Thomas Parry,[6] mentioned above, that the proceedings of the priests were never unknown to Government.

Amongst the papers at Hatfield is a curious note,

---

[1] At a later period (July 20th, 1606) we find that Southwaick ("or Southwell") had lost favour and was warned by Salisbury to leave the country. "I hold him," says the Earl, "to be a very impostor." (*To Edmondes*, Phillipps MS. f. 165.)
[2] Stowe MSS., 168, 39.   [3] *Ibid.* 40.
[4] *Ibid.* 42.   [5] Birch, *Historical View*, p. 234.
[6] P. R. O. *France*, bundle 132, January 25th, 1604-5.

anonymous and undated, giving information of a plot involving murder and treason, which, like the letter to Monteagle, simulates rather too obviously the workmanship of an illiterate person, and artfully insinuates that the design in question is undertaken in the name of religion, and chiefly favoured by the priests.[1]

Another remarkable document is preserved in the same collection. This is a letter written to Sir Everard Digby, June 11th, 1605, and treating of an otter hunt to be undertaken when the hay shall be cut. It has, however, been endorsed by Salisbury, " Letter written to Sir Everard Digby—Powder Treason."[2] Not only is it hard to see how the terms

---

[1] "Who so evar finds this box of letars let him carry hit to the Kings magesty: my mastar litel thinks I knows of this, but yn ridinge wth him that browt the letar to my mastar to a Katholyk gentlemans hows anward of his way ynto lin konsher [Lincolnshire], he told me al his purpos, and what he ment to do; and he beinge a prest absolved me and mad me swar nevar to revel hit to ane man. I confes myself a Katholyk, and do hate the protystans relygon with my hart, and yit I detest to consent ethar to murdar or treson. I have blotyd out sartyn nams in the letars becas I wold not have ethar my mastar or ane of his frends trobyl aboute this; for by his menes I was mad a goud Katholyk, and I wod to God the King war a good Katholyk: that is all the harm I wish him; and let him tak hed what petysons or suplycasons he take of ane man; and I hop this box will be found by som that will giv hit to the King, hit may do him good one day. I men not to com to my mastar any moe, but wil return unto my contry from whens I cam. As for my nam and contry I consel that; and God make the King a goud Katholyk; and let Ser Robart Sesil and my lord Cohef Gustyse lok to them selvse." (Printed in Appendix to *Third Report of Historical MSS. Commission*, p. 148.)

[2] It is signed "G. D.," and was possibly written by a relation of Sir Everard's.

of the document lend themselves to such an interpretation, but the date at which it was written was fully three months prior to Digby's initiation in the conspiracy. The idea is certainly suggested that, far from being passive and indolent, the authorities were sedulously seeking pretexts to entangle as many as possible of those "great of name," concerning whom we have already heard from one of their informers. This much, at any rate, seems clear. Those at the centre of this complex web of espionage, to whom were addressed all these informations and admonitions, cannot have been, as they protested somewhat overmuch, in a state of careless inactivity, depending for security only upon the protection of the Almighty, "who," as the secretary afterwards piously declared, "blessed us in our slumber [and] will not forsake us now that we are awake."[1]

The slumber would at least appear not to have been dreamless. On the one hand, the secretary was evidently much exercised by a threatened *rapprochement* between his royal master and Pope Clement VIII., who, through a Scotch Catholic gentleman, Sir James Lindsay, had sent a friendly message to King James, which had elicited a courteous and almost cordial reply.[2] The significance of this Cecil

[1] To Sir H. Bruncard, March 3rd, 1605-6. P. R. O. *Ireland*, vol. 218.

[2] "Instructions to my trusty servant Sir James Lindsay, for answer to the lettre and Commission brought by him from the Pope unto me." Aº 1604. (P. R. O. *France*, b. 132.)

In these notes the king explains that the things of greatest import cannot be written, but have been imparted "by tongue" to the envoy, to be delivered to his holiness. Moreover he thus charges Lindsay: "You shall assure him that I shall never be

strenuously endeavoured, in a letter to the Duke of Lenox,[1] to explain away, and in February, 1604-5, we find him assuring the Archbishop of York with an earnestness somewhat suspicious,[2] "I love not to procure or yield any toleration; a matter which I well know no creature living durst propound to our religious Sovereign." For himself, he thus declares: "I will be much less than I am, or rather nothing at all, before I shall become an instrument of such a miserable change." Nevertheless, on the 17th of April following, he was fain to acknowledge, in writing to Parry,[3] that the news of Pope Clement's death had much eased him in his mind.

It would, however, appear that the spectre of possible toleration still haunted him, and that he felt it necessary to commit the king to a course of severity. In a minute of September 12th, 1605, addressed to the same ambassador, which has been corrected and amended with an amount of care sufficiently testifying to the importance of the subject,[4] after speaking of "the plots and business of the priests," and the tendency of Englishmen going abroad "in this time

---

forgetful of the continual proof I have had of his courtesy and long inclination towards me, and especially by this his so courteous and unexpected message, which I shall be careful to requite thankfully by all civil courtesies that shall be in my power, the particulars whereof I remit likewise to your declaration." Besides this, he protests that he will ever inviolably observe two points: first, never to dissemble what he thinks, especially in matters of conscience; secondly, never to reject reason when he hears it urged on the other side.

[1] P. R. O. *France*, b. 132.
[2] Lodge, *Illustrations*, iii. 262.
[3] P. R. O. *France*, b. 132.   [4] *Ibid.*

of peace" to become Catholics, he thus continues: "Only this is it wherein my own heart receiveth comfort, that we live under a most religious and understanding Prince, who sticketh not to publish, as well in his own particular, as in the form of his government, how contrary that religion is to his resolution, and how far he will be from ever gracing [it]." He goes on to declare that nothing will so avail to make his Majesty withdraw his countenance from any man as such "falling away."

About the same time as this was written, we are told by a writer, almost a contemporary,[1] that a dependent of Cecil's warned a Catholic gentleman, by name Buck, of a "wicked design" which his master had in hand against the papists.

On the 17th of October, more than a week before the first hint of danger is said to have been breathed, we find the minister writing to Sir Thomas Edmondes, at Brussels,[2] in terms which certainly appear to couple together the growing danger of conversions to Catholicism, of which we have heard above, and the remedy soon to be supplied by the new policy which the discovery of the Plot so effectively established. He speaks of the "insolencies" of the priests and Jesuits, who are doing much injury by infecting with their poison "every youth that cometh amongst them;" ominously adding, "which liberty must, for one cause or another, be retrenched."

There can be no doubt that the issue of the Gunpowder Plot was eminently calculated to work such

---

[1] *The Politician's Catechism*, 1658.
[2] Birch, *Historical View*, p. 234.

an effect; and even more would seem to have been anticipated from it than was actually realized, for the secretary, we are told, promised King James that in consequence of it not a single Jesuit should remain in England.

In the accounts supplied to us as to the manner of the "discovery," we obtain much interesting information from the utterances of the government itself. In studying these we cannot fail to notice an evident effort to reconcile two conflicting interests. On the one hand, that the king and the nation should be properly impressed with a sense of their marvellous deliverance, it was essential to represent the catastrophe as having been imminent, which could not be unless the preparations for it had been altogether unsuspected; and it was likewise desirable to magnify the divine sagacity of the monarch, which had been the instrument of Providence to avert a disaster otherwise inevitable. On the other hand, however, it should not be made to appear that those to whose keeping the public safety was intrusted had shown themselves culpably negligent or incompetent; and it had therefore to be insinuated that, after all, they were not without "sufficient advertisement" of danger, and even of danger specifically connected with the actual conspirators, and directed against the Parliament. But, again, lest such information should appear suspiciously accurate, the actual plotters had to be merged in a larger body of their co-religionists, and their design to be represented in vague and general terms. At the time, no doubt, this was effective enough. Now however that we know, by the light of subsequent investigations, who exactly were engaged, and what was in hand, it is possible to estimate these declarations at their true value.[1]

Except with the aid of such an explanation as this, it seems impossible to understand the endless inconsistencies and contradictions of the official narrative. This we have in four forms, all coming to us on the highest authority, but addressed to different audiences, and hopelessly at variance upon almost every point. One is that given to the world as the "King's Book,"[2] containing, as Mr. Jardine tells us, the version which it was desired that the general public should accept. A second was furnished by Cecil himself to the ambassadors at Madrid and Brussels, and the Lord Deputy in Ireland,[3] and a third to the ambassador at Paris.[4] We have likewise the minute of November 7th, already mentioned as perhaps intended for the information of the Privy Council, which, although it has seemingly served as the basis of the story told in the

---

[1] "If the Priestes and Catholickes, so many thousands in England would have entertayned it, no man can be so malicious and simple to thinke but there would have been a greater assembly than fourscore [in the Midlands] to take such an action in hand, and the Council could not be so winking eyed, but they would have found forth some one or other culpable, which they could never do, though some of them, most powerable in it, tendered and racked forth their hatred against us to the uttermost limites they could extend." *English Protestants' plea*, p. 60.

[2] *Discourse of the manner of the discovery of the Gunpowder Plot.* Printed in the Collected Works of King James, by Bishop Mountague, by Bishop Barlow, in *Gunpowder Treason*, and in Cobbett's *State Trials*, as an appendix to that of the conspirators.

[3] *I.e.*, Cornwallis, Edmondes, and Chichester. The despatch to Cornwallis is printed in Winwood's *Memorials*, ii. 170.

[4] Sir Thoms Parry, P. R. O. *France*, bundle 132.

"King's Book," contradicts that story in various not unimportant particulars.

We shall afterwards have to examine in some detail the divergencies of these several narratives : at present we are concerned only with the intimation which they afford of a previous knowledge of the Plot on the part of the government. In the " King's Book "—which was not only to be disseminated broadcast at home, but to be translated and spread abroad, and, moreover, to be suited to the taste of its supposed author—the preternatural acuteness of the monarch is extolled in terms of most preposterous flattery, and his secretary is represented as altogether incredulous of danger, and unwilling to be convinced even by his royal master's wonderful interpretation of the mysterious warning. Nevertheless, not only is mention parenthetically introduced of the minister's "customable and watchful care of the king and State, boiling within him," of his laying up these things in his heart, "like the Blessed Virgin Mary," and being unable to rest till he had followed the matter farther,—but it is dexterously intimated that, for all his hardness of belief, he was sufficiently well informed before the warning came to hand, and that "this accident did put him in mind of divers advertisements he had received from beyond the seas, wherewith he had acquainted as well the king himself, as divers of his Privy Councillors, concerning some business the Papists were in, both at home and abroad, making combination amongst them for some combination against this Parliament time," their object being to approach the king with a petition for toleration, "which should be delivered in some such order, and so well backed, as the king should be loth to refuse their requests; like the sturdy beggars craving alms with one open hand, but carrying a stone in the other, in case of refusal."

As prepared for the Privy Council, the account, though substantially the same, was somewhat more explicit. The secretary was fully aware, so the Lords were told, "that some practices might be doubted," and he "had, any time these three months, acquainted the King, and some of his Majesty's inward Counsellors, that the priests and laymen abroad and at home were full of the papists of this kingdom, seeking still to lay some *plot* for procuring at this Parliament exercise of their religion."

In his letter to the ambassadors Cecil was able to speak more plainly, for this document was not to meet the eye of James. Accordingly, he not only acknowledges that on seeing the Monteagle letter he at once divined the truth, and understood all about the powder, and moreover reverses the parts played by his Majesty and himself—making the former incredulous in spite of what he himself could urge in support of his opinion—but he goes on to give his previous information a far more definite complexion: "Not but that I had sufficient advertisement that most of these that now are fled [*i.e.* the conspirators]—being all notorious Recusants—with many others of that kind, had a practice in hand for some stir this Parliament." He, moreover, describes the plotters, in terms already cited, as "gentlemen spent in their fortunes and fit for all alterations."

In view of all this it is quite impossible to believe the account given of themselves by those who were responsible for the public safety, and to suppose that they were not only so neglectful of their duty, but so incredibly foolish, and so unlike themselves, as to permit a gross and palpable peril to approach unnoticed. If, on the other hand, as appears to be certain, the information with which they were supplied were copious and minute, erring by excess far more than by defect, if, instead of lethargy and carelessness, we find in their conduct, at every stage of the proceedings, evidence of the extremest vigilance and of constant activity, and if they held it of prime importance to disguise the facts, and were willing to incur the charge of having been asleep at their posts, rather than let it be thought that they knew what they did, it can scarcely be doubted that the history of the Gunpowder Plot given to the world was in its essential features what they wished it to be.[1]

A practical illustration of the methods freely employed by statesmen of the period will serve to throw fuller light upon this portion of our inquiry. In the service of the government was one Thomas Phelippes,[2] by trade a "decipherer," who was employed to "make English" of intercepted letters written in cipher. His services had been largely used in connection with Mary,

---

[1] Mr. Hepworth Dixon observes (*Her Majesty's Tower*, i. 352, seventh edition) that a man must have been in no common measure ignorant of Cecil and Northampton who could dream that such a design could escape the greatest masters of intrigue alive, and that abundant evidence makes it clear that the Council were informed of the Plot in almost every stage, and that their agents dogged the footsteps of those whom they suspected, taking note of all their proceedings. "It was no part of Cecil's policy," adds Mr. Dixon, "to step in before the dramatic time."

[2] Often called Phelipps, or Philipps.

Queen of Scots, some of whose letters he thus interpreted, having it in his power, as Mr. Tytler remarks, to garble or falsify them at pleasure.[1] Moreover, to serve the purposes of his masters, as he himself acknowledges,[2] he had upon occasion forged one side of a correspondence, in order to induce the person addressed to commit himself in reply.[3] At the time of the Gunpowder Plot, however, Phelippes had himself fallen under suspicion, on account of a correspondence with Hugh Owen, of whom we shall hear elsewhere. Accordingly, an attempt was made to hoist him with his own petard, and another agent, named Barnes, was employed by Cecil to write a letter, as coming from Phelippes (who was then in England) and carry it to Owen in Flanders in order to draw him out. At Dover, however, Barnes was arrested, being mistaken for another man for whom a watch was being kept. Thereupon, his papers being seized and sent to the Earl of Northampton, who appears not to have been in the secret of this matter, Cecil was obliged to arrest Phelippes at once, as though the letter were genuine, instead of waiting, as he had intended, in order to worm out more.

The story of this complex and crooked business is frankly told by Cecil himself in a letter to Edmondes,

---

[1] *History of Scotland*, iii. 376, note (ed. Eadie). It was on one of these letters which had been in the hands of Phelippes that Mary was convicted.

[2] *Dom. James I.* xx. 51. April, 1606.

[3] In the fragment cited above, Phelippes says that Queen Elizabeth and the Earl of Essex largely availed themselves of this device of his, and that "My Lord of Salisbury had himself made some use of it in the Queen's time."

English ambassador at Brussels, which, after the above abstract, will be sufficiently intelligible.[1]

"As for Barnes, he is now returning again into Flanders, with many vows and promises to continue to do good service. As he was at Dover with my pass, carrying a letter from Philipps to Owen (of Barnes own handwriting, wherewith I was before acquainted), he was suddenly stayed by order from the Lord Warden, upon suspicion that he was one Acton, a traitor of the late conspiracy. . . . Whereupon, his papers and letters being sent to my Lord of Northampton, I thought fit not to defer any longer the calling of Philipps into question; which till then I had forborne, hoping by Barnes his means to have discovered some further matter than before I could do."

[1] February 12th, 1605-6. (Stowe MSS. 168.)

CHAPTER VI.

THE "DISCOVERY."

WHEN the conspirators first undertook their enterprise, Parliament was appointed to meet on February 7th, 1604-5, but, as has been seen, it was subsequently prorogued till October 3rd, and then again till Tuesday, November 5th. On occasion of the October prorogation, the confederates employed Thomas Winter to attend the ceremony in order to learn from the demeanour of the assembled Peers whether any suspicion of their design had suggested this unexpected adjournment. He returned to report that no symptom could be discerned of alarm or uneasiness, and that the presence of the volcano underfoot was evidently unsuspected. Thus reassured, his associates awaited with confidence the advent of the fatal Fifth.

In the interval occurred the event which forms the official link connecting the secret and the public history of the Plot, namely, the receipt of the letter of warning by Lord Monteagle. That the document is of supreme importance in our history cannot be denied, for the government account clearly stands or falls with the assertion that this was in reality the means whereby the impending catastrophe was averted. That it was so, the official story proclaimed from the first with a vehemence in itself suspicious, and the famous letter was exhibited to the world with a persistence and solicitude not easy to explain; being printed in the "King's Book," and in every other account of the affair; while transcribed copies were

The gallant *Eagle*, foaring vp on high:
Beares in his beake, *Treafons* difcouery.
Movnt, noble Eagle, with thy happy prey,
And thy rich *Price* to th' *King* with fpeed conuay.

MONTEAGLE AND LETTER.

sent to the ambassadors at foreign courts and other public personages.[1] Had a warning really been given, in such a case, to save the life of a kinsman or friend,

---

[1] Copies were sent by Cecil to Cornwallis at Madrid, Parry at Paris, Edmondes at Brussels, and Chichester at Dublin. Also by Chamberlain to Dudley Carleton.

the circumstance, however fortunate, would scarcely have been wonderful, nor can we think that the document would thus have been multiplied for inspection. If, on the other hand, it had been carefully contrived for its purpose, it would not be unnatural for those who knew where the weak point lay, to wish the world to be convinced that there really had been a letter. It is, moreover, not easy to understand the importance attributed to Monteagle's service in connection with it. To have handed to the authorities such a message, evidently of an alarming nature, though he himself did not professedly understand it, does not appear to have entitled him to the extraordinary consideration which he in fact received. The Attorney General was specially instructed, at the trial, to extol his lordship's conduct.[1] Whereever, in the confession of the conspirators, his name was mentioned, it was erased, or pasted over with paper, or the whole passage was omitted before publication of the document. All this is easy to understand if he were the instrument employed for a critical and delicate transaction, depending for success upon his discretion and reticence. On any other supposition it seems inexplicable.

Moreover, Monteagle's services received most substantial acknowledgment in the form of a grant of

[1] "Lastly, and this you must not omit, you must deliver, in commendation of my Lord Mounteagle, words to show how sincerely he dealt, and how fortunately it proved that he was the instrument of so great a blessing, . . . because it is so lewdly given out that he was once of this plot of powder, and afterwards betrayed it all to me."—Cecil to Coke. (Draft in the R. O., printed by Jardine, *Criminal Trials*, ii. 120.)

£700 a year,[1] equivalent, at least, to ten times that amount in money of the present day.[2] There still exists [3] the draft preamble of the grant making this award, which has been altered and emended with an amount of care which sufficiently testifies to the importance of the matter. In this it is said of the letter that by the knowledge thereof " we had the first *and only* means to discover that most wicked and barbarous plot "—the words italicised being added as an interlineation by Cecil himself. Nevertheless, it appears certain that this is not, and cannot be, the truth; indeed, historians of all shades equally discountenance the idea. Mr. Jardine [4] considers it "hardly credible that the letter was really the means by which the plot was discovered," and inclines to the belief [5] that the whole story concerning it "was merely a device of the government ... to conceal the means by which their information had been derived." Similarly Mr. J. S. Brewer [6] holds it as certain that this part, at least, of the story is a fiction designed to conceal the truth. Mr. Gardiner, who is less inclined than others to give up the received story, thinks that, to say the least of it, it is highly probable that Monteagle expected the letter before it came.[7]

For a right understanding of the point it is neces-

---

[1] £500 as an annuity for life, and £200 per annum to him and his heirs for ever in fee farm rents.

[2] See Thorold Rogers, *Agriculture and Prices*, v. 631, and Jessopp, *One Generation of a Norfolk House*, p. 285.

[3] R. O. *Dom. James I*. xx. 56.

[4] *Criminal Trials*, ii. 65.   [5] *Ibid*. 68.

[6] Note on Fuller's *Church History*, x. § 39, and *on The Student's Hume*.

[7] *History*, i. 251.

sary to consider the character of the man who plays so important a part in this episode. Lord Monteagle, the eldest son of Lord Morley, ennobled under a title derived through his mother, was, in Mr. Jardine's opinion,[1] " a person precisely adapted for an instrument on such an occasion;" and the description appears even more applicable than was intended. He had been implicated in all the doings of the turbulent section of the English Catholics [2] for several years, having taken part in the rising of Essex, and in the Spanish negotiations, whatever they were, conducted through the instrumentality of Thomas Winter. With Catesby, and others of the conspirators, he was on terms of the closest and most intimate friendship, and Tresham was his brother-in-law. A letter of his to Catesby is still preserved, which, in the opinion of some, affords evidence of his having been actually engaged in the Powder Plot itself;[3] and Mr. Jardine, though dissenting from the view that the letter proves so much, judges it not at all impossible or improbable that he was in fact privy to the conspiracy. It is likewise certain that up to the last moment Monteagle was on familiar terms with the plotters, to whom, a few days before the final catastrophe, he imparted an important piece of information.[4]

[1] *Criminal Trials*, ii. 69.

[2] On March 13th, 1600-1, Monteagle wrote to Cecil from the Tower, " My conscience tells me that I am no way gilty of these Imputations, and that mearely the blindness of Ignorance lead me into these infamous errors." (Brit. Mus. MSS. Add. 6177).

[3] The letter is printed in *Archæologia*, xxviii. 422, by Mr. Bruce, who argues from it Monteagle's complicity with the Plot. Mr. Jardine's reply is found *ibid.* xxix. 80.

[4] According to T. Winter's famous declaration, Monteagle,

At the same time it is evident that Monteagle was in high favour at Court, as is sufficiently evidenced by the fact that he was appointed to be one of the commissioners for the prorogation of October 3rd, a most unusual distinction for one in his position, as also by the pains taken by the government on behalf of his brother, who had shortly before got himself into trouble in France.[1] A still more remarkable circumstance has been strangely overlooked by historians.[2] Monteagle always passed for a Catholic, turbulent indeed and prone to violence, but attached, even fanatically, to his creed, like his friend Catesby and the rest. There remains, however, an undated letter of his to the king,[3] in which he expresses his determination to become a Protestant; and while in fulsome language extolling his Majesty's zeal for his spiritual welfare, speaks with bitterness and contempt of the faith which, nevertheless, he continued to profess to the end of his life, and that without exciting suspicion of his deceit among the Catholics. Not only must this shake our con-

---

within ten days before the meeting of Parliament, told Catesby and the others that the Prince of Wales was not going to attend the opening ceremony, wherefore they resolved to "leave the Duke alone," and make arrangements to secure the elder brother.

The original of Winter's declaration, dated November 25th, which is at Hatfield, contains these and other particulars, which are altogether omitted in a "copy" of the same in the Record Office, dated, remarkably enough, on November the 23rd. It is from the latter that the version in the "King's Book" was printed.

[1] De Beaumont to Villeroy, September 17th, 1605.

[2] Mr. Gardiner alludes to it, *History*, i. 254 (note), but apparently attaches no importance to it.

[3] Brit. Museum, Add. MSS. 19402 fol. 143. See the letter in full, Appendix H.

fidence in the genuine nature of any transaction in which such a man played a prominent part, it must likewise suggest a doubt whether others may not in like manner have passed themselves off for what they were not, without arousing suspicion.

The precise facts as to the actual receipt of the famous letter are involved, like every other particular of this history, in the obscurity begotten of contradictory evidence. In the published account,[1] it is stated with great precision that it was received by Monteagle on Saturday, October 26th, being but ten days before the Parliament. In his letter to the ambassadors abroad,[2] Cecil dates its receipt "about eight days before the Parliament should have begun." In the account furnished for the benefit of the King of France,[3] the same authority declares that it came to hand "some four or five days before." A doubt is thus unquestionably suggested as to whether the circumstances of its coming to Monteagle's hands are those traditionally described: for our present purpose, however, it will perhaps be sufficient to follow the story as formally told by authority in the king's own book.

On Saturday, October 26th, ten days before the assembly of Parliament, Monteagle suddenly, and without previous notice, ordered a supper to be pre-

---

[1] *Discourse of the Manner of the Discovery* (the "King's Book."

[2] Winwood, *Memorials*, ii. 170, etc. (November 9th). In the entry book of the Earl of Salisbury's letters (Phillipps' MSS. 6297, f. 39) this is described as "being the same that was sent to all his Majestie's Embassadors and Ministers abroad." To Parry, however, quite a different account was furnished.

[3] Cecil to Sir T. Parry, P. R. O. *France*, bundle 132 (November 6th).

pared at his house at Hoxton "where he had not supped or lain of a twelvemonth and more before that time."[1] While he was at table one of his pages brought him a letter which had been given to him by a man in the street, whose features he could not distinguish, with injunctions to place it in his master's own hands. It is undoubtedly a singular circumstance, which did not escape notice at the time, that the bearer of this missive should have thus been able to find Monteagle at a spot which he was not accustomed to frequent, and the obvious inference was drawn, that the arrival of the letter was expected. On this point, indeed, there is somewhat more than inference to go upon, for in Fulman's MS. collection at Corpus Christi College, Oxford, among some interesting notes concerning the Plot, of which we shall see more, occurs the statement that "the Lord Monteagle knew there was a letter to be sent to him before it came."[2]

[1] Gerard, *Narrative*, p. 101.
[2] Vol. ii. 15. The partisans of the government at the time appear to have solved the difficulty by invoking the direct guidance of Heaven :

> "For thus the Lord in's all-protecting grace,
> Ten days before the Parliament began,
> Ordained that one of that most trayterous race
> Did meet the Lord Mounteagles Serving-man,
>   Who about Seven a clocke at night was sent
>   Upon some errand, and as thus he went,
> Crossing the street a fellow to him came,
> A man to him unknowen, of personage tall,
> In's hand a Letter, and he gave the same
> Unto this Serving-man, and therewithall
>   Did strictly charge him to take speciall heede
>   To give it into 's Masters hand with speede."
>   *Mischeefes Mystery* (1617).

Monteagle opened the letter, and, glancing at it, perceived that it bore neither date nor signature, whereupon he handed it to a gentleman of his household, named Ward, to read aloud, an apparently unnatural and imprudent proceeding not easy to explain, but, at least, inconsistent with the conduct of one receiving an obviously important communication in such mysterious circumstances. The famous epistle must be given in its native form.

My lord out of the love i beare to some of youere frends i have a caer of youer preseruacion therfor i would advyse yowe as yowe tender youer lyf to devys some excuse to shift of youer attendance at this parleament for god and man hath concurred to punishe the wickednes of this tyme and think not slightlye of this advertisment but retyre youre self into youre contri wheare yowe may expect the event in safti for thowghe theare be no apparence of anni stir yet i saye they shall receyve a terrible blowe this parleament and yet they shall not seie who hurts them this cowncel is not to be contemned because it maye do yowe good and can do yowe no harme for the dangere is passed as soon as yowe have burnt the letter and i hope god will give yowe the grace to mak good use of it to whose holy proteccion i comend yowe

(Addressed) *to the ryht honorable the lord moūteagle*

Monteagle, though he saw little or nothing in this strange effusion, resolved at once to communicate with the king's ministers, his Majesty being at the time engaged at Royston in his favourite pastime of the chase, and accordingly proceeding at once to town, he placed the mysterious document in the hands of the Earl of Salisbury.[1]

As to what thereafter followed and the manner in which from this clue the discovery was actually accomplished, it is impossible to say more than this, that the accounts handed down cannot by any possibility be true, inasmuch as on every single point they are utterly and hopelessly at variance. We can do no more than set down the particulars as supplied to us on the very highest authority.

A.—*The account published in the "King's Book."*

1. The letter was received ten days before the meeting of Parliament, *i.e.*, on October 26th.

2. The Earl of Salisbury judged it to be the effusion of a lunatic, but thought it well, nevertheless, to communicate it to the king.

3. This was done five days afterwards, November 1st, when, in spite of his minister's incredulity, James insisted that the letter could intend nothing but the blowing up of the Parliament with gunpowder, and that a search must be made, which, however, should be postponed till the last moment.

4. Accordingly, on the afternoon of Monday, No-

---

[1] Here again evidence was found of the direct guidance of Heaven :

> "And thus with loyall heart away he goes,
> Thereto resolved whatever should betide,
> To th' Court he went this matter to disclose,
> To th' Earle of Salsb'ryes chamber soone he hide,
>   Whither heavens finger doubtless him directed,
>   As the best meanes to have this fact detected."
>   *Mischeefes Mystery.*

vember 4th, the Lord Chamberlain going on a tour of inspection, visited the "cellar" and found there "great store of billets, faggots, and coals," and moreover, "casting his eye aside, perceived a fellow standing in a corner ... Guido Fawkes the owner of that hand which should have acted that monstrous tragedy." Coming back, the chamberlain reported that the provision of fuel appeared extraordinary, and that as to the man, "he looked like a very tall and desperate fellow."

5. Thereupon the king insisted that a thorough scrutiny must be made, and that "those billets and coals should be searched to the bottom, it being most suspicious that they were laid there only for covering of the powder." For this purpose Sir Thomas Knyvet, a magistrate, was despatched with a suitable retinue.

6. Before his entrance to the house, Knyvet found Faukes "standing without the doors, his boots and clothes on," and straightway apprehended him. Then, going into the cellar, he removed the firewood and at once discovered the barrels.

B.—*The Account sent by Salisbury to the Ambassadors abroad, and the Deputy in Ireland, November 9th, 1605.*

1. The letter was received about *eight* days before the Parliament.

2. Upon perusal thereof, Salisbury and Suffolk, the chamberlain, "both conceived that it could not be more proper than the time of Parliament, nor by any other way to be attempted than with powder, while the King was sitting in that Assembly." With this interpreta-

tion other Lords of the Council agreed; but they thought it well not to impart the matter to the king till three or four days before the session.

3. His Majesty was "hard of belief" that any such thing was intended, but his advisers overruled him and insisted on a search, not however till the last moment.

ARREST OF GUY FAUKES.

4. About 3 o'clock on the afternoon of Monday, November 4th, the Lord Chamberlain, Suffolk, visited the cellar, and found in it only firewood and not Faukes.

5. The lords however insisting, in spite of the king, that the matter should be probed to the bottom, Knyvet was despatched with orders to "*remove all the wood, and so to see the plain ground underneath.*"

6. Knyvet, about midnight, "going unlooked for into the vault, found that fellow Johnson [*i.e.*, Faukes] *newly come out of the vault*," and seized him. Then, having removed the wood, he perceived the barrels.

C.—*The Account furnished by Salisbury for the information of the King of France, November 6th, 1605. (Original draft, in the P. R. O.)*

1. The letter was received *some four or five days* before the Parliament.
2. This being shown to the king and the lords, "their lordships found not good ... to give much credit to it, nor yet so to contemn it as to do nothing at all."
3. It was accordingly determined, the night before, "to make search about that place and to appoint a watch in the old Palace, to observe what persons might resort thereabouts."
4. Sir T. Knyvet, being appointed to the charge thereof, *going by chance, about midnight, into the vault, by another door, found Faukes within*. Thereupon he caused some few faggots to be removed, and so discovered some of the barrels, "*merely, as it were, by God's direction, having no other cause but a general jealousy.*"[1]

---

[1] In the account forwarded to the ambassadors, there is a curious contradiction. In the general sketch of the discovery with which it opens, it is said that Faukes was captured "in the place itself," with his lantern, "making his preparations." Afterwards, in the detailed narrative of the proceedings, that he was taken outside. The fact is, that the first portion of this

Never, assuredly, was a true story so hard to tell. Contradictions like these, upon every single point of the narrative, are just such as are wont to betray the author of a fiction when compelled to be circumstantial.

To say nothing of the curious discrepancies as to the date of the warning, it is clearly impossible to determine the locality of Guy's arrest. The account officially published in the "King's Book" says that this took place in the street. The letter to the ambassadors assigns it to the cellar and afterwards to the street; that to Parry, to the cellar only. Faukes himself, in his confession of November 5th, says that he was apprehended neither in the street nor in the cellar, but in his own room in the adjoining house. Chamberlain writes to Carleton, November 7th, that it was in the cellar. Howes, in his continuation of Stowe's *Annals*, describes two arrests of Faukes, one in the street, the other upstairs in his own chamber. This point, though seemingly somewhat trivial, has been invested with much importance. According to the time-honoured story, the baffled desperado roundly declared that had he been within

letter is taken bodily from that of November 6th to Parry, wherein the arrest of Faukes in the vault was a principal point. Between the 6th and the 9th this part of the story had been altered, but it does not seem to have been noticed that a remnant of the earlier version still existed in the introductory portion.

It will be remarked that the account of November 6th makes no mention of the visit of the chamberlain to the vault, nor that of November 9th to the presence of Faukes at the time of this visit. The minute of November 7th says that Faukes admitted the chamberlain to the vault.

reach of the powder when his captors appeared, he would have applied a match and involved them in his own destruction. This circumstance is strongly insisted on not only in the "King's Book," but also in his Majesty's speech to Parliament on November 9th, which declared, "and in that also was there a wonderful providence of God, that when the party himself was taken he was but new come out of his house from working, having his fire-work for kindling ready in his pocket, wherewith, as he confesseth, if he been taken immediately before, he was resolved to have blown up himself with his takers." We learn, however, from Cecil's earliest version of the history, that Faukes was apprehended in the very situation most suitable for such a purpose, "in the place itself, as he was busy to prepare his things for execution," while Chamberlain adds that he was actually engaged in "making his trains."

Far more serious, to say nothing of the episode of the chamberlain's visit, are the divergencies of the several versions as to the very substance of the story. We are told that King James was the first to understand and interpret the letter which had baffled the sagacity of his Privy Council; that the Lords of the Council had fully interpreted it several days before the king saw it; that the said lords would not credit the king's interpretation; that the king would not believe their interpretation; and that neither the one nor the other ever interpreted it at all; that his Majesty insisted on a search being made in spite of the reluctance of his ministers; that they insisted on the search in spite of the reluctance of their royal master; and that no such search was ever proposed by either; that Knyvet was despatched expressly to look for gunpowder, with instructions to rummage the firewood to the bottom, leaving no cover in which a barrel might lie hid; and that having no instructions to do anything of the kind, nor any reason to suspect the existence of any barrels, he discovered them only by a piece of luck, so purely fortuitous as to be clearly providential. On this last point especially the contradictions are absolutely irreconcilable.

It is abundantly evident that those who with elaborate care produced these various versions were not supremely solicitous about the truth of the matter, and varied the tale according to the requirements of circumstances. As Mr. Jardine acknowledges,[1] the great object of the official accounts was to obtain credence for what the government wished to be believed, or, as Father Gerard puts it,[2] these accounts were composed "with desire that men should all conceive this to be the manner how the treason came to light." If from time to time the details were altogether transformed, it was clearly not through any abstract love of historical accuracy, but rather that there were difficulties to meet and doubts to satisfy, which had to be dealt with in order to produce the desired effect.

That, from the beginning, there was whispered disbelief, which it was held all-important to silence, is sufficiently attested by Cecil himself, when, on the very morrow of the discovery, he sent to Parry his first draft of the history. "Thus much," he wrote, "I have thought necessary to impart unto you in haste, to the end that you may deliver as much to the

---

[1] *Criminal Trials*, ii. 3-5. [2] *Narrative*, p. 100.

French king, for prevention of false bruits, which I know, as the nature of fame is, will be *increased*,[1] perverted, and disguised according to the disposition of men."

It does not appear why the appearance of erroneous versions of so striking an event should have been thus confidently anticipated if the facts were undeniably established ; while, on the other hand, it is not a little remarkable that the narrative thus expressly designed to establish the truth, should have been forthwith abandoned and contradicted by its author in every single particular.

Important information upon the same point is furnished by Cecil in another letter, written in the following January.[2] He undertakes to explain to his correspondent how it came to pass that a circumstance of supreme importance, of which the government were fully cognizant,[3] was not mentioned in the official account. This he does as follows : " And although in his Majesty's book there is not any mention made of them [the Jesuits], and of many

---

[1] This word is cancelled in the original draft.

[2] To Sir T. Edmondes, January 22nd, 1605-6.—Stowe MSS., 168, 73, f. 301.

[3] *Viz.*, the complicity of the Jesuits, "not only as being casually acquainted with the Plot," but as having been "principall comforters, to instruct the consciences of some of these wicked Traytors, in the lawfulnesse of the Act and meritoriousnesse of the same."

On this it is enough to remark that when Father Garnet, the chief of the said Jesuits, came afterwards to be tried, no attempt whatever was made to prove any such thing. Cecil therefore wrote thus, and made so grave an assertion, without having any evidence in his hands to justify it.

things else which came to the knowledge of the State, yet is it but a frivolous inference that thereby [they] seek to serve their turn, considering the purpose of his Majesty was not to deliver unto the world all that was confessed concerning this action, *but so much only of the manner and form of it, and the means of the discovery*, as might make it apparent, both how wickedly it was conceived by those devilish instruments, and *how graciously it pleased God to deal with us in such an extraordinary discovery thereof.*"

Turning to the details of the story which survive the struggle for existence in the conflict of testimony, if any can be said to do so, there is abundant matter deserving attention, albeit we may at once dismiss the time-honoured legend concerning the sagacity of the British Solomon, and his marvellous interpretation of the riddling phrases which baffled the perspicacity of all besides himself.[1]

[1] That King James alone solved the enigma was put forth as an article of faith. In the preamble to the Act for the solemnization of the 5th of November, Parliament declared that the treason "would have turned to utter ruin of this whole kingdom, had it not pleased Almighty God, by inspiring the king's most excellent Majesty with a divine Spirit, to discover some dark phrases of a letter . . ." In like manner, the monarch himself, in his speech to the Houses, of November 9th, informed them: "I did upon the instant interpret and apprehend some dark phrases therein, contrary to the ordinary grammar construction of them, and in another sort, than I am sure any divine or lawyer in any university would have taken them."

This "dark phrase" was the sentence—"For the danger is past as soon as you have burnt the letter," which the royal sage interpreted to mean "as quickly," and that by these words "should be closely understood the suddenty and quickness of

More important is Cecil's admission that the presence of the powder under the Parliament House was at least suspected for several days before anything was done to interfere with the proceedings of those who had put it there. The reasons alleged for so extraordinary a course are manifestly absurd. It was resolved, he told the ambassadors, "that, till the night before, nothing should be done to interrupt any purpose of theirs that had any such devilish practice, but rather to suffer them to go on to the end of their day." In like manner he informed the Privy Council[1] that it was determined to make no earlier search, that "such

the danger, which should be as quickly performed and at an end as that paper should be of blazing up in the fire."

Of this famous interpretation Mr. Gardiner says that it is "certainly absurd;" while Mr. Jardine is of opinion that the words in question "must appear to every common understanding mere nonsense."

When it was proposed in the House of Commons (January 31st, 1605-6,) to pass a vote of thanks to Lord Monteagle for his share in the "discovery," one Mr. Fuller objected that this would be to detract from the honour of his Majesty, for "the true discoverer was the king."

The reader will perhaps be reminded of Sir Walter Scott's inimitable picture of the king's satisfaction in this notable achievement.

"Do I not ken the smell of pouther, think ye? Who else nosed out the Fifth of November, save our royal selves? Cecil, and Suffolk, and all of them, were at fault, like sae mony mongrel tikes, when I puzzled it out; and trow ye that I cannot smell pouther? Why, 'sblood, man, Joannes Barclaius thought my ingine was in some manner inspiration, and terms his history of the plot, *Series patefacti divinitus parricidii;* and Spondanus, in like manner, saith of us, *Divinitus evasit.*"—*Fortunes of Nigel,* c. xxvii.

[1] *Relation* . . . , November 7th, 1605 (P. R. O.).

as had such practice in hand might not be scared before they had let the matter run on to a full ripeness for discovery." It certainly appears that, at least, it would have been well before the eleventh hour to institute observations as to who might be coming and going about the cellar. On the other hand, can it be imagined that any minister in his right senses would have allowed the existence of a danger so appalling to continue so long, and have suffered a desperado like Faukes to have gone on knocking about with his flint and steel and lantern in a powder magazine beneath the House of Parliament? Accidents are proverbially always possible, and in the circumstances described to us there would have been much more than a mere possibility, for the action said to have been taken by the authorities, in sending the chamberlain to "peruse" the vault, seems to have been expressly intended to give the alarm; and had the conspirators been scared it would evidently have been their safest plan to have precipitated the catastrophe, that in the confusion it would cause they might escape. How terrible such a catastrophe would have been is indicated by Father Greenway:[1] "Over and above the grievous loss involved in the destruction of these ancient and noble buildings, of the archives and national records, the king himself might have been in peril, and other royal edifices, though situate at a distance, and undoubtedly many would have perished who had come up to attend the Parliament." Moreover, the loss of life in so thickly populated a spot must have been frightful, and especially amongst the official classes.

---

[1] *Narrative*, f. 68 b.—Stonyhurst MSS.

Father Greenway expresses his utter disbelief in the incident of the chamberlain's visit:[1] "To speak my own mind," he writes, "I do not see in this portion of the story any sort of probability." He adds another remark of great importance. If the Lord Chamberlain,—and, we may add, Sir T. Knyvet,—could get into the cellar without the assistance of Faukes, to say nothing of the "other door" which makes its appearance in Cecil's first version, there is an end of the secret and hidden nature of the place, and some one else must have had a key. How, then, about the months during which the powder had been lying in it; during much of which time it had been, apparently, left to take care of itself? Did no man ever enter and inspect it before?

But questions far more fundamental inevitably suggest themselves. If, during ten, or even during five days, a minister so astute and vigilant was willing to risk the danger of an explosion, it certainly does not appear that he was much afraid of the powder, or thought there was any harm in it. We have already remarked on the strangeness of the circumstance that the plotters were able so easily to procure it. It may be observed that they appear themselves to have

[1] F. 66. It will be remembered that this episode is not mentioned by Cecil in his version of November 6th. Bishop Goodman's opinion is that this and other points of the story were contrived for stage effect: "The King must have the honour to interpret that it was by gunpowder; and the very night before the parliament began it was to be discovered, to make the matter the more odious, and the deliverance the more miraculous. No less than the lord chamberlain must search for it and discover it, and Faux with his dark lantern must be apprehended." (*Court of King James*, p. 105.)

been disappointed with its quality, for we are told [1] that late in the summer they added to their store "as suspecting the former to be dank." Still more remarkable, however, was the conduct of the government. Immediately upon the "discovery" they instituted the most minute and searching inquiries as to every other particular connected with the conspirators. We find copious evidence taken about their haunts, their lodgings, and their associates: of the boatmen who conveyed them hither and thither, the porters who carried billets, and the carpenters who worked for them: inquiries were diligently instituted as to where were purchased the iron bars laid on top of the barrels, which appear to have been considered especially dangerous; we hear of sword-hilts engraved for some of the company, of three beaver hats bought by another, and of the sixpence given to the boy who brought them home. But concerning the gunpowder no question appears ever to have been asked, whence it came, or who furnished it. Yet this would appear to be a point at least as important as the rest, and if it was left in absolute obscurity, the inference is undoubtedly suggested that it was not wished to have questions raised. It may be added that no mention is discoverable of the augmentation of the royal stores by so notable a contribution as this would have furnished.

Neither can it escape observation that whereas the powder was discovered only on the morning [2] of

[1] T. Winter, November 23rd, 1605.
[2] There is, of course, abundant contradiction upon this point, as all others, but the balance of evidence appears to point to 2 a.m. or thereabouts.

November 5th, the peers met as usual in their chamber that very day.[1] It cannot be supposed either that four tons of powder could have been so soon removed, or that the most valuable persons in the

DISCOVERY OF GUNPOWDER PLOT, AND COINS OF JAMES I.

State would have been suffered to expose themselves to the risk of assembling in so perilous a situation.[2]

[1] The customary hour for the meeting of the Houses was 9 a.m., or even earlier. (*Journals of Parliament.*)
[2] The list of those present is given in the *Lords' Journals*; it is headed by the Lord Chancellor (Ellesmere), and includes the

However this may be, from the moment of the "discovery" the discovered gunpowder disappears from history.[1]

There is another point which must be noticed. It might naturally be supposed that after so narrow an escape, and in accordance with their loud protestations of alarm at the proximity of a shocking calamity from which they had been so providentially delivered, the official authorities would have carefully guarded against the possibility of the like happening again. Their acts, however, were quite inconsistent with their words, for they did nothing of the kind. For more than seventy years afterwards the famous "cellar" continued to be leased in the same easy-going fashion to any who chose to hire it, and continued to be the receptacle of

Archbishop of Canterbury, fourteen bishops, and thirty-one peers, of whom Lord Monteagle was one. In 1598, as Mr. Atkinson tells us in his preface to the lately published volume of the *Calendar of Irish State Papers*, the cellars of the Dublin Law Courts were used as a powder magazine. The English Privy Council, startled to hear of this remarkable arrangement, pointed out that it might probably further diminish the number of loyal subjects in that kingdom, but were quaintly reassured by the Irish Lords Justices, who explained that, in view of the troublous state of the times, the sittings of the courts had been discontinued, and were not likely to be resumed for the present.

[1] The only allusion to it I have been able to find occurs in the *Politician's Catechism* (1658), p. 95: "Yet the barells, wherein the powder was, are kept as reliques, and were often shown to the king and his posterity, that they might not entertain the least thought of clemency towards the Catholique Religion. There is not an ignorant Minister or Tub-preacher, who doth not (when all other matter fails) remit his auditors to the Gunpowder Treason, and describe those tubs very pathetically, the only reliques thought fit by them to be kept in memory."

all manner of rubbish and lumber, eminently suited to mask another battery. Not till the days of the mendacious Titus Oates, and under the influence of the panic he had engendered, did the Peers bethink themselves that a project such as that of Guy Faukes might really be a danger, and command that the "cellar" should be searched.[1] This was done, in November, 1678, by no less personages than Sir Christopher Wren and Sir Jonas Moore, who reported that the vaults and cellars under and near the House of Lords were in such a condition that there could be no assurance of safety. It was accordingly ordered that they should be cleared of all timber, firewood, coals, and other materials, and that passages should be made through them all, to the end that they might easily be examined. At this time, and not before, was instituted the traditional searching of the cellars on the eve of Parliament.[2]

What then, it will be asked, really did occur? What was done by the conspirators? and what by those who discovered them?

Truth to tell, it is difficult, or rather impossible, to answer such questions. That there was a plot of some kind cannot, of course, be doubted; that it was of such a nature as we have been accustomed to believe, can be affirmed only if we are willing to ignore difficulties which are by no means slight. There is, doubtless, a mass of evidence in support of the traditional story upon these points, but while its value has yet to be discussed, there are other considerations, hitherto overlooked, which are in conflict with it.

Something has been said of the amazing contradic-

[1] *Journals of the House of Lords*, November 1st and 2nd, 1678.
[2] *Ibid.*, November 2nd, 1678.

tions which a very slight examination of the official story reveals at every turn, and much more might be added under the same head.[1]

On the other hand it is clear that even as to the material facts there was not at the time that unanimity which might have been expected. We have seen how anxious was the Secretary of State that the French

"GUY FAUKES' LANTERN."

court should at once be rightly informed as to all particulars. We learn, however, from Mr. Dudley

---

[1] I have already remarked upon Faukes' statement that he was arrested in quite a different place from any mentioned in the government accounts. It should be added, that as to the person who arrested him, there is a somewhat similar discrepancy of evidence. The honour is universally assigned by the official accounts to Sir T. Knyvet, who in the following year was created a peer, which shows that he undoubtedly rendered some valuable service on the occasion. An epitaph, however, in St. Anne's Church, Aldersgate (printed in Maitland's *History of London*, p. 1065, 3rd ed.), declares that it was Peter Heiwood, of Heywood, Lancashire, "who apprehended Guy Faux, with his dark Lanthorn; and for his zealous Prosecution of Papists, as Justice of Peace, was stabbed, in Westminster Hall, by John James, a Dominican Friar, A.D. 1640." No trace of this assassination can be found, nor does the name of John James occur in the Dominican records. It is, however, a curious coincidence that the "Guy Faukes' Lantern," exhibited in the Ashmolean

Carleton, then attached to the embassy at Paris,[1] that in spite of Cecil's promptitude he was anticipated by a version of the affair sent over from the French embassy in London, giving an utterly different complexion to it. According to this, the design had been, "That the council being set, and some lords besides in the chamber, a barrel of gunpowder should be fired underneath them, and the greater part, if not all, blown up." According to this informant, therefore, it was not the Parliament House but the Council Chamber which was to have been assailed, there is no mention of the king, and we have one barrel of powder instead of thirty-six. It is not easy to understand how in such a matter a mistake like this could have been made, for it is the inevitable tendency of men to begin by exaggerating, and not by minimizing, a sudden and startling peril.[2]

Museum at Oxford, bears the inscription: "*Laterna illa ipsa quâ usus est, et cum qua deprehensus Guido Faux in cryptâ subterraneâ, ubi domo* [sic] *Parliamenti difflandae operam dabat. Ex dono Robti. Heywood nuper Academiae Procuratoris, Ap.* 4°, 1641." See the epitaph in full, Appendix I.

[1] To J. Chamberlain, 10th-20th November, 1605. P. R. O. *France*, b. 132, f. 335 b.

[2] The Council appears at this time to have met in the Painted Chamber, and, without at all wishing to lay too much stress upon this point, I cannot but remark that the supposition that this was the original scene assigned to the operations of Faukes would solve various difficulties:

1. Beneath the Painted Chamber was a vaulted cellar, answering to the description we have so frequently heard, whereas under the House of Lords was neither a cellar nor a vault.

2. This crypt beneath the Painted Chamber has been constantly shown as "Guy Faukes' Cellar."

3. In prints of the period, Faukes is usually represented as going to blow up this chamber, never the House of Lords.

Moreover, even this modest version of the affair was not suffered to pass unchallenged. Three days later Carleton again wrote :[1] "The fire which was said to have burnt our king and council, and hath been so hot these two days past in every man's mouth, proves but *ignis fatuus*, or a flash of some foolish fellow's brain to abuse the world; for it is now as confidently reported there was no such matter, nor anything near it more than a barrel of powder found near the court."

It must here be observed that the scepticism thus early manifested appears never to have been exorcised from the minds of French writers, many of whom, of all shades of thought, continue, down to our day, to assume that the real plotters were the king's government.[2]

Neither can we overlook sundry difficulties, again suggested by the facts of the case, which make it hard to understand how the plans of the plotters can in reality have been as they are represented.

We have already observed on the nature of the house occupied in Percy's name. If this were, as Speed tells us, and as there is no reason to doubt, at

[1] To Chamberlain, November 13th (O. S.), 1605. P. R. O.

[2] Thus M. Bouillet, in the latest edition of his *Dictionnaire d'histoire et géographie*, speaks as follows : " Le ministre cupide et orgueilleux, Cécil, semble avoir été l'âme du complot, et l'avoir découvert lui même au moment propice, après avoir présenté à l'esprit faible de Jacques I. les dangers auxquels il était en but de la part des Catholiques."

Gazeau and Prampain (*Hist. Mod.*, tome i.) speak of the conspiracy as " cette plaisanterie ; " and say of the conspirators, " Dans une cave, ils avaient déposé 36 barils contenant (ou soi-disant tels) de la poudre."

the service of the Peers during a session, for a withdrawing-room, and if the session was to begin on November 5th, how could Faukes hope not only to remain in possession, but to carry on his strange proceedings unobserved, amid the crowd of lacqueys and officials with whom the opening of Parliament by the Sovereign must needs have flooded the premises? How was he, unobserved, to get into the fatal "cellar"?

This difficulty is emphasized by another. We learn, on the unimpeachable testimony of Mrs. Whynniard, the landlady, that Faukes not only paid the last instalment of rent on Sunday, November 3rd, but on the following day, the day immediately preceding the intended explosion, had carpenters and other workfolk in the house "for mending and repairing thereof."[1] To say nothing of the wonderful honesty of paying rent under the circumstances, what was the sense of putting a house in repair upon Monday, which on Tuesday was to be blown to atoms? And how could the practised eyes of such workmen fail to detect some trace of the extraordinary and unskilled operations of which the house is said to have been the theatre? If, indeed, the truth is that on the Tuesday the premises were to be handed over for official use, it is easy to understand why it was thought necessary to set them in order, but on no other supposition does this appear comprehensible.

Problems, not easy to solve, connect themselves, likewise, with the actual execution of the conspirators' plan. If it would have been hard for Guy Faukes to get into the "cellar," how was he ever to get out of it

---

[1] P. R. O. *Gunpowder Plot Book*, 39 (November 7).

again? We are so accustomed to the idea of darkness and obscurity in connection with him and his business, as perhaps to forget that his project was to have been executed in the very middle of the day, about noon or shortly afterwards. The king was to come in state with retinue and guards, and attended by a large concourse of spectators, who, as is usual on such occasions, would throng every nook and corner whence could be obtained a glimpse of the building in which the royal speech was being delivered.[1] It cannot be doubted, in particular, that the open spaces adjacent to the House itself would be strictly guarded, and the populace not suffered to approach too near the sacred precincts, more especially when, as we have seen, so many suspicions were abroad of danger to his sacred Majesty, and to the Parliament.

On a sudden a door immediately beneath the spot where the flower of the nation were assembled, would be unlocked and opened, and there would issue therefrom a man, "looking like a very tall and desperate fellow," booted and spurred and equipped for travel. He was to have but a quarter of an hour to save himself from the ruin he had prepared.[2] What possible chance was there that he would have been allowed to pass?

[1] In Herring's *Pietas Pontificia* (1606) the king is described as coming to the House:

"Magna cum Pompa, stipatorumque Caterva,
Palmatisque, Togis, Gemmis, auroque refulgent:
Ingens fit Populi concursus, compita complens,
Turbis se adglomerant densis, spectantque Triumphum."

[2] Faukes himself says—examination of November 16th—that the touchwood would have burnt a quarter of an hour.

As to his further plans, we have the most extravagant and contradictory accounts, some obvious fabulous.[1] According to the least incredible, a v[essel] was lying below London Bridge ready at once to proceed to sea and carry him to Flanders; while a [boat] awaiting him at the Parliament stairs, was to convey him to the ship.[2] If this were so, it is not clear why he equipped himself with his spurs, which, however, are authenticated by as good evidence as any other feature of the story. It would also appear that, here again, the plan proposed was altogether impracticable, for at the time of his projected flight the tide would have been flowing,[3] and it is well known that to attempt to pass Old London Bridge against it would have been like trying to row up a waterfall. Neither does it seem probable that the vessel would have been able to get out of the Thames for several hours, before which time all egress would doubtless have been stopped.

Such considerations must at least avail to make us pause before we can unhesitatingly accept the tradi-

---

[1] See Appendix K, *Myths of the Powder Plot*.
[2] In connection with this appears an interesting example of the natural philosophy of the time, it being said that Faukes selected this mode of escape, hoping that water, being a non-conductor, would save him from the effects of the explosion.
[3] I am informed on high authority that on the day in question it was high water at London Bridge between five and six p.m. In his *Memorials of the Tower of London* (p. 136) Lord de Ros says that the vessel destined to convey him to Flanders was to be in waiting for Faukes at the river side close by, and that in it he was to drop down the river with the ebb tide. It would, of course, have been impossible for any sea-going craft to make its way up to Westminster; nor would the ebb tide run to order.

...tional history, even in those broad outlines which appear to be best established. The main point is, however, independent of their truth. Though all be excepted as has been affirmed concerning the "cellar" and its contents, and the plan of operations agreed upon by the traitors, the question remains as to the real nature of the "discovery." We have seen, on the one hand, that the official narrative bristles with contradictions, and, whatever be the truth, with falsehoods. On the other hand, the said narrative was avowedly prepared with the object of obtaining credence for the picturesque but unveracious assertion that the plotters' design was detected "very miraculously, even some twelve hours before the matter should have been put in execution." On the Earl of Salisbury's own admission, it had been divined almost as many days previously, and it was laid open at the last moment only because he deliberately chose to wait till the last moment before doing anything. No doubt a dramatic feature was thus added to the business, and one eminently calculated to impress the public mind: but they who insist so loudly on the miraculousness of an event which they alone have invested with the character of a miracle, must be content to have it believed that they knew still more than in an unguarded moment they acknowledged, and arranged other things concerning the Plot than its ultimate disclosure.[1]

---

[1] It is frequently said that the testimony of Bishop Goodman, who has been so often cited, is discredited by the fact that he probably died a Catholic, for he was attended on his death-bed by the Dominican Father, Francis à S. Clara (Christopher Davenport), chaplain to Queen Henrietta Maria, a learned man who indulged in the dream of corporate reunion between England

and Rome, maintaining that the Anglican articles were in accordance with Catholic doctrine.

In his will Goodman professed that as he lived, so he died, most constant in all the articles of the Christian Faith, and in all the doctrine of God's holy Catholic and Apostolic Church, "whereof," he says, "I do acknowledge the Church of Rome to be the Mother Church. And I do verily believe that no other church hath any salvation in it, but only so far as it concurs with the faith of the Church of Rome." On this, Mr. Brewer, his editor, observes that a sound Protestant might profess as much, the question being what meaning is to be given to the terms employed. Moreover, the same writer continues, Goodman cannot have imagined that his life had been a constant profession of Roman doctrine, inasmuch as he advanced steadily from one preferment to another in the Church of England, and strongly maintaining her doctrines formally denounced those of Rome. What is certain, however, is this, that in the very work from which his evidence is quoted he speaks in such a manner as to show that whatever were his religious opinions, he was a firm believer in the Royal Supremacy and a lover of King James, whom he thus describes: "Truly I did never know any man of so great an apprehension, of so great love and affection, —a man so truly just, so free from all cruelty and pride, such a lover of the church, and one that had done so much good for the church." (*Court of King James*, i. 91.)

CHAPTER VII.

PERCY, CATESBY, AND TRESHAM.

ON occasion of a notorious trial in the Star Chamber, in the year 1604,[1] Bancroft, the Archbishop of Canterbury, made the significant observation[2] that nothing was to be discovered concerning the Catholics "but by putting some Judas amongst them." That amongst the Powder Plot conspirators there was some one who played such a part, who perhaps even acted as a decoy-duck to lure the others to destruction, has always been suspected, but with sundry differences of opinion as to which of the band it was. Francis Tresham has most commonly been supposed at least to have sent the warning letter to Monteagle, which proved fatal to himself and his comrades: some writers have conjectured that he did a good deal more.[3] Monteagle himself, as we have seen, has been supposed by others to have been in the Plot and to have betrayed it. It would appear, however, that neither of these has so strong a claim to this equivocal distinction as one whose name has been scarcely mentioned hitherto in such a connection.

The part played in the conspiracy by Thomas

[1] That of Mr. Pound.
[2] Jardine, *Criminal Trials*, ii. 38, n.
[3] *E.g.*, the author of the *Politician's Catechism*.

Percy is undoubtedly very singular, and the more so when we learn something of the history and character of the man. Till within some three years previously [1] he had been a Protestant, and, moreover, unusually wild and dissolute. After his conversion, he acquired the character of a zealous, if turbulent, Catholic, and is so described, not only by Father Gerard and Father Greenway, but by himself. In a letter written so late as November 2nd, 1605,[2] he represents that he has to leave Yorkshire, being threatened by the Archbishop with arrest, "as the chief pillar of papistry in that county."

It unfortunately appears that all the time this zealous convert was a bigamist, having one wife living in the capital and another in the provinces. When his name was published in connection with the Plot, the magistrates of London arrested the one, and those of Warwickshire the other, alike reporting to the secretary what they had done, as may be seen in the State Paper Office.[3]

Gravely suspicious as such a fact must appear in connection with one professing exceptional religious fervour, it by no means stands alone. Father Greenway, in describing the character of Percy,[4] dwells much on his sensitiveness to the suspicion of having played false to his fellow Catholics in his dealings with King

---

[1] "About the time of my Lord Essex his enterprise he became Catholic" (*i.e.* 1601). Father Gerard, *Narrative*, p. 58.

[2] P. R. O. *Gunpowder Plot Book*, n. 4.

[3] Justice Grange, of St. Giles-in-the-Fields, to Salisbury, November 5th, 1605. Justices of Warwickshire, to the same, November 12th.

[4] MS., f. 31-32.

Hæc est vera & prima originalis editio Thoæ Perci
Os vultumq̅ vides Thomæ cognomine Percy   A ThomasIchnp Capitaneus
    Inter Britannos nobileis notissimi   B Tho:Iehnso Regi adhære̅
Quis rebus fœdat ambitione superstitioso   C Tho:Persi in Arce fugit
    Animo nefandam machinatur dum nectem, D Thomas Persi sagittatus
Regi Reginæ Ordinibus diripiendus: ipsum   mortuus
    Deo volente scelus in auctorem vult

THOMAS PERCY.

James in Scotland, coupled with protestations of his determination to do something to show that he as well as they had been deceived by that monarch. We find evidence that as a fact some Catholics distrusted him, as in the examination of one Cary, who, being interrogated concerning the Powder Plot, protested that "Percy was no Papist but a Puritan."[1] There is likewise in the king's own book a strange and obscure reference to Percy as the possible author of the letter to Monteagle, one of the chief grounds for suspecting him being "his backwardness in religion." It would moreover appear that he was not a man who always impressed those favourably who had to do with him, for Chamberlain reminds his friend Carleton that the latter had ever considered him "a subtle, flattering, dangerous knave."[2]

We have seen something of the extraordinary manner in which Percy transacted the business of hiring the house and "cellar," wholly unlike what we should expect from one whose main object was to escape observation, and that he brought to bear the influence of sundry Protestant gentlemen, amongst them Dudley Carleton himself,[3] in order to obtain the desired lease.

---

[1] Tanner MSS., *ut sup.*, f. 167.
[2] P. R. O. *Dom. James I.*, November 7th, 1605.
[3] The case of Carleton is not without mystery. At the time of the discovery he was at Paris, as secretary to the English ambassador, but about the middle of the month was ordered home in hot haste and placed "in restraint." On February 28th, 1605-6, he wrote to his friend Chamberlain that he was airing himself on the Chilterns to get rid of the scent of powder, asking his correspondent to consult a patron as to his best means of promotion (*Dom. James I.* xviii. 125). Far from being injured by any suspicion that he might seem to have incurred,

We know, moreover, that various unfortunate accidents prevented the history of these negotiations from ever being fully told.

Yet more remarkable is a piece of information supplied by Bishop Goodman, his authority being the eminent lawyer Sir Francis Moore, who, says he, "is beyond all exception."[1] Moore, having occasion during the period when the Plot was in progress to be out on business late at night, and going homeward to the Middle Temple at two in the morning, "several times he met Mr. Percy coming out of the great statesman's house, and wondered what his business should be there." Such wonder was certainly not unnatural, and must be shared by us. That a man who was ostensibly the life and soul of a conspiracy directed against the king's chief minister, even more than against the sovereign himself, should resort for conference with his intended victim at an hour when he was most likely to escape observation, is assuredly not the least extraordinary feature in this strange and tangled tale.

Not less suspicious is another circumstance. Immediately before the fatal Fifth of November, Percy had been away in the north, and he returned to London only on the evening of Saturday, the 2nd. Of this return, Cecil, writing a week later,[2] made a great mystery, as though the traitor's movements had been of a most stealthy and secret character, and declared

---

he subsequently rose rapidly in favour, was intrusted with most important diplomatic missions, and was finally created Viscount Dorchester.

[1] *Court of King James*, i. 105.
[2] To the ambassadors, November 9th.

that the fact had been discovered from Faukes only with infinite difficulty, and after many denials. It happens, however, that amongst the State Papers is preserved a pass dated October 25th, issued by the Commissioners of the North, for Thomas Percy, posting to Court upon the king's especial service, and charging all mayors, sheriffs, and postmasters to provide him with three good horses all along the road.[1] It is manifestly absurd to speak of secrecy or stealth in connection with such a journey, or to pretend that the Chief Secretary of State could have any difficulty in tracing the movements of a man who travelled in this fashion; and protestations of ignorance serve only to show that to seem ignorant was thought desirable.

Considerations like these, it will hardly be denied, countenance the notion that Percy was, in King James's own phrase, a tame duck employed to catch wild ones. Against such a supposition, however, a grave objection at once presents itself. Percy was amongst the very first victims of the enterprise, being one of the four who were killed at Holbeche when the conspirators were brought to bay.

This, unquestionably, must at first sight appear to be fatal to the theory of his complicity, and the importance of such a fact should not be extenuated. At the same time, on further scrutiny, the argument which it supplies loses much of its force.

It must, in the first place, be remembered, that according to the belief then current, it was no uncommon thing, as Lord Castlemaine expresses it [2] the game being secured, to hang the spaniel which caught

---

[1] *Dom. James I.* xv. 106.   [2] *Catholique Apology*, p. 415.

it, that its master's art might not appear, and, to cite no other instance, we have the example of Dr. Parry, who, as Mr. Brewer acknowledges,[1] was involved in the ruin of those whom he had been engaged to lure to destruction.

There are, moreover, various remarkable circumstances in regard to the case of Percy in particular. It was observed at the time as strange and suspicious that any of the rebels should have been slain at all, for they were almost defenceless, having no fire-arms; they did not succeed in killing a single one of their assailants, and might all have been captured without difficulty. Nevertheless, the attacking party were not only allowed to shoot, but selected just the wrong men as their mark, precisely those who, being chiefly implicated in the beginnings of the Plot, could have afforded the most valuable information,[2] for besides Percy, were shot down Catesby and the two Wrights,[3] all deeply

---

[1] Goodman's *Court of King James*, i. 121, note.

[2] See Goodman's remarks on this subject (*Court of King James*, i. 106). The author of the *Politician's Catechism* writes: "It is very certaine that Percy and Catesby might have been taken alive, when they were killed, but Cecil knew full well that these two unfortunate Gentlemen would have related the story lesse to his owne advantage, than himself caused it to be published: therefore they were dispatched when they might have been made prisoners, having no other weapons, offensive or defensive, but their swords."

[3] About the death of the Wrights there are extraordinary contradictions. In the "original" of his famous confession T. Winter says: "The next shot was the elder Wright, stone dead; after him the younger Mr. Wright." In *Mischeefes Mystery* we read that Percy and Catesby were killed "with a gunne," the two Wrights "with Halberts." The day after the attack, November 9th, Sir Edward Leigh wrote to the Council,

implicated from the first. So unaccountable did such a course appear as at once to suggest sinister interpretations—especially as regarded the case of Percy and Catesby, who were always held to be the ringleaders of the band. As Goodman tells us,[1] "Some will not stick to report that the great statesman sending to apprehend these traitors gave special charge and direction for Percy and Catesby, 'Let me never see them alive;' who it may be would have revealed some evil counsel given." A similar suspicion seems to be insinuated by Sir Edward Hoby, writing to Edmondes, the Ambassador at Brussels[2]: "Percy is dead: who it is thought by some particular men could have said more than any other."

More suspicious still appears the fact that the king's government thought it necessary to explain how it had come to pass that Percy was not secured alive, and to protest that they had been anxious above all for his capture, but had been frustrated by the inconsiderate zeal of their subordinates. In the "King's Book" we read as follows: "Although divers of the King's Proclamations were posted down after those Traitors with all speed possible, declaring the odiousness of that bloody attempt, and the necessity to have Percy preserved alive, if it had been possible, . . . yet the far distance of the way (which was above an hundred miles), together with the extreme deepness thereof, joined also with the shortness of the day, was

that the Wrights were not slain, as reputed, but wounded. Not till the 13th was their death certified by Sir Richard Walsh.

[1] *Court of King James*, i. 106.
[2] Nichols, *Progresses of King James I.* i. 588.

the cause that the hearty and loving affection of the King's good subjects in those parts prevented the speed of his Proclamations."

Such an explanation cannot be deemed satisfactory. The distance to be covered was about 112 miles, and there were three days to do it, for not till November 8th were the fugitives surrounded. They in their flight had the same difficulties to contend with, as are here enumerated, yet they accomplished their journey in a single day, and they had not, like the king's couriers, fresh horses ready for them at every post.

But we have positive evidence upon this point. Father Greenway, who was at the time in the Midlands, close to the scene of action, incidentally mentions, without any reference to our present question,[1] that while the rebels were in the field, messengers came post haste continually, one after the other, from the capital, all bearing proclamations mentioning Percy by name.

It must also be observed that though the couriers, we are told, could not in three days get from London to Holbeche to hinder Percy's death, they contrived to ride in one from Holbeche to London with news that he was dead.[2]

Another circumstance not easy to explain is, that the man who killed Percy and Catesby,[3] John Streete by name, received for his service the handsome pension of two shillings a day for life, equal at least to a pound of our present money.[4] This is certainly a large

[1] MS., f. 70, b.
[2] Cecil writing to the ambassadors, November 9th, mentions in a postscript the fate of the rebels.
[3] They were slain by two balls from the same musket.
[4] Warrant, P. R. O.

reward for having done the very thing that the government most desired to avoid, and for an action, moreover, involving no sort of personal risk, killing two practically unarmed men from behind a tree.[1] If, however, he had silenced a dangerous witness, it is easy to understand the munificence of his recompense.

Against Catesby, likewise, there are serious indictments, and it seems impossible to believe him to have been, as commonly represented, a man, however blinded by fanaticism, yet honest in his bad enterprise, who would not stoop to fraud or untruth. It is abundantly evident that on many occasions he deliberately deceived his associates, and those whom he called his spiritual guides, making promises which he did not mean to keep, and giving assurances which he knew to be false.[2] It will be sufficient to quote one or two examples quite sufficient to stamp him as a man utterly unscrupulous about the means employed to gain his ends.

On the 5th of November, when, after the failure of the enterprise, he arrived at Dunchurch, in Warwickshire, Catesby, in order to induce Sir Everard Digby to commit himself to the hopeless campaign now to be undertaken, assured him,[3] that though the powder was discovered, yet the king and Salisbury were killed; all were in "a pother;" the Catholics were sure to rise in a body, one family alone, the Littletons, would bring in one thousand men the next day; and so on,—

---

[1] Father Gerard mentions this circumstance (*Narrative*, p. 110).

[2] This point is well developed in the recent *Life of a Conspirator*, pp. 120-126.

[3] *Dom. James I.* xvi. 97.

all this being absolutely untrue. That he had previously employed similar means on a large scale to inveigle his friends into his atrocious and senseless scheme, there is much evidence, strongest of all that of Father Garnet;[1] "I doubt not that Mr. Catesby hath feigned many such things for to induce others."

Worst of all, we learn from another intercepted letter of Garnet's, Catesby had for his own purposes circulated an atrocious slander against Garnet himself, although passing as his devoted disciple and friend: "Master Catesby," he wrote,[2] "did me much wrong, and hath confessed that he told them he asked me a question in Q. Elizabeth's time of the powder action,[3] and that I said it was lawful. All which is most untrue. He did it to draw in others."

In view of this, and much else of a similar kind, it is difficult to read Father Gerard's *Narrative*, and more particularly Father Greenway's additions thereto, without a growing feeling that if Catesby sought counsel it was with no intention of being guided by it, and that his sole desire was to get hold of something which might serve his own purposes.

---

[1] *Dom. James I.*, March 4th, 1605-6.
[2] *Gunpowder Plot Book*, 242.
[3] The strange story of a powder-plot under Elizabeth is variously told. According to one of the mysterious confessions attributed to Faukes, which have disappeared from the State Papers, Owen told him in Flanders that one Thomas Morgan had proposed to blow up her majesty (Abbot, *Antilogia*, 137). The *Memorial to Protestants* by Bishop Kennet (1713) says that the man's name was Moody, who wanted the French ambassador to subsidise him. The idea was to place a 20 lb. bag of powder under the queen's bed, and explode it in the middle of the night, but how this was to be managed is not explained.

We have already seen that a great deal of mystery attaches to Francis Tresham, who is generally supposed to have written the letter to Monteagle, and was clearly suspected by some of having done a great deal more; for the author of the *Politician's Catechism* speaks of him as having access to Cecil's house even at midnight, along with another whose name is not given, these two being therefore supposed to have been the secretary's instruments in all this business. What is certain is, that Tresham did not fly like the rest when the "discovery" had taken place, not only remaining in London, and showing himself openly in the streets, but actually presenting himself to the council, and offering them his services. Moreover, though his name was known to the government, at least on November 7th, as one of the accomplices, it was for several days omitted from their published proclamations, and not till the 12th was he taken into custody. Being confined in the Tower, he was shortly attacked by a painful malady, and on December 23rd he died, as was officially announced, of a "strangury," as Salisbury assures Cornwallis "by a natural sickness, such as he hath been a long time subject to."[1] Throughout his sickness he himself and his friends loudly declared that should he survive it "they feared not the course of justice."[2] Such confidence, as Mr. Jardine remarks, could be grounded only on his possession of knowledge which the authorities would not venture to reveal, and it is not surprising that his death should have been attributed, by the enemies of the government, to poison. It is no doubt an argument against

[1] Winwood, *Memorials*, ii. 189.
[2] Wood to Salisbury, December 23rd, 1605.

such a supposition that during his illness Tresham was allowed to be attended by his wife and a confidential servant. On the other hand, not only does Bishop Goodman inform us [1] that "Butler, the great physician of Cambridge," declared him to have been poisoned; but the author of *Mischeefes Mystery*, a violent government partisan, contradicts the notion of a natural death, by asserting that "Tresham murthered himself in the Tower."

It thus appears, once again, that the more its details are scrutinized, the less does the traditional history of the Plot commend itself to our acceptance. It is hard to believe that within the ranks of the conspirators themselves, there was no treachery, no one who, lending himself to work the ruin of his associates, unwittingly wrought his own.

The evidence hitherto considered may fitly conclude with the testimony of a witness living near the time in question, who had evidently been at pains to make inquiries amongst those most likely to give information. This is an anonymous correspondent of Anthony à Wood, whose notes are preserved in Fulman's collection in the library of Corpus Christi College, Oxford. These remarkable notes have been seen by Fulman, who inserted in the margin various questions and objections, to which the writer always supplied precise and definite replies. In the following version this supplementary information is incorporated in the body of his statement, being distinguished by italics. The writer, who explains that his full materials are in the country, speaks thus: [2]

[1] *Court of King James*, i. 107.   [2] *Collection*, vol. ii. 15.

"I should be glad to understand what your friend driveth at about the Fifth of November. It was, without all peradventure, a State Plot. I have collected many pregnant circumstances concerning it.

"'Tis certain that the last Earl of Salisbury[1] confessed to William Lenthal[2] it was his father's contrivance, which Lenthal soon after told one Mr. Webb (*John Webb, Esq.*), a person of quality, and his kinsman, yet alive.

"Sir Henry Wotton says 'twas usual with Cecil to create plots, that he might have the honour of the discovery, or to such effect.

"The Lord Mounteagle knew there was a letter to be sent to him before it came. (*Known by Edmund Church, Esq., his confidant.*)

"Sir Everard Digby's sons were both knighted soo after, and Sir Kenelm would often say it was a Stat design, to disengage the king of his promise to tl Pope and the King of Spain, to indulge the Catholi· if ever he came to be king here; and somewhat to h purpose was found in the Lord Wimbledon's pape after his death.[3]

"Mr. Vowell, who was executed in the Rump tim did also affirm it so.[4]

"Catesby's man (*George Bartlet*),[5] on his death-bc

---

[1] William, second earl (born 1591, died 1668), son of ؟ minister of James I.

[2] Speaker of the Long Parliament.

[3] Edward Cecil, Viscount Wimbledon, third son of Thor first Earl of Exeter (the elder brother of Robert Cecil, first of Salisbury), died 1638.

[4] Peter Vowell, a Protestant, executed with Colonel J Gerard for an alleged plot against Cromwell, July 10th, 165

[5] "George Bartlett, Mr. Catesby's servant,' appears amc

confessed his master went to Salisbury House several nights before the discovery, and was always brought privately in at a back door."

Then, in answer to an objection of Fulman's, is added: "Catesby, 'tis like, did not mean to betray his friends or his own life—he was drawn in and made believe strange things. All good men condemn him and the rest as most desperate wretches; yet most believed the original contrivance of the Plot was not theirs."

Whatever else may be thought of the above statements, they at least serve to contradict Mr. Jardine's assertion,[2] that the notion of Cecil's complicity,—which he terms a strange suggestion, scarce worthy of notice, was first heard of long after the transaction, and was adopted exclusively by Catholics. Clearly it was not unknown to Protestants who were contemporaries, or personally acquainted with contemporaries, of the event. Yet the document here cited was known to Mr. Jardine, who mentions one of its statements, that relating to Lord Monteagle, but says nothing of its more serious allegations.

It must also be remarked that we find some traces of the evidence which remains of certain mysterious conspirators of great importance, concerning whom no investigation whatever appears to have been made, they being at once permitted to drop into the profoundest obscurity, in a manner quite contrary to the habitual practice of the authorities.

[1] The suspected persons whose names were sent up to Cecil by the Justices of Warwickshire, November 12th, 1605. (*Gunpowder Book*, 134.)

[2] *Criminal Trials*, ii. 188.

One such instance is afforded by the testimony of a mariner, Henry Paris, of Barking,[1] that Guy Faukes, *alias* Johnson, hired a boat of him, "wherein was carried over to Gravelines a man supposed of great import : he went disguised, and would not suffer any one man to go with him but this Vaux, nor to return with him. This Paris did attend for him back at Gravelines six weeks. If cause require there are several proofs of this matter." None of these, however, seem to have been sought.

[1] *Gunpowder Plot Book*, 130.

CHAPTER VIII.

THE GOVERNMENT'S CASE.

WE have hitherto confined our attention to sources of information other than those with which the authors of the official narrative have supplied us, and upon which they based the same. It remains to inquire how far the evidence presented by them can avail to substantiate the traditional history, and to rebut the various arguments against its authenticity which have been adduced.

For brevity and clearness' sake it will be advisable to divide this investigation under several heads.

i. *The Trial of the Conspirators.*

On the threshold of our inquiry we are met by a most singular and startling fact. As to what passed on the trial of the conspirators, what evidence was produced against them, how it was supported,—nay, even how the tale of their enterprise was told—we have no information upon which any reliance can be placed. One version alone has come down to us of the proceedings upon this occasion—that published "by authority"—and of this we can be sure only that it is utterly untrustworthy. It was issued under the title of the *True and Perfect Relation*, but, as Mr.

Jardine has already told us, is certainly not deserving of the character which its title imports. "It is not *true*, because many occurrences on the trial are wilfully misrepresented; and it is not *perfect*, because the whole evidence, and many facts and circumstances which must have happened, are omitted, and incidents are inserted which could not by possibility have taken place on the occasion. It is obviously a false and imperfect relation of the proceedings; a tale artfully garbled and misrepresented . . . to serve a State purpose, and intended and calculated to mislead the judgment of the world upon the facts of the case."[1] Again the same author remarks,[2] "that every line of the published trial was rigidly weighed and considered, not with reference to its accuracy, but its effect on the minds of those who might read it, is manifest."

Moreover, the narrative thus obviously dishonest, was admittedly issued in contradiction of divers others already passing "from hand to hand," which were at variance with itself in points of importance, and which it stigmatized as "uncertain, untrue, and incoherent;" it justified its appearance on the ground that it was supremely important for the public to be rightly informed in such a case:[3] and so successful were the efforts made to secure for it a monopoly, that no single document has come down to us by which its state-

---

[1] *Criminal Trials*, ii. 235. Mr. Jardine is here speaking expressly of the trial of Father Garnet, as reported in the book, but evidently intends his observations to extend to that of the conspirators as well.

[2] *Ibid.* 105.

[3] *True and Perfect Relation*, Introduction.

ments might be checked. In consequence, to quote Mr. Jardine once more,[1] there is no trial since the time of Henry VIII. in regard of which we are so ignorant as to what actually occurred.[2]

The employment of methods such as these would in any circumstances forfeit all credit on behalf of the story thus presented. In the present instance the presumption raised against it is even stronger than it would commonly be. If the Gunpowder Plot were in reality what was represented, why was it deemed necessary, in Cecil's own phrase, to pervert and disguise its history in order to produce the desired effect? A project so singular and diabolical in its atrocity, prepared for on so large a scale, and so nearly successful, should, it would appear, have needed no fictitious adjuncts to enhance its enormity; and for the conviction of miscreants caught red-handed in such an enterprise no evidence should have been so effectual as that furnished by the facts of the case, which of their nature should have been patent and unquestionable. When we find, on the contrary, a web

---

[1] *Criminal Trials*, ii. 113.
[2] The contemporary, Hawarde (*Les Reportes del Cases in Camera Stellata*) gives a report of the trial of the conspirators, under the curious title "*Al le arraignemente del Traitors por le grande treason of blowinge up the Parliamente Howse*," which, although evidently based upon the official account, differs in two remarkable particulars. In the first place it gives a different list of the commissioners by whom the trial was conducted, omitting Justice Warburton, and including instead, Lord Chief Baron Flemming, Justices Yelverton and Williams, and Baron Saville. Moreover, Hawarde says that the king and queen "were both there in pryvate," an important circumstance, of which the *True and Perfect Relation* says nothing.

of falsehood and mystery woven with elaborate care over the whole history of the transaction, it is not unnatural to infer that to have told the simple truth would not have suited the purpose of those who had the telling of the tale; and it is obviously necessary that the evidence whereby their story was supported should be rigorously sifted.

What has been said, though in great measure true of the trial of Father Garnet, at the end of March, is especially applicable to that of the conspirators, two months earlier, for in regard of this we have absolutely no information beyond that officially supplied. The execution of Faukes and his companions following close upon their arraignment,[1] all that had been elicited, or was said to have been elicited, at their trial, became henceforth evidence which could not be contradicted, the prosecution thus having a free hand in dealing with their subsequent victim.[2] In view of this circumstance it has been noted as remarkable that whereas the conspirators had been kept alive and untried for nearly three months, they were thus summarily dealt with at the moment when it was known that the capture of Father Garnet was imminent, and, as a matter of fact, he was taken on the very day on which the first company were executed.[3] It would

---

[1] Viz., on January 30th and 31st: not January 31st and February 1st, as Mr. Gardiner has it.

[2] Father Garnet clearly believed that this advantage was used unscrupulously against him, for when certain evidence attributed to Bates was cited, he replied that "Bates was a dead man," and would testify otherwise if he were alive. (Brit. Mus. MSS. Add. 21203. *Foley's Records*, iv. p. 188.)

[3] It is frequently said that the search at Hendlip was undertaken not for Garnet but for Oldcorne, whose presence there was

appear that nothing should have seemed more desirable than to confront the Jesuit superior with those whom he was declared to have instigated to their crime, instead of putting them out of the way at the very moment when there was a prospect of doing so.

ii. *The Fundamental Evidence.*

Amongst all the confessions and "voluntary declarations" extracted from the conspirators, there are two of exceptional importance, as having furnished the basis of the story told by the government, and ever since generally accepted. These are a long declaration made by Thomas Winter, and another by Guy Faukes, which alone were made public, being printed in the "King's Book," and from which are gathered the essential particulars of the story as we are accustomed to hear it.

Of Winter's declaration, which is in the form of a letter to the Lords Commissioners, there is found in the State Paper Office only a copy, bearing date November 23rd, 1605, in the handwriting of Levinus Munck, Cecil's private secretary. This copy has been shown to the King, who in a marginal note objects to a certain "uncleare phrase," which has accordingly been altered in accordance with the royal criticism:

known by the confession of Humphrey Littleton. But this confession was made several days after the search had been begun, and the directions for it given by Cecil to the sheriff, Sir H. Bromley, clearly indicate that he had in view some capture of prime importance. (See Gardiner's *History*, i. 271, and Brit. Mus. MSS. Add. 6178, f. 693.)

and from it has evidently been taken the printed version, which agrees with it in every respect, including the above-mentioned emendation of the phraseology.

It must strike the reader as remarkable that, whereas, as has been said, the body of the letter is in the handwriting of the secretary, Munck, the names of the witnesses who attest it[1] are added in that of his master, Cecil himself.

The "original" document, in Winter's own hand, is at Hatfield, and agrees in general so exactly with the copy, as to demonstrate the identity of their origin.[2] But while, as we have seen, the "copy" is dated November 23rd, the "original" is dated on the 25th.[3] On a circumstance so singular, light is possibly thrown by a letter from Waad, the Lieutenant of the Tower,

---

[1] Viz.: Nottingham, Suffolk, Worcester, Devonshire, Northampton, Salisbury, Marr, Dunbar, Popham, Coke, and Waad.

[2] In the "original," however, there are some passages which do not appear in the copy, notably one in which Lord Monteagle is mentioned. It appears, therefore, that the "copy" is not the first version produced, but has been edited from another still earlier.

[3] That this is not a slip of the pen is evidenced by the fact that Winter first wrote 23, and then corrected it to 25.

to Cecil, on the 21st of the same month.¹ "Thomas Winter," he wrote, " doth find his hand so strong, as after dinner he will settle himself to write that he hath verbally declared to your Lordship, adding what he shall remember." The inference is certainly suggested that torture had been used until the prisoner's spirit was sufficiently broken to be ready to tell the story required of him, and that the details were furnished by those who demanded it. It must, moreover, be remarked that although Winter's "original" declaration is witnessed only by Sir E. Coke, the Attorney General, it appears in print attested by all those whom Cecil had selected for the purpose two days before the declaration was made.² It may be said that the inference drawn above is violent and unfair, and, perhaps, were there no other case to go upon but that of Winter, so grave a charge as it implies should not be made. There remains, however, the companion case of Faukes, which is yet more extraordinary.

His declaration first makes its appearance as " The examination of Guy Fawkes, taken the 8th of November."³ The document thus described is manifestly a draft, and not a copy of a deposition actually taken. It is unsigned: the list of witnesses is in the same handwriting as the rest, and in no instance is a witness indicated by such a title as he would employ for his signature.⁴ Throughout this paper Faukes is made to

[1] Brit. Mus. MSS. Add. 6178, 84.
[2] The document is headed in the printed version : "Thomas Winter's Confession, taken the Twenty-third of November, 1605, in the Presence of the Counsellors, whose Names are underwritten."
[3] *Gunpowder Plot Book*, 49.
[4] The list stands thus: " L. Admyrall—L. Chamberlayn—

speak in the third person, and the names of accomplices to whom he refers are not given.

What, however, is most remarkable is the frank manner in which this document is treated as a draft. Several passages are cancelled and others substituted, sometimes in quite a contrary sense, so that the same deponent cannot possibly have made the statements contained in both versions. Other paragraphs are "ticked off," as the event proves, for omission.

Nine days later, November 17th,[1] Faukes was induced to put his name to the substance of the matter contained in the draft.[2] The document is headed "The declaration[3] of Guy Fawkes, prisoner in the Tower of London." Faukes speaks throughout in the first person, and supplies the names previously omitted.[4] Most noteworthy is the manner in which this

Erle of Devonshire—Erle of Northampton—Erle of Salisbury—Erle of Marr—L. Cheif Justice—attended by Mr. Attorney Generall."

The Lord Admiral was the Earl of Nottingham, better known as Lord Howard of Effingham, the commander-in-chief against the Spanish Armada. There appears to be no foundation for the supposition that he was a Catholic. Northampton (Henry Howard) was a professing Catholic. The chamberlain was the Earl of Suffolk, the Chief Justice, Popham.

[1] The *Calendar of State Papers* assigns this document, like the other, to the 8th, a mistake not easy to understand, for not only is the date clearly written, but the printed version in the "King's Book" gives it correctly.

[2] *Gunpowder Plot Book*, 101.

[3] This was originally written "deposition;" the title is altered in Coke's hand, who also added the words, "taken the 17· of Nov. 1605 : acknowledged before the Lords Commissioners."

[4] Thus the *examination* of November 8th begins as follows : "He confesseth that a Practise in generall was first broken unto him, agaynst his Majesty, for the Catholique cause, and not in-

version is adapted to the emendations of the draft. The passages ticked off have disappeared entirely, amongst them the remarkable statements that "they [the confederates] meant also to have sent for the prisoners in the Tower, of whom particularly they had some consultation,"—that "they had consultation for the taking of the Lady Mary [the infant daughter of King James] into their possession"—and that "provision was made by some of the conspiracy of armour of proof this last summer, for this action." Where an alteration has been made in the draft, great skill is shown in combining what is important in both versions.[1]

vented, or propounded by himself: and this was first propounded unto him, about Easter last was twelvemonth, beyond the seas, in the Low Countreyes, by an English Lay-man, and that English man came over with him in his company, into England, and they tow and three more were the first five, mencioned in the former examination," etc.

The *declaration* of November 17th opens: "I confesse that a practise in general was first broken unto me against his Majesty, for releife of the Catholique cause, and not invented or propounded by myself. And this was first propounded unto me about Easter last was twelvemonth, beyond the Seas, in the Low Countries of the Archdukes obeysance, by Thomas Winter, who came thereupon with me into England, and there wee imparted our purpose to three other Englishmen more, namely Robt Catesby, Thos Percy, and John Wright, who all five consulting together," etc. See both documents in full, Appendix N.

[1] Thus, in the confession of November 8th, we read as follows: "He confesseth, that it was resolved amonge them, that the same day that this detestable act should have been performed, the same day [*sic*] should other of their confederacye have surprised the person of the Lady Elizabeth and presently have proclaimed her queen [to which purpose a Proclamation was drawne, as well to avow and justifye the Action, as to have protested against the Union, and in noe sort to have meddled with

As to the means which were employed to compel Faukes to sign the declaration there can be no doubt; his signature bearing evidence that he had been tortured with extreme severity. The witnesses are but two, Coke, the Attorney General, and Waad, the Lieutenant of the Tower. When, however, the document came to be printed, as in the other case, a fuller list was appended, but not exactly that previously indicated, for to Faukes were assigned the same witnesses as to Winter, including the Earls of Worcester and Dunbar over and above his own list.[1]

The printed version exhibits other points of interest. There was in the Archduke's service, in Flanders, an

---

Religion therein. And would have protested all soe against all strangers,] and this Proclamation should have been made in the name of the Lady Elizabeth."

The portion within brackets is cancelled, and the following substituted: "He confesseth that if their purpose had taken effect, untill they had power enough, they would not have avowed the deed to be theirs; but if their power ... had been sufficient, they thereafter would have taken it upon them."

The corresponding portion of the declaration of November 17th runs thus: "It was further resolved amongst us, that the same day that this action should have been performed, some other of our confederates should have surprised the person of the L. Elizabeth, the King's eldest daughter, . . . and presently proclaimed her for Queene, having a *project* of a Proclamation ready for the purpose, wherein we made no mention of altering of Religion, nor would have avowed the deed to be ours, untill we should have had power enough to make our partie good, and then we would have avowed both."

[1] The printed version of Fauke's declaration is headed: "The true Copy of the Deposition of Guido Fawkes, taken in the Presence of the Counsellors, whose Names are under written."

English soldier, Hugh Owen,[1] whom the government were for some reason, excessively desirous to incri-

Guido Fawkes

Guido Fawkes

Guido

Edwarde Oldcorne

Edwarde Oldcorne

Edward Oldcorne

SIGNATURES OF FAUKES AND OLDCORNE.[2]

minate, and get into their hands. For this purpose, a

[1] In the *Calendar of State Papers* he is continually styled "Father Owen," or "Owen the Jesuit," without warrant in the original documents. That he was a soldier and not a priest there is no doubt.

[2] See Appendix K., *The Use of Torture*.

passage was artfully interpolated in the statement of Faukes, whereof no trace is found in the original. In the "King's Book," the passage in question stands thus, the words italicised being those fraudulently introduced:

"About Easter, the parliament being prorogued till October next, we dispersed ourselves, and I retired into the Low-countries, *by advice and direction of the rest; as well to acquaint Owen with the particulars of the plot, as also,* lest, by my longer stay, I might have grown suspicious." But of Owen we shall see more in particular. It must not be forgotten that on several other days besides those named above, Faukes made declarations, still extant, viz., November 5th, 6th, 7th, 9th, and 16th, and January 9th and 20th. The most important items of information furnished by that selected for publication were not even hinted at in any of these.

Farther light appears to be thrown on the manner in which this important declaration was prepared by another document found amongst the State Papers. This is an "interrogatory" drawn up by Sir E. Coke on November 8th, the very day of the "draft," expressly for the benefit of Faukes.[1] That the "draft" was composed from this appears to be shown by a curious piece of evidence. We have already noticed the strange phraseology of one of the passages attributed to Faukes: "He confesseth that the same day that this detestable act should have been performed the same day should other of their confederacy have surprised the person of the Lady Elizabeth," etc.

[1] *Dom. James I.* xvi. 38.

Precisely the same repetition occurs in the sixth of Mr. Attorney's suggested questions. "*Item*, was it not agreed that the same day that the act should have been done, the same day or soon after the person of the Lady Elizabeth should have been surprised," etc.?

Moreover, it is apparent that this interrogatory is not founded on information already obtained, but is, in fact, what is known as a "fishing" document, intended to elicit evidence of some kind. In the first place, some of its suggestions are mutually incompatible. Thus in another place it implies that not Elizabeth but her infant sister Mary was the choice of the queen-makers :—" Who should have been protector of the Lady Mary, who, being born in England, they meant to prefer to the crown. With whom should she have married?" (She was then seven months old.) Again it asks: " What should have become of the Prince?" as though he might after all be the sovereign intended.

Besides this, many points are raised which are evidently purely imaginary, inasmuch as no more was ever heard of them though if substantiated, they would have been supremely important.[1]

---

[1] E.g. *Item*. Where you have confessed that it was discoursed between you that the prisoners in the Tower should have had intelligence after the act done, declare the particularity of that discourse, and whether some prisoners in the Tower should not have been called to office or place, or have been employed, etc.

Item. Where you have confessed that the L. Elizabeth should have succeeded, and that she should have been brought up as a Catholic, and married to an English Catholic. (1) Who should have had the government of her? (2) Who was nominated to be the fittest to have married her?

Item. Was it not resolved amongst you that after the act done

The above details will not appear superfluous if the importance of these documents be fully understood. It is upon these narratives, stamped with features so incompatible with their trustworthiness, that we entirely depend for much of prime importance in the history of the conspiracy, in particular for the notab episode of the mine, which they alone relate, a: which is not even mentioned, either in the oth: numerous confessions of Faukes and Winter them selves, or by any of the other confederates. Save for an incidental remark of Keyes, that he helped to work in the mine, we hear nothing else of it; while not only is this confession quite as strange a document as the two others, but, to complicate the matter still more, Keyes is expressly described by Cecil[1] himself as one of those that "wrought not in the mine."

It is hard to understand how so remarkable an operation should have been totally ignored in all the other confessions and declarations, numerous and various as they are; while, on the other hand, should

you would have taken the Tower, or any other place of strength, and meant you not to have taken the spoil of London, and whom should you have instantly proclaimed?

Item. By what priests or Jesuits were you resolved that it was godly and lawful to execute the act?

Item. Whether was it not resolved that if it were discovered Catesby and others should have killed the king coming from Royston?

Item. Were not Edw. Neville, calling himself Earl of Westmorland, Mr. Dacre, calling himself Lord Dacre, or any of the Nobility, privy to it? How many of the Nobility have you known at Mass? What persons in the Tower were named to be partakers with you?

[1] To Edmondes, November 14th, 1605. (Stowe MSS.)

this striking feature of the Plot prove to be a fabrication, what is there of which to be certain?

iii. *The Confession of Thomas Bates (December 4th, 1605).*

There is another piece of evidence to which exceptional prominence has been given, the confession of Thomas Bates, Catesby's servant, dated December 4th, 1605. This is the only one of the conspirators' confessions specifically mentioned in the government account of their trial, and it is mentioned twice over— a circumstance not unsuspicious in view of the nature of that account as already described.[1]

It is not necessary at present to enter upon the large question of the attitude of the Jesuits towards the Plot, nor to discuss their guilt or innocence. This is, however, beyond dispute, that the government were above all things anxious to prove them guilty,[2] and no document ever produced was so effective for this purpose as the said confession, for, if it were true, there could be no question as to the guilt of one Jesuit, at least, Father Greenway *alias* Tesimond. The substance of Bates' declaration was as follows:

That being introduced and sworn into the conspiracy by his master, Catesby, he was then told that, as a pledge of fidelity, he must receive the sacrament upon his oath, and accordingly he went to confession to Greenway, the Jesuit.

---

[1] *Viz., The True and Perfect Relation.* The confession of Bates is mentioned but not textually quoted. It is in the "King's Book" that the confessions of Winter and Faukes are given.

[2] "The great object of the government now was to obtain evidence against the priests."— Gardiner, *History of England*, i. 267.

That in his confession he fully informed Greenway of the design, and that Greenway bade him obey his master, because it was for a good cause, and be secret, and mention the matter to no other priest.

That he was absolved by Greenway, and afterwards received Holy Communion.

It will be observed that the second paragraph, here italicized, is of supreme importance. We have evidence that although the conspirators, during the course of their operations, frequented the sacraments, they expressly avoided all mention of their design to their confessors, Catesby having required this of them, assuring them that he had fully satisfied himself that the project, far from being sinful, was meritorious, but that the priests were likely to give trouble.[1] We are even told by some authors that Catesby exacted of his confederates an oath of secrecy in this regard. It is clear that his authority must have had special weight with his own servant, who was, moreover, devotedly attached to his master, as he proved in the crisis of his fate. We might, therefore, naturally be prepared to learn that Bates, though confessing to Greenway, never acquainted him with the Plot ; and, that in fact he never did so, there is some interesting evidence.

It cannot escape observation as a suspicious circum-

---

[1] See Rokewood's examination, December 2nd, 1605. (*Gunpowder Plot Book*, 136.) In the confession of Keyes, November 30th, 1605 (*Gunpowder Plot Book*, 126) we read : "He sayth that the reason that he revealed not the project to his ghostly father was for that Catesby told him that he had good warrant and authoritie that it might safely and with good conscience be done," etc.

stance that this most important confession, upon which so much stress was laid, exists amongst the State Papers only in a copy.[1] Moreover, this copy has been treated as though it were an original, being officially endorsed, and it has on some occasion been used in Court.[2] If, however, this version were not genuine, but prepared for a purpose, it is clear that it could not have been produced while Bates was alive to contradict it, and there appears to be no doubt that it was not heard of till after his death.

This appears, in the first place, from a manuscript account of the Plot,[3] written between the trial of the conspirators and that of Father Garnet, that is, within two months of the former. The author sets himself expressly to prove that the priests must have been cognizant of the design, for, he argues, Catholics, when they have anything of the kind in hand, always consult their confessors about it, and it cannot be supposed that on this occasion only did they omit to do so. In support of his assertion, he quotes the instances of Parry, Babington, and Squires, but says nothing of Bates. He mentions Greenway as undoubtedly one of the guilty priests, but only because "his Majesty's proclamation so speaks it." Had the confession of Bates, as we have it, been so prominently adduced at the trial, as the official narrative represents, it is quite impossible that such a writer should have been content with these feeble inferences.

---

[1] *Gunpowder Plot Book*, 145.

[2] This is shown by a mark (§) in the margin opposite the important passage, attention being called to this by the same mark, and the name "Greenway" in the endorsement.

[3] Brit. Mus., Harleian 360, f. 96.

Still more explicit is the evidence furnished by another MS. containing a report of Father Garnet's trial.[1] In this the confession of Bates is cited, but precisely without the significant passage of which we have spoken, as follows: "Catesby afterwards discovered the project unto him; shortly after which discovery, Bates went to Mass to Tesimond [Greenway], and there was confessed and had absolution."

Here, again, it is impossible to suppose that the all-important point was the one omitted. It is clear, however, that the mention of a confession made to Greenway would *primâ facie* afford a presumption that this particular matter had been confessed, thus furnishing a foundation whereon to build; and, knowing as we do how evidence was manipulated, it is quite conceivable that the copy now extant incorporates the improved version thus suggested.

Such an explanation was unmistakably insinuated by Father Garnet, when, on his trial, this evidence was urged against him; for he significantly replied that "Bates was a dead man."[2] Greenway himself afterwards, when beyond danger, denied on his salvation that Bates had ever on any occasion mentioned to him any word concerning the Plot. It is still more singular that Bates himself appears to have known nothing of his own declaration. He had apparently said, in some examination of which no record remains, that he thought Greenway "knew of the business." This statement he afterwards retracted as having been

[1] Brit. Mus., Harleian 360, f. 109, etc. The reporter had clearly been present.
[2] Brit. Mus., MSS. Add. 21,203; Plut. ciii. F. Printed by Foley, *Records*, iv. 164 *seq*.

elicited by a vain hope of pardon, in a letter which is given in full by Father Gerard,[1] and of which Cecil himself made mention at Garnet's trial.[2] But of the far more serious accusation we are considering he said never a word.

There is, however, evidence still more notable. On the same day, December 4th, on which Bates made his declaration, Cecil wrote a most important letter to one Favat,[3] who had been commissioned by King James to urge the necessity of obtaining evidence without delay against the priests. This document is valuable as furnishing explicit testimony that torture was employed with this object. "Most of the prisoners," says the secretary, "have wilfully forsworn that the priests knew anything in particular, and obstinately refuse to be accusers of them, yea, what torture soever they be put to."

He goes on, however, to assure his Majesty that the desired object is now in sight, particularly referring to a confession which can be none other than that of Bates, but likewise cannot be that afterwards given to the world; for it is spoken of as affording promise, but not yet satisfactory in its performance.

"You may tell his Majesty that if he please to read privately what this day we have drawn from a voluntary and penitent examination, the point I am persuaded (but I am no undertaker) shall be so well cleared, if he forbear to speak much of this but few days, as we shall see all fall out to the end whereat his Majesty shooteth."

It seems clear, therefore, that the famous declara-

---

[1] *Narrative*, p. 210.   [2] Plut. ciii. F. § 39.
[3] Brit. Mus. MSS. Add. 6178, § 625.

tion of Bates, like those of Faukes and Winter, tends to discredit the story which in particulars so important rests upon such evidence.

It may be farther observed that if the confession of Bates, as officially preserved, were of any worth, it would have helped to raise other issues of supreme importance. Thus its concluding paragraph runs as follows:

"He confesseth that he heard his master, Thomas Winter, and Guy Fawkes say (presently upon the coming over of Fawkes) that they should have the sum of five-and-twenty thousand pounds out of Spain."

This clearly means that the King of Spain was privy to the design, for a sum equivalent to a quarter of a million of our money could not have been furnished by private persons. The government, however, constantly assured the English ambassadors abroad of the great satisfaction with which they found that no suspicion whatever rested upon any foreign prince.

iv. *Robert Winter.*

There are various traces of foul play in regard of this conspirator in particular, which serve to shake our confidence as to the treatment of all. Robert Winter was the eldest brother of Thomas, and held the family property, which was considerable. Whether this motive, as Mr. Jardine suggests, or some other, prompted the step, certain it is that the government in their published history falsified the documents in order to incriminate him more deeply. Faukes, in the confession of Nov. 17th, mentioned Robert Keyes as amongst the first seven of the conspirators who worked in the mine, and Robert Winter as one of the five introduced at a later period. The names of these two were deliberately interchanged in the published version, Robert Winter appearing as a worker in the mine, and Keyes, who was an obscure man of no substance, among the gentlemen of property whose resources were to have supported the subsequent rebellion. Moreover, in the account of the same confession sent to Edmondes by Cecil three days before Faukes signed it (*i.e.*, Nov. 14th), the same transposition occurs, Keyes being explicitly described as one of those " who wrought not in the mine," although, as we have seen, he is one of the three who alone make any mention of it.

Still more singular is another circumstance. About November 28th, Sir Edward Coke, the attorney-general, drew up certain farther notes of questions to be put to various prisoners.[1] Amongst these we read: "Winter to be examined of his brother. For no man else can accuse him." But a fortnight or so before this time the Secretary of State had officially informed the ambassador in the Low Countries that Robert Winter was one of those deepest in the treason, and, to say nothing of other evidence, a proclamation for his apprehension had been issued on November 18th. Yet Coke's interrogatory seems to imply that nothing had yet been established against him, and that he was not known to the general body of the traitors as a fellow-conspirator.

[1] *Dom. James I.* xvi. 116.

v. *Captain Hugh Owen, Father William Baldwin, and others.*

We have seen something of the extreme anxiety evinced by the English government to incriminate a certain Hugh Owen, a Welsh soldier of fortune serving in Flanders under the archduke.[1] With him were joined Father Baldwin, the Jesuit, and Sir William Stanley, who, like Owen, was in the archduke's service. The measures taken in regard of them are exceedingly instructive if we would understand upon what sort of evidence the guilt of obnoxious individuals was proclaimed as incontrovertible.

[1] In the *Calendar of State Papers*, Mrs. Everett Green, as has been said, quite gratuitously and without warrant from the original documents, uniformly describes him as "Father Owen," or "Owen the Jesuit." Mr. Gardiner (*Hist.* i. 242) has been led into the same error.

It is not impossible that Owen had some knowledge of the conspiracy, though the course adopted by his enemies seems to afford strong presumption to the contrary. It must, moreover, be remembered that, as Father Gerard tells us, he and others similarly accused, vehemently protested against the imputation, while in his case in particular we have some evidence to the same effect. Thomas Phelippes, the "Decipherer," of whom we have already heard, was on terms of close intimacy with Owen, and in December, 1605, wrote to him about the Plot in terms which certainly appear to imply a strong conviction that his friend had nothing to do with it.

"There hath been and yet is still great paynes taken to search to the bottom of the late damnable conspiracy. The Parliamente hit seemes shall not be troubled with any extraordinarie course for their exemplarye punishment, as was supposed upon the Kinges speeche, but onlye with their attaynder, the more is the pitye I saye."—*Dom. James I.* xvii. 62.

No time was lost in commencing operations. On November 14th, three days before Faukes signed the celebrated declaration which we have examined, and in which Owen was not mentioned, the Earl of Salisbury wrote to Edmondes, ambassador at Brussels,[1] that Faukes had now directly accused Owen, whose extradition must therefore be demanded. In proof of this assertion he inclosed a copy of the declaration, in which, however, curiously enough, no mention of Owen's name occurs.[2]

Edmondes on his side was equally prompt. He at once laid the matter before the archduke and his ministers, and on November 19th was able to write to Salisbury that Owen and his secretary were apprehended and their papers and ciphers seized, and that, "If there shall fall out matter to charge Owen with partaking in the treason, the archduke will not refuse the king to yield him to be answerable to justice,"[3] though venturing to hope that he would be able to clear himself of so terrible an accusation.

On "the last of November" the subject was pursued in an epistle from the King himself to the "Archdukes,"[4]

---

[1] Stowe MSS. 168, 54.

[2] This version of the deposition is interesting as being a form intermediate between the draft of November 8th and the finished document of November 17th. The passages cancelled in the former are simply omitted without any attempt to complete the sense of the passages in which they occurred. Those "ticked off" are retained.

[3] Stowe MSS. 168, 58.

[4] *I.e.*, the Archduke Albert, and his consort the Infanta, daughter of Philip II., who, as governors of the Low Countries, were usually so designated.

in which the undoubted guilt of both Owen and Baldwin was roundly affirmed.[1]

On December 2nd, 1605, Salisbury wrote to Edmondes:[2] "I do warrant you to deliver upon the forfeiture of my judgment in your opinion that it shall appear as evident as the sun in the clearest day, that Baldwin by means of Owen, and Owen directly by himself, have been particular conspirators."

In spite of this, the authorities in Flanders asked for proofs of the guilt of those whom they were asked to give up. Wherefore Edmondes wrote (December 27th) to secure the co-operation of Cornwallis, his fellow-ambassador, at Madrid. After declaring that Owen and Baldwin were now found to have been "principal dealers in the late execrable treason," with remarkable *naïveté* he thus continues:[3]

"I will not conceal from your lordship that they have been here so unrespective as to desire for their better satisfaction to have a copy of the information against the said persons to be sent over hither; which I fear will be very displeasing to his Majesty to understand."

In January (1605-6), Salisbury sending, in the King's name, instructions to Sir E. Coke as to the trial of the conspirators, concluded with this admonition:[4] "You must remember to lay Owen as foul in this as you

---

[1] "Nous avons bien voulu aussy par ces presentes, nous mesmes vous asseurer que ce qu'il [Edmondes] vous en a desja declaré, est fondé sur tout verité; et vous dire en oultre, que ces meschantes Creatures d'Owen et Baldouin, gens de mesme farine, ont eu aussi leur part en particulier a ceste malheureuse conspiration de Pouldre."—*Phillipps' MS.* 6297, f. 129.

[2] Stowe, 168, 65.   [3] Winwood, ii. 183.

[4] *Dom. James I.* xix. 94.

can," which certainly does not suggest that the case against him was overwhelmingly strong.

After the execution of the traitors, an Act of Attainder passed by Parliament included Owen amongst them.[1]

The archdukes remaining unconvinced, another and very notable argument was brought into play. On February 12th, 1605-6, Salisbury wrote to Edmondes:[2]

"As for the particular depositions against Owen and Baldwin, which the archdukes desire to have a sight of, you may let them know that it is a matter which can make but little to the purpose, considering that his Majesty already upon his royal word hath certified the archdukes of their guilt."

As to Owen's own papers which had been seized, the archduke assured the English ambassador,[3] "that if there had been anything to have been discovered out of the said papers touching the late treason (as he was well assured of the contrary), he would not have failed to have imparted the same to his Majesty."

At a later date the Spanish minister De Grenada wrote from Valladolid[4] that men could not be de-

[1] 3° *Jac. I.* c. 3. On the 21st of June following, Salisbury forwarded to Edmondes a fresh copy of this Act, "because in the former there was a great error committed in the printing." (Phillipps, f. 157.) It would be highly interesting to know what the first version was. In that now extant it is only said regarding Owen, that inasmuch as he obstinately keeps beyond the seas, he cannot be arraigned, nor can evidence and proofs be produced against him. (*Statutes at large.*)

[2] Stowe, 168, 76; Phillipps, f. 141.

[3] Edmondes to Salisbury, January 23rd, 1605(6). P. R. O., Flanders, 38.

[4] April 19th, 1606, *ibid.*

livered up on mere suspicion, which might prove groundless, but that the archduke had received orders to sift the matter to the bottom, in order that justice might be done " very fully."

About the same time President Richardot informed Edmondes [1] that Owen strenuously denied the charges against him, "and that there is the more probability of his innocency for that his papers having been carefully visited, there doth not appear anything in them to charge him concerning the said matter."

On April 21st Salisbury informed Edmondes of a conference on the subject between the king and the archduke's ambassador.[2] The latter declared that his master was ready to prosecute the accused in his own courts if evidence was furnished him, but in reply King James explained that this was impossible, and that he "was loth to send any papers or accusations over, not knowing how they might be framed or construed there by the formalities of their laws." He added that it was useless now to talk of evidence, "seeing the wretch is already condemned by the public sentence of the whole Parliament, which sentence the archdukes might see if they would." The ambassador thereupon asked to have a copy, but was curtly told that it would presently be printed, when he could buy one for twelve pence and send it to his masters, but that the king was not disposed to make a present of it.

In these circumstances the archdukes determined to detain Owen no longer, and he was presently discharged. The news of this proceeding produced a

---

[1] Edmondes to Salisbury, April 5th, 1606, *ibid.*
[2] Phillipps, f. 150.

remarkable change in the tone of his accusers. On June 18th, the secretary wrote to Edmondes[1] that Owen's enlargement "seemed to give too much credit to his innocency;" moreover, that " though his Majesty showed no great disposition (for many considerations specified unto you) to send over the papers and accusations against him, . . . yet this proceeded not out of any conscience of the invalidity of the proofs, but rather in respect that his process being made here, and the caitiff condemned by the public sentence of the Parliament, it would have come all to one issue, seeing they have proceeded when his Majesty left it to themselves to do as they thought fit."

To reinforce this lucid explanation Salisbury sent six days later what had before been refused, an abstract of "confessions against Owen," and a corrected copy of the Act of Attainder. These documents deserve some consideration.

We have seen how much stress was laid upon the action of Parliament in regard of Owen, although the Act of Attainder which it passed affords no information whatever to assist our judgment of his case. In moving for this attainder, Sir E. Coke appeared at the bar of the House of Commons (April 29th, 1606) to exhibit the evidence on which the charge rested. His notes of this evidence, which are extant,[2] clearly show that the government possessed no proofs at all beyond surmise and inference.[3] Three testimonies were cited

---

[1] Phillipps, f. 152.   [2] *Dom. James I.* xx. 52.
[3] This is obvious from a marginal note in Coke's own hand, arguing that Owen must be guilty in this instance, as he has been guilty on former occasions, and "Qui semel malus est semper præsumitur esse malus in eodem genere mali."

which were quite inconsistent and mutually destructive: (1) An extract from a confession of Guy Faukes, January 20th, 1605-6, declaring that he had himself initiated Owen in the Plot in May, 1605. (2) An information of one Ralph Ratcliffe, to the effect that Owen and Baldwin were busy with the Plot in April, 1604. (3) T. Winter's testimony—from his famous confession of November 23rd, or 25th, 1605—that in the spring of 1604 Owen had assisted him to secure the services of Faukes.

In Salisbury's letter to Edmondes, the first and the last of these alone were cited,[1] probably because it had by this time been perceived that Ratcliffe's evidence flatly contradicted that of Faukes.

Winter's confession has already been discussed, and moreover affords no proof that Owen was acquainted with the purpose for which the services of Faukes were required. There remains the very circumstantial story of Faukes himself, which belongs to a curious and interesting class of documents, containing matter of the highest importance, whereof no trace, not even a copy, is to be found amongst the State Papers. These comprise various confessions of Faukes, dated November 19th, 25th, and 30th, 1605, and January 20th, 1605-6, all dealing with information of a sensational nature, concerning which we learn nothing from the eleven depositions of the same conspirator preserved in the Record Office.[2] For our knowledge of these

[1] It will be noticed that the confession of Faukes cited against Owen is dated two months after he had first been declared to be proved guilty by Faukes' testimony.
[2] These are dated November 5th, 6th [bis], 7th, 8th [the "draft"], 9th, 16th, 17th, January 9th, 20th, 26th.

mysterious documents we have to depend on transcripts of portions of them among the Tanner MSS. in the Bodleian Library, on fragmentary Latin versions in the *Antilogia* of Bishop Abbot, and on the extract cited from the last amongst them by Sir Edward Coke, which exactly agrees with that sent by Salisbury to Edmondes, as above mentioned.

It cannot escape notice that although these versions all profess to be taken from the originals under Faukes' hand, they are so utterly different as to preclude the belief that they have been copied from the same documents.[1]

---

[1] Thus, to confine ourselves to the confession of January 20th, with which we are particularly concerned, we have the following variations:

Tanner transcript. "At my going over Mr Catesby charged me two things more : the one to desire of Baldwin & Mr Owen to deal with the Marquis [Spinola] to send over the regiment of which he [Catesby] expected to have been Lieutenant Colonel under Sir Charles [Percy]. . . . He wished me secondly to be earnest with Baldwin to deal with the Marquis to give the said Mr Catesby order for a Company of Horse, thinking by that means to have opportunity to buy Horses and Arms without suspition."

According to *Abbot*, Faukes was to give instructions that when the time of Parliament approached, Sir Wm. Stanley was on some pretext to lead the English forces in the archduke's service towards the sea, and with them any others he could manage to influence. He also mentions the conspiracy of Morgan, as spoken of by Coke.

In addition to all this, Abbot cites from the same confession the following extraordinary particulars (p. 160): Faukes, when he came to London, with T. Winter, went to Percy's house and found there Catesby and Father Gerard. They talked over matters, and agreed that nothing was to be hoped from foreign aid, nor from a general rising of Catholics, and that the on'y

It must farther be observed that we hear nothing of important matters contained in these confessions till the supposed author and his confederates were all dead, whereas these are such as would certainly have been

plan was to strike at the king's person: whereupon Catesby, Percy, John Wright, Winter, and himself, were sworn in by Gerard.

[This is in absolute contradiction to Winter's evidence (November 23rd) that Percy was initiated in the middle of the Easter term, the other four having agreed on the scheme at the beginning of the same term; and to that of Faukes himself (November 17th) that he and Winter first resolved on a plot for the benefit of the Catholic cause, and afterwards imparted their idea to Catesby, Wright, and Percy.]

Sir E. Coke's Version. "After the powder treason was resolved upon by Catesbye, Thomas Winter, the Wrightes, my self, and others, and preparation made by us for the execution of it, by their advise and direction I went into fflanders and had leave given unto me to discover our project in every particular to Hughe Owen and others, but with condicion that they should sweare first to secrecie as we our selves had done. When I arryved in fflanders I found Mr Owen at Bruxelles to whom after I had given the oathe of secrecye I discovered the whole busines, howe we had layed 20 whole barrells of powder in the celler under the parliament howse, and howe we ment to give it fire the first day of the parliament when the King, the prince, the duke, the Lords spirituall and temporall, and all the knights, citizens, and burgesses of parliament should be there assembled. And that we meant to take the Ladye Elizabeth and proclaime hir for we thought most like that the prince and duke would be there with the king. Mr Owen liked the plott very well, and said that Thomas Morgan had once propounded the very same in quene Elizabeth's time, and willed me that by ani meanes we should not make any mencion of religion at the first, and assured me that so soone as he should have certaine newes that this exploit had taken effect that he would give us what assistance he could and that he would procure that Sir Wm Stanley should

produced on their trial had this been possible.[1] Some of the evidence thus afforded is, in fact, too good, for the Government's purpose, to be true, for if authentic, it would have secured results which, though much desired, were never obtained. In particular it would have established beyond question the guilt of the Jesuits abroad, and especially of Father Baldwin.[2] It is this Father, however, whose case conclusively proves the utter worthlessness of the evidence. Having been proclaimed and branded by the English government

have leave to come with those English men which be there and what other forces he could procure."

The confession of Faukes in the Record Office, dated the same, January 20th, is thus summarized in the *Calendar of State Papers* (*Dom. James I.* xviii. 28) : "Talked with Catesby about noblemen being absent from the meeting of Parliament ; he said Lord Mordaunt would not be there, because he did not like to absent himself from the sermons, as the king did not know he was a Catholic ; and that Lord Stourton would not come to town till the Friday after the opening."

[1] The powder design of Morgan is an instance in point. The Thomas Morgan in question was doubtless the same as the partisan of Mary Queen of Scots.

[2] *E.g.*: " Winter came over to Owen, by him and the Fathers to be informed of a fit and resolute man for the execution of the enterprise. This examinate (being by the Fathers and Owen recommended to be used and trusted in any action for the Catholicks) came into England with Winter."—Faukes, November 19th, 1605 (Tanner MSS.).

Abbot, whose whole object is to incriminate the Jesuits, does not mention this remarkable statement.

Again we read, November 30th (*ibid.*) : "Father Baldwin told this examinate that about 2,000 horses would be provided by the Catholicks of England to join with the Spanish forces . . . and willed this examinate to intimate so much to Father Creswell, which this examinate did."

as a convicted traitor, he, five years later, fell into their hands, being delivered up, in 1610, by their ally the Elector Palatine. He was at once thrown into the Tower, where he was frequently and rigorously examined, it is said even on the rack.[1] After a confinement of eight years he was discharged " with honour," his innocence being attested by the respect with which he was treated by men of all parties.[2] In view of this unquestionable acquittal the famous proofs of his criminality, though certified on the royal word of King James himself, forfeit all claim to consideration.

A word may be added concerning Father Cresswell, an English Jesuit residing in Spain. He, too, was assumed to have been deeply implicated in this and other treasons. In November, 1605, Cecil included his name in a list of traitors against whom proofs were to be procured.[3] It was even asserted that at the time of the intended explosion he came over to England " to bear his part with the rest of his Society in a victorial song of thanksgiving."[4] He was, moreover, loudly denounced as the principal agent in the notorious Spanish Treason.

After all this it is somewhat surprising to find Sir Charles Cornwallis, the English Ambassador, while the excitement of the Powder Plot was at its height, testifying in the most cordial terms to his esteem for the said Cresswell. The latter having been called to Rome by his superiors, Cornwallis (December

---

[1] Oliver, *Collectanea*, sub nom. ; Foley, *Records*, iv. 120, note.
[2] Foley, *Records*, iii. 509 ; *English Protestants' Plea*, p. 59.
[3] *Dom. James I.* xvi. 115.
[4] *Englands Warning Peece*, by T. S. [Thomas Spencer], p. 73.

23rd, N. S. 1605,) addressed to him the following letter.[1]

"Sir, although in matter of religion well you know that there are many discords between us, yet sure in your duty and loyalty to my King and Country I find in you so good a concordance I cannot but much reverence and love you, and wish you all the happiness that a man of your sort upon the earth can desire.

"Much am I (I assure you) grieved at your departure, and the more that I was put in so good hope that your journey should have been stayed. The time of the year unpleasant to travel in, your body, as I think, not much accustomed to journeys of so great length, and the great good you did here to your poor countrymen (which now they want) are great motives to make your friends to wish your will in that voyage had been broken.

"If it be not, I shall not believe in words, for many here do greatly desire you for causes spiritual, and some for temporal. In the latter number am I, who, not affecting your spiritualities (for that these in you abound to superfluity), do much reverence and respect your temporal abilities, as wherein I acknowledge much wisdom, temper, and sincerity. So no friends you have shall ever more desire good unto you than myself. And therefore I wish I were able to make so good demonstration as willingly I would that I ever will here and in all places in this world rest

"Your very assured loving friend,
CH. Co."

[1] Cotton MSS. *Vespasian C.*, ix. f. 259.

About the same time, in an undated letter to Lord Salisbury,[1] Cornwallis again expresses his regret on account of the removal of Cresswell from Spain.

vi. *Other Documents.*

It is impossible to analyze in detail the evidence supplied by the several conspirators after their capture, or to examine the endless inconsistencies and contradictions with which it abounds. One or two points must, however, be indicated.

1. As we have seen, it is clear that at the beginning an effort was made to invest the Plot with a far wider political significance than was afterwards attempted, and to introduce elements which were soon quietly laid aside. In the interrogatories prepared by Sir E. Coke and Chief Justice Popham, we find it suggested that the death of the Earl of Salisbury was a main feature of the scheme, "absolutely agreed upon" among the conspirators. Also that the titular Earl of Westmoreland, the titular Lord Dacre, the Earl of Northumberland, Sir Walter Raleigh, and others were mixed up in the business.

Nor were such endeavours altogether fruitless, for, supposing the testimony extorted from the prisoners to be worthy of credit, information was obtained altogether changing the character and complexion of the design. This was, however, presently buried in oblivion and treated as of no moment whatever.

Thus in Sir Everard Digby's declaration of Nov. 23rd,[2] we find him testifying that the Earls of West-

---

[1] Winwood, *Memorials*, ii. 178.
[2] *Dom. James I.* xvi. 104.

moreland and Derby,[1] were to have been sent to raise forces in the north. Faukes, in the famous confession which we have so fully discussed, was made to say "They meant also to have sent for the prisoners in the Tower to have come to them, of whom particularly they had some consultation," and although this important clause was omitted from the finished version finally adopted, it appears in that of Nov. 14th, sent by Cecil to the ambassador at Brussels. Again, in his examination of November 9th, famous for the ghastly evidence of torture afforded by his signature, we find Faukes declaring, "He confesseth also that there was speech amongst them to draw Sir Walter Rawley to take part with them, being one that might stand them in good stead, *as others in like sort were named*."[2]

With regard to Raleigh it must be remembered that he was in a very special manner obnoxious to Salisbury, who, however, was at great pains to disguise his hostility. On occasion of Sir Walter's trial, in 1603, he vehemently protested that it was a great grief to him to have to pronounce against one whom he had hitherto loved.[3] But two years earlier, in his secret correspondence with James, he had not only described

[1] William Stanley.
[2] The last words are added in another hand.
[3] "I am in great dispute with myself to speak in the case of this gentleman. A former dearness between me and him tied so firm a knot of my conceit of his virtues, now broken by discovery of his imperfections, that I protest, did I serve a king that I knew would be displeased with me for speaking, in this case I would speak, whatever came of it; but seeing he is compacted of piety and justice, and one that will not mislike of any man for speaking a truth, I will answer," etc.—*State Trials.*

Raleigh to the future king as one of the diabolical triplicity hatching cockatrice eggs, but had solemnly protested that if he feigned friendship for such a wretch, it was only with the purpose of drawing him on to discover his real nature.[1]

2. Even more worthy of notice is the shameless manner in which evidence was falsified. That produced in court consisted entirely of the written depositions of the prisoners themselves, and of those who had been similarly examined. It was, however, carefully manipulated before it was read; all that told in favour of those whose conviction was desired being omitted, and only so much retained as would tell against them. On this subject Mr. Jardine well remarks:[2] "This mode of dealing with the admissions of an accused person is pure and unmixed injustice; it is in truth a forgery of evidence; for when a qualified statement is made, the suppression of the qualification is no less a forgery than if the whole statement had been fabricated."

It will be sufficient to cite one notorious and com-

[1] "For this do I profess in the presence of Him that knoweth and searcheth all men's harts, that if I did not some tyme cast a stone into the mouth of these gaping crabbs, when they are in their prodigall humour of discourses, they wold not stick to confess dayly how contrary it is to their nature to be under your soverainty; though they confess (Ralegh especially) that (*rebus sic stantibus*) naturall pollicy forceth them to keep on foot such a trade against the great day of mart. In all which light and soddain humours of his, though I do no way check him, because he shall not think I reject his freedome or his affection ... yet under pretext of extraordinary care of his well doing, I have seemed to dissuade him from ingaging himself so farr," etc.— *Hatfield MSS.*, cxxxv. f. 65.

[2] *Criminal Trials*, ii. 358.

They five did meete at a House in the fields, beyond St. Clements Inn, where they did Confer, and Agree upon the Plott, they went to undertake, and put in Execucion; and there they tooke a solemne Oath and vowe, by all their force and Powers to Execute the same, and of secrecy not to bewraie anie of their fellowes, but to such as should be thought fitt persons to enter into that Acton. And in the same House they did receave the Sacrament of Gerrard the Iesuit: to performe their vowe, and of secrecy as is aforesaid. But he saith that Gerrard was not acquainted or of their purpose

FROM FAUKES' CONFESSION OF NOVEMBER 9, 1605.

pendious example. In regard of the oath of secrecy taken by the conspirators, Faukes (Nov. 9th, 1605) and Thomas Winter (Jan. 9th, 1605-6) related how they administered it to one another, "in a chamber," to quote Winter, "where no other body was," and afterwards proceeded to another chamber where they heard Mass and received Communion at the hands of Father Gerard.[1] Both witnesses, however, emphatically declared that the Father knew nothing of the oath that had been taken, or of the purpose of the associates.

Such testimony in favour of one whom they were anxious above all things to incriminate, the government would not allow to appear. Accordingly, Sir E. Coke, preparing the documents to be used in court as evidence, marked off the exculpatory passages, with directions that they were not to be read.[2] Having thus suppressed the passage which declared that the Jesuit was unaware of the conspirators' purpose, and of their oath, Coke went on to inform the jury, in his speech, "This oath was by Gerard the Jesuit given to Catesby, Percy, Christopher Wright, and Thomas Winter, and by Greenwell [Greenway] the Jesuit to Bates at another time, and so to the rest."[3]

---

[1] Father Gerard (*Narrative*, p. 201) denies in the most emphatic terms that he was the priest who said mass on this occasion. The point is fully discussed by the late Father Morris, S. J., in his Life of Father Gerard, pp. 437-438.

[2] The accompanying facsimile of this portion of Faukes' confession exhibits the marks made by Coke, and his added direction in the margin, *hucusque* ("thus far"). In the original his additions are in red ink.

[3] It is singular that he should not mention Faukes himself as

FALSIFICATION OF EVIDENCE. 201

3. Neither must it be forgotten that even apart from these manifest instances of tampering, the confessions themselves, obtained in such circumstances, are open to much suspicion. In an intercepted letter to Father Baldwin, of whom we have heard, Father Schondonck, another Jesuit, then rector of St. Omers, speaks thus:[1] " I much rejoice that, as I hear, there is no confession produced, by which, either in court or at the place of execution, any of our society is accused of so abominable a crime. This I consider a point of prime importance. *Of secret confessions, or those extorted by violence or torture, less account must be made; for we have many examples whereby the dishonesty of our enemies in such matters has been fully displayed."*

Father John Gerard in his Autobiography[2] relates an experience of his own which illustrates the methods employed to procure evidence such as was required.

one of those who received the oath from Gerard. There is no mention in any document of Greenway as giving the oath to Bates, or anyone else.

The facsimile of Faukes' signature, appended to his confession of November 9th, though affording unmistakable evidence of torture, gives no idea of the original, wherein the letters are so faintly traced as to be scarcely visible. It is evident that the writer had been so severely racked as to have no strength left in his hands to press the pen upon the paper. He must have fainted when he had written his Christian name, two dashes alone representing the other.

This signature, with other of the more sensational documents connected with the Plot, is exhibited in the newly established museum at the Record Office.

[1] *Dom. James I.* xviii. 97, February 27th, 1606, N. S. (Latin).

[2] *Narratio de rebus a se in Anglia gestis* (Stonyhurst MSS.). Published in Father G. R. Kingdon's translation under the title of *During the Persecution.*

When, in Queen Elizabeth's time, he had himself been taken and thrown into prison, the notorious Topcliffe, the priest-hunter, endeavoured to force him into an acknowledgment of various matters of a treasonable character. Father Gerard undertook to write what he had to say on the subject, and proceeded to set down an explicit denial of what his questioner suggested. What followed he thus relates.[1]

"While I was writing this, the old man waxed wroth. He shook with passion, and would fain have snatched the paper from me.

"'If you don't want me to write the truth,' said I, I'll not write at all.'

"'Nay,' quoth he, 'write so and so, and I'll copy out what you have written.'

"'I shall write what *I* please,' I answered, 'and not what *you* please. Show what I have written to the Council, for I shall add nothing but my name.'

"*Then I signed so near the writing, that nothing could be put in between.* The hot-tempered man, seeing himself disappointed, broke out into threats and blasphemies: 'I'll get you into my power, and hang you in the air, and show you no mercy: and then I shall see what God will rescue you out of my hands.'"

It was not by Catholics alone that allegations of this sort were advanced. Sir Anthony Weldon tells us[2] that on the trial of Raleigh and Cobham, the latter protested that he had never made the declaration attributed to him incriminating Raleigh. "That

---

[1] *During the Persecution*, p. 83.
[2] *Court and Character of King James*, p. 350 (ed. 1811).

villain Wade," [1] said he, "did often solicit me, and, not prevailing, got me, by a trick, to write my name on a piece of white paper, which I, thinking nothing, did ; so that if any charge came under my hand, it was forged by that villain Wade, by writing something above my hand, without my consent or knowledge."

Moreover, there exists undoubted evidence that the king's chief minister availed himself upon occasion of the services of such as could counterfeit handwriting and forge evidence against suspected persons. One Arthur Gregory [2] appears to have been thus employed, and he subsequently wrote to Salisbury reminding him of what he had done.[3] After acknowledging that he owes his life to the secretary who knows how to appreciate "an honest desire in respect of his Majesty's public service," Gregory thus continues :

"Your Lordship hath had a present trial of that which none but myself hath done before, *to write in another man's hand*, and, discovering the secret writing being in blank, to abuse a most cunning villain in his own subtlety, leaving the same at last in blank again, wherein although there be difficulty their answers show they have no suspicion."

This the calendarer of State Papers believes to refer to the case of Father Garnet, and it is certain from

---

[1] Sir William Waad, Lieutenant of the Tower, to whose charge the Powder Plot conspirators were committed, was afterwards dismissed from his office on a charge of embezzling the jewels of the Lady Arabella Stuart.

[2] Presumably the same Arthur Gregory who at an earlier period had counterfeited the seals of Mary Queen of Scots' correspondence.

[3] *Dom. James I.* xxiv. 38.

Gregory's own letter that at one time he held a post in the Tower. Is it not possible that an explanation may here be found of the strange circumstance, that perhaps the most important of Father Garnet's examinations[1] bears an endorsement, "This was forbydden by the King to be given in evidence"?

Gregory's letter, of which we have been speaking, has appended to it an instructive postscript:

"Mr. Lieutenant expecteth something to be written in the blank leaf of a Latin Bible, which is pasted in already for the purpose. I will attend it, and whatsoever else cometh."[2]

vii. *Catholic Testimony.*

It will not improbably be urged that the government history is confirmed in all essential particulars by authorities to whom no exception can be taken, namely, contemporary Catholic writers, and especially the Jesuits Gerard and Greenway, whose narratives of the conspiracy corroborate every detail concerning which doubts have been insinuated.

This argument is undoubtedly deserving of all consideration, but upon examination appears to lose much of its force. If the narratives in question agree with that furnished by the government, it is because they are based almost entirely upon it, and upon those published confessions of Winter and Faukes with which we are familiar.

---

[1] March 3rd, 1605-6 (Hatfield MSS.).
[2] Eudaemon Joannes cites the renegade Alabaster as testifying to having seen a letter seemingly of his own to Garnet, which he had never written. (*Answer to Casaubon*, p. 159.)

On this point Father Gerard is very explicit:[1] "Out of [Mr. Thomas Winter's] examination, with the others that were made in the time of their imprisonment, I must gather and set down all that is to be said or collected of their purposes and proceedings in this heady enterprize. For that, as I have said, they kept it so wholly secret from all men, that until their flight and apprehension it was not known to any that such a matter was in hand, and then there could none have access to them to learn the particulars. But we must be contented with that which some of those that lived to be examined, did therein deliver. Only for that some of their servants that were up in arms with them in the country did afterwards escape, somewhat might be learned by them of their carriage in their last extremities, and some such words as they then uttered, whereby their mind in the whole matter is something the more opened."

Elsewhere he writes, exhibiting more confidence in government documents than we can feel:[2]

"[The prisoners'] examinations did all agree in all material points, and therefore two only were published in print, containing the substance of the rest. And indeed [this is] the sum of that which I have been able to say in this narration touching either their first intentions or the names or number of the conspirators, or concerning the course they took to keep the matter so absolutely secret, or, finally, touching the manner of their beginning and proceeding in the whole matter; for that—as I noted before—it being kept a vowed secret in the heads and hearts of so few, and those also

[1] *Narrative*, p. 54.   [2] *Ibid.* p. 113.

afterwards apprehended before they could have means to declare the particulars in any private manner, therefore no more can be known of the matter or manner of this tragedy than is found or gathered out of their examinations."

As for Greenway, it should not be forgotten that for the most part he confined himself to translating Gerard's narrative from English into Italian, though he supplemented it occasionally with items furnished by his own experience as to the character and general conduct of the conspirators on previous occasions, or during their last desperate rally. Of this he was able to speak with more authority, as he not only chanced to be in the immediate neighbourhood, but actually visited them at Huddington House (the seat of Robert Winter) on November 6th, being summoned thither by Catesby through his servant Bates.[1] Greenway, like Gerard, constantly refers to the published confessions of Winter and Faukes as the sources of his information.

It may here be observed that the practical identity

[1] Though we have not now to consider the question of Father Greenway's connection with the conspirators, it may not be out of place to cite his own account of this visit (*Narrative*, Stonyhurst MSS., f. 86 b):

"Father Oswald [Greenway] went to assist these gentlemen with the Sacraments of the Church, understanding their danger and their need, and this with evident danger to his own person and life: and all those gentlemen could have borne witness that he publicly told them how he grieved not so much because of their wretched and shameful plight, and the extremity of their peril, as that by their headlong course they had given the heretics occasion to slander the whole body of Catholics in the kingdom, and that he flatly refused to stay in their company, lest the heretics should be able to calumniate himself and the other Fathers of the Society."

of the narratives of these two fathers was unknown to Mr. Jardine, who having seen only that of Father Greenway, and believing it to be an original work, founded upon this erroneous assumption an argument which loses its force when we learn the real author to have been Gerard. Mr. Jardine maintains that the narrator must, from internal evidence, have been an active and zealous member of the conspiracy, "approving, promoting and encouraging it with the utmost enthusiasm."[1] It so happens, however, that the real author, Father Gerard, is just the one of the incriminated Jesuits whose innocence is held by historians certainly not partial to his Order, to be beyond question. Mr. Gardiner considers[2] that there is "strong reason" to believe him not to have been acquainted with the Plot. Dr. Jessopp is still more emphatic, and declares[3]

---

[1] In this, as in some other respects, Mr. Jardine shows himself rather an advocate than an impartial historian. He holds that the complicity of the writer of the *Narrative* with the plotters is proved by the intimate knowledge he displays concerning them, "their general conduct—their superstitious fears—their dreams—'their thick coming fancies'—in the progress of the work of destruction." (*Criminal Trials*, ii. xi.)

There is here an evident allusion to the silly story of the "bell in the wall" (related by Greenway and not by Gerard), to which Mr. Jardine gives extraordinary prominence. He does not, however, inform us that Greenway relates this (*Narrative*, f. 58 b) and some similar matters, on the authority of "an acquaintance to whom Catesby told it shortly before his death," and that he leaves it to the judgment of his readers.

Greenway's frequent and earnest protestations of innocence Mr. Jardine summarily dismisses with the observation that they are "entitled to no credit whatever" (p. xii).

[2] *History*, i. 243.

[3] *Dictionary of National Biography* (Digby, Sir E.).

that it is impossible for any candid reader of all the evidence to doubt that Gerard must be exonerated.

What has been said of Gerard and Greenway may serve also for Father Garnet, who in his various examinations and other utterances assumes the truth of the government story, for neither had he materials to go upon except those officially supplied.

It is obvious that the conclusion to be drawn from the above considerations is chiefly negative. That the conspirators embarked on a plot against the state, is, of course unquestionable. What was the precise nature of that plot is by no means clear, and still less what were the exact circumstances of its initiation and its collapse. This only appears to be certain, that things did not happen as they were officially related, while the elaborate care expended on the falsification of the story seems to indicate that the true version would not have served the purposes to which that story was actually put.

CHAPTER IX.

THE SEQUEL.

As we have already seen, the Gunpowder Plot formed no exception to the general law observable in conspiracies of its period, proving extremely advantageous to those against whom it was principally directed. No single individual was injured by it except those concerned in it, or accused of being so concerned. On the other hand, it marked an epoch in public policy, and irrevocably committed the king and the nation to a line of action towards Catholics, which up to that time they had hoped, and their enemies had feared, would not be permanently pursued.

"The political consequences of this transaction," says Mr. Jardine,[1] "are extremely important and interesting. It fixed the timid and wavering mind of the king in his adherence to the Protestant party, in opposition to the Roman Catholics; and the universal horror, which was naturally excited not only in England but throughout Europe by so barbarous an attempt, was artfully converted into an engine for the suppression of the Roman Catholic Church: so that the ministers of James I., having procured the reluctant acquiescence of the king, and the cordial assent of public opinion, were enabled to continue in full force

[1] *Criminal Trials*, ii. 1.

the severe laws previously passed against Papists, and to enact others of no less rigour and injustice."

Such was the effect in fact produced, and the calm deliberation displayed in dealing with the crisis appears to indicate that no misgivings were entertained as to the chance of anything but advantage resulting from it. We have already seen with what strange equanimity the presence of the powder beneath the Parliament House was treated. Not less serene was the attitude of the minister chiefly responsible for the safety of the State in face of the grave dangers still declared to be threatening, even after the "discovery." Preparations, it was officially announced, had been made for an extensive rising of the Catholics, and this had still to be reckoned with. As the king himself informed Sir John Harington, the design was not formed by a few, the "whole legion of Catholics" were implicated: the priests had been active in preaching the holy war, and the Pope himself had employed his authority on behalf of the cause.[1]

Moreover, the conspirators, except Faukes, escaped from London, and hurried to the intended scene of action, where, though no man voluntarily joined them, they were able at first to collect a certain force of their own retainers and domestics, and began to traverse the shires in which their influence was greatest, committing acts of plunder and violence, and calling on all men to join them for God and the country. For a couple of days the local magistrates did not feel strong enough to cope with them, and forwarded to the capital reports capable, it might be

[1] *Nugæ Antiquæ*, i. 374.

supposed, of alarming those who were bewildered by so totally unexpected an assault, for which the evidence in hand showed preparations of no ordinary magnitude to have been made. The numbers of the insurgents, it was said, were constantly increasing; only a feeble force could be brought against them; they were seizing horses and ammunition, and all this in "a very Catholic country."

In his famous speech to Parliament, delivered on November 9th, the king dwelt feelingly on the danger of the land, left exposed to the traitors, in the absence of the members of the legislature, its natural guardians. "These rebels," he declared,[1] "that now wander through the country could never have gotten so fit a time of safety in their passage, or whatsoever unlawful actions, as now; when the country, by the aforesaid occasions, is, in a manner, left desolate and waste unto them."[2]

Meanwhile, however, the secretary remained imperturbably tranquil as before, and so well aware of the true state of the case that he could afford to make merry over the madcap adventurers. On the same 9th of November he wrote to the ambassadors: "It is also thought fit that some martial men should presently repair down to those countries where the Robin Hoods are assembled, to encourage the good and to terrify the bad. In which service the Earl of Devon-

---
[1] *Harleian Miscellany*, iv. 249.
[2] This terrible state of things was alleged as a principal reason for the prorogation of the Parliament for two months and a half. As a matter of fact, the rebels had been overthrown and captured the day before that on which the king's speech was delivered, and news of that event was received that same evening.

shire is used, a commission going forth for him as general: although I am easily persuaded that this Faggot will be burnt to ashes before he shall be twenty miles on his way."

His prescience was not at fault, for before despatching the letter the minister was able to announce the utter collapse of the foolish and unsupported enterprise.

No time was lost in turning the defeated conspiracy to practical account. On the very 5th of November[1] itself the Commons proceeded, before all other business, to the first reading of a bill for the better execution of penal statutes against Recusants. On the following day this was read a second time. The house next met on the 9th, to hear the king's speech, and was then prorogued to January 21st following. On that day, the foremost article on the programme was the first reading of a bill (whether the same or another) for the better execution of penal statutes; another was likewise proposed for prevention of the danger of papistical practices; and a committee was appointed "to consider of some course for the timely and severe proceeding against Jesuits, Seminaries, and other popish agents and practisers, and for the prevention and suppression of their plots and practices."[2] On the 22nd there was a motion directed against the seminaries beyond the seas, and the bill for better execution of penal statutes was read a second time. On the 23rd the bill for a public thanksgiving was read twice, being finally

---

[1] *Commons' Journals.*
[2] In the preamble of the Act so passed we read: "Forasmuch as it is found by daily experience, that many his Majesty's subjects that adhere in their hearts to the popish religion, by the

passed on the 25th. Its preamble runs thus : " Forasmuch as ... no nation of the earth hath been blessed with greater benefits than this kingdom now enjoyeth, having the true and free profession of the gospel under our most gracious sovereign lord King James, the most great, learned, and religious king that ever reigned therein ... the which many malignant and devilish papists, jesuits, and seminary priests, much envying and fearing, conspired most horribly ..." and so forth.

Thus did the Commons set to work, and the other House, though they declined to sanction all that was proposed in the way of exceptional severity towards the actual conspirators, were no wise lacking in zeal against the Catholic body.

The course of legislation that ensued is thus described by Birch :[1]

"The discovery of the Plot occasioned the Parliament to enjoin the oath of allegiance to the king, and to enact several laws against Popery, and especially against the Jesuits and Priests who, as the Earl of Salisbury observed,[2] sought to bring all things into

infection drawn from thence, and by the wicked and devilish counsel of jesuits, seminaries, and other like persons dangerous to the church and state, are so perverted in the point of their loyalties and due allegiance unto the King's majesty, and the Crown of England, as they are ready to entertain and execute any treasonable conspiracies and practices, as evidently appears by that more than barbarous and horrible attempt to have blown up with gunpowder the King, Queen . . ." etc., etc.

[1] *Negotiations*, p. 256.
[2] " Our parliament is prorogued till the 18th of next November. Many things have been considerable in it, but especially the zeal of both Houses for the preservation of God's true religion, by

confusion.... In passing these laws for the security of the Protestant religion, the Earl of Salisbury exerted himself with distinguished zeal and vigour, which gained him great love and honour from the kingdom, as appeared, in some measure, in the unusual attendance upon him at his installation into the Order of the Garter, on the 20th of May, 1606,[1] at Windsor."

It is, indeed, abundantly clear that beyond all others this statesman benefited by the Plot, in consequence of which he obtained, at least for a time, a high degree of both power and popularity. His installation at Windsor, above mentioned, was an almost regal triumph. Baker notes[2] that he was attended on the occasion "beyond ordinary promotion." Howes writes[3] that he "set forward from his house in the Strand, being almost as honourably accompanied, and with as great a train of lords, knights, gentlemen, and officers of the Court, with others besides his peculiar servants, very richly attired and bravely mounted, as was the King when he rid in state through London."

Neither were there wanting to the secretary other advantages which, if less showy, were not less substan-

---

establishing many good laws against Popery and those firebrands, Jesuits, and Priests, that seek to bring all things into confusion. His Majesty resolveth once more by proclamation to banish them all; and afterwards, if they shall not obey, then the laws shall go upon them without any more forbearance."
—Cecil to Winwood, June 7th, 1606 (Winwood, *Memorials*, ii. 219).

[1] In the *Dictionary of National Biography*, and Doyle's *Official Baronage*, this installation is erroneously assigned to 1605.

[2] *Chronicle*, p. 408.

[3] Continuation of Stowe's *Annals*, p. 883.

tial. It will be remembered how, in his secret correspondence with the King of Scots before the death of Elizabeth, Cecil had constantly endeavoured to turn

THE POWDER PLOT. III.

the mind of his future sovereign against the Earl of Northumberland, whom he declared to be associated with Raleigh and Cobham in a "diabolical triplicity," and to be "a sworn enemy of King James."[1] These

[1] Letter iii.

efforts had not been altogether successful, and though Cobham and Raleigh had been effectually disposed of in connection with the conspiracy known as the "Main," Northumberland was still powerful, and was thought by many to be Cecil's most formidable rival. As one result of the Gunpowder Plot, he now disappeared for ever from public life.

When we remember the terms in which the secretary had previously described him, as well as the result about to ensue, it is not a little startling to remark with what emphasis it was protested, in season and out, that a ruling principle of the government's action was to do nothing which might even seem to cast a slur upon the earl's character, while at the same time the very point is artfully insinuated which was to be turned against him.[1] Thus in the "King's Book," in explanation of the curious roundabout courses adopted in connection with the "discovery," we are told that a far-fetched excuse was devised for the search determined upon, lest it might "lay an ill-favoured imputation upon the Earl of Northumberland, one of his Majesty's greatest subjects and counsellors; this Thomas Percy being his kinsman and most confident familiar." So again Cecil wrote to the ambassadors: "It hath been thought meet in policy of State (all circumstances considered) to commit the Earl of North-

---

[1] At Northumberland's trial Lord Salisbury thus expressed himself: "I have taken paines in my nowne heart to clear my lord's offences, which now have leade me from the contemplation of his virtues; for I knowe him vertuous, wyse, valiaunte, and of use and ornamente to the state.... The cause of this combustion was the papistes seekinge to restore their religion. Non libens dico, sed res ipsa loquitur."—Hawarde, *Les Reportes*, etc.

umberland to the Archbishop of Canterbury, there to be honourably used, until things be more quiet. Whereof if you shall hear any judgment made, as if his Majesty or his council could harbour a thought of such a savage practice to be lodged in such a nobleman's breast, you shall do well to suppress it as a malicious discourse and invention, this being only done to satisfy the world that nothing be undone which belongs to policy of State, when the whole monarchy was proscribed to dissolution ; and being no more than himself discreetly approved when he received the sentence of the council for his restraint."

Yet what was the issue ? A series of charges were brought against Northumberland, all of which broke down except that of having, as Captain of the Royal Pensioners, admitted Percy amongst them without exacting the usual oath. He in vain demanded an open trial, and was brought before the Star Chamber, by which, after he had been assailed by Coke in the same violent strain previously employed against Raleigh, he was sentenced to forfeit all offices which he held under the Crown, to be imprisoned during the king's pleasure, and to pay a fine of £30,000, equal to at least ten times that sum at the present day.

As if this were not enough, fresh proceedings were taken against him six years later, when he was again subjected to examination, and again, says Lingard,[1] foiled the ingenuity or malice of his persecutor.

[1] *History*, vii. 84, note. On this subject Mr. Sawyer, the editor of Winwood (1715), has the following remark : " We meet with some account of his [Northumberland's] offence, though couched in such tender terms, that 'tis a little difficult to con-

It seems, therefore, by no means extraordinary that men, as we have heard from the French ambassador, should have commonly attributed the earl's ruin to the resolution of his great rival to remove from his own path every obstacle likely to be dangerous, or that Cecil should himself bear witness,[1] in 1611, to the "bruites" touching Northumberland which were afloat, and should be anxious, as "knowing how various a discourse a subject of this nature doth beget," to "prevent any erroneous impression by a brief narrative of the true motive and progress of the business."

As to Northumberland's own sentiments, he, we are told by Osborne,[2] declared that the blood of Percy would refuse to mix with that of Cecil if they were poured together in the same basin.

It is, moreover, evident not only that the great statesman, to use Bishop Goodman's term, actually profited largely by the powder business, but that from the first he saw in it a means for materially strengthening his position; an opportunity which he lost no time in turning to account by making it appear that in such a crisis he was absolutely necessary to the State. This is shown by the remarkable manifesto which he promptly issued, a document which appears to have been almost forgotten, though well deserving attention.

A characteristic feature of the traitorous proceedings of the period was the inveterate habit of conspirators to drop compromising documents in the street, or to throw

ceive it deserved so heavy a punishment as a fine of £30,000 and perpetual imprisonment." (*Memorials*, iii. 287, note.)

[1] To Winwood, *Memorials*, iii. 287.
[2] *Traditional Memoirs*, p. 214.

them into yards and windows. In the court of Salisbury House was found, in November, 1605, a threatening letter, more than usually extraordinary. It purported to come from five Catholics, who began by unreservedly condemning the Gunpowder Plot as a work abhorred by their co-religionists as much as by any Protestants. Since, however, his lordship, beyond all others, seemed disposed to take advantage of so foul a scandal, in order to root out all memory of the Catholic religion, they proceeded to warn him that they had themselves vowed his death, and in such fashion that their success was certain. None of the accomplices knew who the others were, but it was settled who should first make the attempt, and who, in order, afterwards. Moreover, death had no terrors for any of them, two being stricken with mortal sickness, which must soon be fatal; while the other three were in such mental affliction as not to care what became of them.

As a reply to this strange effusion Cecil published a tract,[1] obviously intended as a companion to the famous "King's Book," in which with elaborate modesty he owned to the impeachment of being more zealous than others in the good cause, and protested his resolution, at whatever peril to himself, to continue his services to

[1] *An Answere to certaine Scandalous Papers, scattered abroad under colour of a Catholicke Admonition.* "Qui facit vivere, docet orare." Imprinted at London by Robert Barker, Printer to the King's most Eccellent Majestie. Anno 1606.

This was published in January, 1605-6, on the 28th of which month Sir W. Browne, writing from Flushing, mentions that "my lord of Salisbury hath lately published a little booke as a kynd of answer to som secrett threatning libelling letters cast into his chamber." (Stowe MSS., 168, 74, f. 308.)

his king and country. The sum and substance of this curious apology is as follows.

Having resolved to recall his thoughts from the earthly theatre to higher things, which statesmen are supposed overmuch to neglect, he had felt he could choose no better theme for his meditations than the "King's Book," wherein so many lively images of God's great favour and providence are represented, every line discovering where Apelles' hand hath been; so that all may see there needs now no Elisha to tell the King of Israel what the Aramites do in their privatest councils.

While in this most serious and silent meditation, divided between rapture at God's infinite mercy and justice, and thought of his own happiness to live under a king pleasing to God for his zealous endeavours to cleanse the vessels of his kingdom from the dregs and lees of the Romish grape,—and while his heart was not a little cheered to observe any note of his own name in the royal register, for one that had been of any little use in this so fortunate discovery,—as the poor day labourer who taketh contentment when he passeth that glorious architecture, to the building whereof he can remember to have carried some few sticks and stones,—while thus blissfully engaged, he is grieved to find himself singled out from the honourable body of the council,—why, he knows not, for with it he would be content to be identified—as the author of the policy which is being adopted; and, conscious that in his humble person the Body of Authority is assailed, he thinks it well, for once, to make a reply.

Having recited the threatening letter in full, he presently continues:

"Though I participate not in the follies of that fly who thought herself to raise the dust because she sat on the chariot-wheel, yet I am so far from disavowing my honest ambition of my master's favour, as I am desirous that the world should hold me, not so much his creature, by the undeserved honours I hold from his grace and power, as my desire to be the shadow of his mind, and to frame my judgment, knowledge, and affections according to his. Towards whose Royal Person I shall glory more to be always found an honest and humble subject, than I should to command absolutely in any other calling."

Of those who threaten him he says very little, assuming, however, as self-evident, that they are set on by some priest, who, after the manner of his tribe, doth "carry the unlearned Catholics, like hawks hooded, into those dangerous positions."

But, as for himself, let the world understand that he is not the man to neglect his duty on account of the personal danger it entails. "Far I hope it shall be from me, who know so well in whose HOLY BOOK my days are numbered, once to entertain a thought to purchase a span of time, at so dear a rate, as for the fear of any mortal power, in my poor talent, *Aut Deo, aut Patriæ, aut Patri patriæ deesse.*" [1]

---

[1] On this subject Cornwallis wrote to Salisbury (Winwood, ii. 193) : "Many reports are here spread of the Combination against your Lordship, and that five English Romanists would resolve your death. It seems that since they cannot be allowed *Sacrificium incruentum*, they will now altogether put in use their sacrifices of blood. But I hope and suppose that their hearts and their hands want much of the vigour that rests in their wills and their pens. Your Lordship doth take especial courage

In spite of the singular ability of this manifesto, the art of the writer is undoubtedly somewhat too conspicuous to permit us to accept it as the kind of document which would be produced by one who felt himself confronted by a serious peril. An interesting and most pertinent commentary is supplied by a contemporary Jesuit, Giles Schondonck, Rector of St. Omers College, in a letter to Father Baldwin, the same of whom we have already heard in connection with the Plot.[1]

Schondonck has, he says, read and re-read Cecil's book, which Baldwin had lent him. If his opinion be required, he finds in it many flowers of wit and eloquence, and it is a composition well adapted for its object; but the original letter which has evoked this brilliant rejoinder is a manifest fraud, not emanating from any Catholic, but devised by the enemies of the Church for her injury. The writers plainly contradict themselves. They begin by denouncing the Powder Plot as impious and abominable, and they do so most righteously, and they declare its authors to have been turbulent spirits and not religious, in which also they are right. But they go on to approve the design of murdering Cecil. What sense is there in this? If the one design be impious and detestable, with what

in this, that they single you out as the chief and principal watch Tower of your Country and Commonwealth, and turn the strength of their malice to you whom they hold the discoverer of all their unnatural and destructive inventions against their prince and country," etc.

[1] P. R. O. *Dom. James I.* xviii. 97, February 27th, N.S., 1606. The original, which is in Latin, has been utterly misunderstood by the Calendarer of State Papers.

colour or conscience can the other be approved? There is no difference of principle, though in the one case many were to be murdered, in the other but a single man. No one having in him any spark of religion could defend either project, much less approve it. Moreover, much that is set down is simply ridiculous. Men in the last extremity of sickness, or broken down by sorrow, are not of the stuff whereof those are made by whom desperate deeds are done.

From another Jesuit we obtain instructive information which at least serves to show what was the opinion of Catholics as to the way in which things were being managed. This is conveyed in a letter addressed December 1st, 1606, to the famous Father Parsons by Father Richard Blount, Father Garnet's successor as superior of the English mission.[1] It must be remembered that this was not meant for the public eye, and in fact was never published. It cannot have been intended to obtain credence for a particular version of history, and it was written to him who, of all men, was behind the scenes so far as the English Jesuits were concerned. Much of it is in cipher which, fortunately, has been interpreted for us by the recipient.

Blount begins with a piece of intelligence which is startling enough. Amongst the lords of the council none was a more zealous enemy of Popery than the chamberlain, the Earl of Suffolk,[2] who was more than once on the commission for expelling priests and Jesuits, and had in particular been so energetic in the matter of the Powder Plot that Salisbury modestly

---

[1] Stonyhurst MSS., *Anglia*, iii. 72.
[2] Thomas Howard, cr. 1603.

confessed that in regard of the "discovery" he had himself been "much less forward."[1] Now, however, we are told, only a twelvemonth later, that this nobleman and his wife are ready for a sufficient fee to procure "some kind of peace" for the Catholics. The needful sum may probably be raised through the Spanish Ambassador, but the issue is doubtful "because Salisbury will resist."—"Yet such is the want of money with the chamberlain at this time—whose expenses are infinite—that either Salisbury must supply, or else he must needs break with him."[2]

After some particulars concerning the jealousy against the Scots, and the matter of the union (which "sticketh much in the Parliament's teeth") Blount goes on to relate how Cecil has been attempting to float a second Powder Plot—the scene being this time the king's court itself. He has had another letter brought in, to set it going, and had seemingly calculated on capturing the writer himself and some of his brethren in connection with it. In this, however, he has been foiled, and the matter appears to have been dropped. In Blount's own words:[3]

---

[1] To the ambassadors.

[2] Father Blount's account is undoubtedly in keeping with what we know of the Earl, and especially of his Countess, who was a sister of Sir Thomas Knyvet, the captor of Guy Faukes. Suffolk, in 1614, became Lord High Treasurer, but four years afterwards grave irregularities were discovered in his office; he was accused of embezzlement and extortion, in which work his wife was proved to have been even more active than himself. They were sentenced to restore all money wrongfully extorted, to a fine of £30,000, and to imprisonment during pleasure.

[3] In this letter all proper names are in cipher, as well as various other words.

"Now these last days we expected some new stratagem, because Salisbury pretended a letter to be brought to his lordship found by chance in St. Clement's Churchyard, written in ciphers, wherein were many persons named, and a question asked, whether there were any concavity under the stage in the court. But belike the device failed, and so we hear no words of it. About this time this house was ransacked, where by chance Blount came late the night before, finding four more, Talbot, N. Smith, Wright, Arnold; being all besieged from morning to night. If things had fallen out as was expected, then that letter would have haply been spoken of, whereas now it is very secret, and only served to pick a thanks of King James, with whom Salisbury keepeth his credit by such tricks, as upon whose vigilancy his majesty's life dependeth."

One other feature of the after history demands consideration. As Fuller tells us,[1] "a learned author, making mention of this treason, breaketh forth into the following rapture:

> 'Excidat illa dies aevo, ne postera credant
> Saecula; nos certe taceamus, et obruta multâ
> Nocte tegi propriae patiamur crimina gentis.'
>
> 'Oh, let that day be quite dashed out of time,
>   And not believ'd by the next generation;
> In night of silence we'll conceal the crime,
>   Thereby to save the credit of the nation.'"

"A wish," he adds, "which in my opinion, hath more of poetry than of piety therein, and from which I must be

---
[1] *Church History*, x. 40.

forced to dissent." Assuredly if it were judged that silence and oblivion should be the lot of the conspiracy, no stranger means were ever adopted to secure the desired object. A public thanksgiving was appointed to be held every year, on the anniversary of the "discovery;" a special service for that day was inserted in the Anglican liturgy, and Gunpowder Plot Sermons kept the memory of the Treason green in the mind not of one but of many generations.

Moreover, the country was flooded with literature on the subject, in prose and rhyme, and the example of Milton is sufficient to show how favourite a topic it was with youthful poets essaying to try their wings.[1]

In regard of the history, one line was consistently adopted. The Church of England in its calendar marked November 5th, as the *Papists' Conspiracy*, and in the collect appointed for the day the king and estates of the realm were described as being "by Popish treachery appointed as sheep to the slaughter, in a most barbarous and savage manner, beyond the examples of former ages." Similarly, preachers and writers alike concurred in saying little or nothing about the actual conspirators, but much about the iniquity of Rome; the official character of the Plot, and its sanction, even its first suggestion, by the highest authorities of the Church, being the chief feature of

---

[1] We have four Latin epigrams of Milton's, *In proditionem Bombardicam*, which, though pointless, are bitterly anti-Catholic. A longer poem, of 226 lines, *In quintum Novembris*, is still more virulent.

It is somewhat remarkable that the universal Shakespeare should make no allusion to the Plot, beyond the doubtful reference to equivocation in *Macbeth* (ii. 3). He was at the time of its occurrence in the full flow of his dramatic activity.

the tale hammered year after year into the ears of the English people. The details of history supplied are frequently pure and unmixed fables.[1]

THE POWDER PLOT. IV.

Nor was the pencil less active than the pen in popularizing the same belief. Great was the ingenuity spent in devising and producing pictures which should im-

[1] See Appendix L, *Myths and Legends of the Powder Plot*.

press on the minds of the most illiterate a holy horror of the Church which had doomed the nation to destruction. One of the most elaborate of these was headed by an inscription which admirably summarizes the moral of the tale.

THE POWDER TREASON.—Propounded by *Satan:* Approved by *Antichrist* [*i.e.* the Pope]: Enterprised by *Papists:* Practized by *Traitors:* Revealed by an *Eagle* [Monteagle]: Expounded by an *Oracle* [King James]: Founded in *Hell:* Confounded in *Heaven.*

Accordingly we find representations of Lucifer, the Pope, the King of Spain, the General of the Jesuits, and other such worthies, conspiring in the background while the redoubtable Guy walks arm in arm with a demon to fire the mine, the latter grasping a papal Bull (unknown to the Bullarium), expedited to promote the project: or again, Faukes and Catesby stand secretly conspiring in the middle of the street, while Father Garnet, in full Jesuit habit (or what is meant for such) exhorts them to go on : or a priest gives the conspirators " the sacrament of secrecy ;" or representative Romish dignitaries blow threats and curses against England and her Parliament House,—or the Jesuits are buried in Hell in recompense of their perfidy.

It cannot, however, escape remark that while the limners have been conscientiously careful in respect of these details, they have one and all discarded accuracy in regard of another matter in which we might naturally have expected it. In no single instance is Guy Faukes represented as about to blow up the right house. Sometimes it is the House of Commons that he is going to destroy, more frequently the Painted

THE POWDER PLOT. V.

Chamber, often a nondescript building corresponding to nothing in particular,—but in no single instance is it the House of Lords.

The most extraordinary instance of so strange a vagary is afforded by a plate produced immediately after the occurrence it commemorates, in the year 1605 itself.[1] In this, Faukes with his inseparable lantern, but without the usual spurs, is seen advancing to the door of the "cellar," which stands conspicuous above ground. Aloft is seen the crescent moon, represented in exactly the right phase for the date of the discovery.[2] The accuracy exhibited as to this singular detail makes it more than ever extraordinary that the building to which he directs his steps is unquestionably St. Stephen's Chapel—The House of Commons.

One point of the history, in itself apparently insignificant, was at the time invested with such extravagant importance, as to suggest a question in its regard, namely the day itself whereon the marvellous deliverance took place. A curious combination of circumstances alone assigned it to the notorious Fifth of November. Parliament, as we have seen, was originally appointed to meet on the 3rd of October, but was suddenly adjourned for about a month, and so little reason did there seem to be for the prorogation[3] as to

---

[1] Brit. Mus. Print Room, Crace Collection, portf. xv. 28. This is reproduced, as our frontispiece.

[2] There was a new moon at 11.30 p.m. on October 31st.

[3] The reasons assigned in the proclamation for this prorogation are plainly insufficient: viz., "That the holding of it [the Parliament] so soone is not convenient, as well for that the ordinary course of our subjects resorting to the citie for their usuall affaires at the Terme is not for the most part till All-

fill the conspirators with alarm lest some suspicion of their design had prompted it; wherefore they sent Thomas Winter to attend the prorogation ceremony, and observe the demeanour of those who took part in it. Afterwards, though the discovery might have easily been made any time during the preceding week, nothing practical was done till the fateful day itself had actually begun, when, as the acute Lingard has not failed to observe, a remarkable change at once came over the conduct of the authorities, who discarding the aimless and dilatory manner of proceeding which had hitherto characterized them, went straight to the point with a promptitude and directness leaving nothing to be desired.

Whatever were their motive in all this, the action of the government undoubtedly brought it about that the great blow should be struck on a day which not a little enhanced the evidence for the providential character of the whole affair. Tuesday was King James' lucky day, more especially when it happened to be the 5th of the month, for on Tuesday, August the 5th, 1600, he had escaped the mysterious treason of the Gowries.

This coincidence evidently created a profound impression. "Curious folks observe," wrote Chamberlain to Carleton,[1] "that this deliverance happened on the fifth of November, answerable to the fifth of August, both Tuesdays; and this plot to be executed by Johnson [the assumed name of Faukes], and that at Johnstown [*i.e.*, Perth]." On the 27th of November, Lake

hallowtide or thereabouts." Why, then, had the meeting been fixed for so unsuitable a date?

[1] November 7th, 1605. (*Dom. James I.*)

suggested to the Archbishop of Canterbury,[1] that as a perpetual memorial of this so providential circumstance, the anniversary sermon should always be delivered upon a Tuesday. Two days later, the Archbishop wrote to his suffragans,[2] reminding them how on a Tuesday his majesty had escaped the Gowries, and now, on another Tuesday, a peril still more terrible, which must have ruined the whole nation, had not the Holy Ghost illumined the king's heart with a divine spirit. In remembrance of which singular instance of God's governance, there was to be an annual celebration.[3]

Most important of all, King James himself much appreciated the significance of this token of divine protection, and not only impressed this upon his Parliament, but proroguing it forthwith till after Christmas, selected the same propitious day of the week for its next meeting, as a safeguard against possible danger. "Since it has pleased God," said his majesty,[4] "to grant me two such notable deliveries upon one day of the week, which was Tuesday, and likewise one day of the month, which was the fifth, thereby to teach me that as it was the same devil that still persecuted me, so it was one and the same God that still mightily delivered me, I thought it therefore not

[1] Tanner MSS. lxxv. 44.
[2] *Ibid.*
[3] On his arrival in England, as Osborne tells us (*Memoirs*, p. 276), King James "brought a new holiday into the Church of England, wherein God had publick thanks given him for his majestie's deliverance out of the hands of Earle Goury;" but the introduction was not a success, Englishmen and Scots alike ridiculing it. Gunpowder Plot Day was more fortunate.
[4] *Harleian Miscellany*, iv. 251.

amiss, that the twenty-first day which fell to be upon Tuesday, should be the day of meeting of this next session of parliament, hoping and assuring myself, that the same God, who hath now granted me and you all so notable and gracious a delivery, shall prosper all our affairs at that next session, and bring them to an happy conclusion."

Whatever may be thought of this particular element of its history, it is perfectly clear that the fashion in which the Plot was habitually set before the English people, and which contributed more than anything else to work the effect actually produced, was characterized from the first by an utter disregard of truth on the part of those whose purposes it so opportunely served, and with such lasting results.

A Summary.

The evidence available to us appears to establish, principally two points,—that the true history of the Gunpowder Plot is now known to no man, and that the history commonly received is certainly untrue.

It is quite impossible to believe that the government were not aware of the Plot long before they announced its discovery.

It is difficult to believe that the proceedings of the conspirators were actually such as they are related to have been.

It is unquestionable that the government consistently falsified the story and the evidence as presented to the world, and that the points upon which they most insisted prove upon examination to be the most doubtful.

There are grave reasons for the conclusion that the whole transaction was dexterously contrived for the purpose which in fact it opportunely served, by those who alone reaped benefit from it, and who showed themselves so unscrupulous in the manner of reaping.

APPENDIX A.

NOTES ON THE ILLUSTRATIONS.

Frontispiece. The Powder Plot. I.

FROM the Crace Collection, British Museum, *Portf.* xv. 20. Thus described in the catalogue of the collection:

"A small etching of the House of Lords. Guy Fawkes in the foreground. W. E. exc. 1605."

This plate is of exceptional interest as having been executed within five months of the discovery of the Plot, *i.e.*, previously to March 25th, 1606, the first day of the year, Old Style.

Guy Faukes is represented as approaching the House of Commons (St. Stephen's Chapel), not the House of Lords, as the catalogue says.

Title-Page.

Obverse, or reverse, of a medal struck, by order of the Dutch senate, to commemorate the double event of the discovery of the Gunpowder Plot and the expulsion of the Jesuits from Holland. Drawn from a copy of the medal in pewter, by Paul Woodroffe. The design here exhibited is thus described in Hawkins and Frank's *Medallic Illustrations:*

"The name of Jehovah, in Hebrew, radiate, within a crown of thorns.

"Legend, chronogrammatic,
  NON DORMITASTI ANTISTES IACOBI"
[which gives the date 1605]
 On its other face the medal bears a snake gliding amid roses and lilies [symbolizing Jesuit intrigues in England and France], with the legend *Detectus qui latuit. S.C.* [Senatus Consulto]."
 This is reproduced on the cover.

Group of Conspirators (p. 3).

From a print published at Amsterdam.
 Eight conspirators are represented, five being omitted, viz., Grant, Keyes, Digby, Rokewood, and Tresham.
 Bates, as a servant, wears no hat.

The Houses of Parliament in the time of James I.
(pp. 56-7).

Restored from the best authorities, and drawn for the author by H. W. Brewer.

Ground Plan of House of Lords and adjacent Buildings
(p. 59).

Extracted from the "Foundation plan of the Ancient Palace of Westminster; measured, drawn and engraved by J. T. Smith" (*Antiquities of Westminster*, p. 125)

The House of Lords in 1807 (p. 61).

From J. T. Smith's *Antiquities of Westminster.*
 This sketch, made from the east, or river, side, was taken during the demolition of the buildings erected

against the sides of the Parliament House. These were put up previously to the time when Hollar made his drawing of the interior (temp. Charles II.), which shows the walls hung with tapestry, the windows having been blocked up.

According to a writer in the *Gentleman's Magazine* (No. 70, July, 1800), who signs himself "Architect," in a print of the time of James I. the tapestry is not seen, and the House "appears to have preserved much of its original work." The only print answering to this description which I have been able to find exhibits the windows, but is of no value for historical purposes, as it is a reproduction of one of the time of Queen Elizabeth, the figure of the sovereign alone being changed. This engraving is said to be "taken from a painted print in the Cottonian Library," of which I can find no trace. [B. Mus., K. 24. 19. b.]

To the left of our illustration is seen the gable of the Prince's Chamber. The door to the right of this opened into the cellar, and by it, according to tradition, Faukes was to have made his exit.

In front of this is seen part of the garden attached to Percy's lodging.

Interior of "Guy Faukes' Cellar" (p. 71).

Two views of the interior of the "cellar," drawn by H. W. Brewer, from elevations in J. T. Smith's *Antiquities of Westminster*, p. 39.

The remains of a buttery-hatch, at the southern end, testify to the ancient use of the chamber as the palace kitchen; of which the Earl of Northampton made mention at Father Garnet's trial.

The very ancient doorway in the eastern wall, seen on the left of the picture, was of Saxon workmanship, and, like the foundations beneath, probably dated from the time of Edward the Confessor, who first erected this portion of the palace, most of which had been rebuilt about the time of Henry III. By this doorway, according to some accounts, Faukes intended to escape after firing the train, though others assign this distinction to one near the other end.

These two illustrations were originally prepared for the *Daily Graphic* of November 5th, 1894, and it is by the courtesy of the proprietors of that journal that they are here reproduced.

Vault under the East End of the Painted Chamber
(p. 73).

From Brayley and Britton's *Palace of Westminster*, p. 247.

This has been constantly depicted and described as "Guy Faukes' Cellar."

Arches from Guy Faukes' Cellar (p. 75).

Drawn for the author by H. W. Brewer.

Sir John Soane, who in 1823 took down the old House of Lords, removed the arches from the " cellar " beneath it, to his own house in Lincoln's Inn Fields, now the Soane Museum, where they are still to be seen in a small court adjoining the building. They do not, however, appear to have been set up precisely in their original form, being dwarfed by the omission of some stones, presumably that they might occupy less space. In our illustration they are represented exactly as they now stand, with the modern building behind them. Some incongruous relics of other stonework which have been introduced amongst them have, however, been omitted.

The architecture of these arches, and of the adjacent Prince's Chamber, assigns them to the best period of thirteenth century Gothic.

Cell at S.E. corner of Painted Chamber (p. 83).

Often styled "Guy Faukes' Cell."
From Brayley and Britton, *op. cit.*, p. 360.
There appears to be no reason for associating this with Faukes.

The Powder Plot. II. (p. 90).

"Invented by Samuel Ward, Preacher, of Ipswich. Imprinted at Amsterdam, 1621." [British Museum, *Political and Personal Satires*, i. 41.]

This is the portion to the right of a composition representing on the left the Spanish Armada, and in the centre a council table at which are gathered the Devil, the Pope, the King of Spain, the General of the Jesuits, and others. An eye above is fixed on the cellar. Faukes in this case is going to blow up the Painted Chamber.

Interior of the old House of Lords (Scene on occasion of the King's Speech, 1755) (p. 97).

This plate represents the House in the reign of George II. In the century and a half since the time of the Powder Plot it is probable that the windows in the side walls had been blocked up, and the tapestry hung. The latter represented the defeat of the Armada.

[From Maitland's *London* (1756), ii. 1340.]

Lord Monteagle and the Letter (p. 115).

From *Mischeefes Mystery*.

King James enthroned, with crown and sceptre, upon a daïs, at the foot of which stands the Earl of Salisbury. An eagle bears a letter in its beak, to receive which the king and his minister extend their left hands.

The English poem, by John Vicars, embellished with this woodcut, was published in 1617, being a much expanded version of one in Latin hexameters, entitled *Pietas Pontificia*, by Francis Herring, which appeared in 1606.

Arrest of Guy Faukes (p. 125).

From *Mischeefes Mystery*.

Guy Faukes booted and spurred, and with his lantern, prepares to open a door at the extremity of the Painted Chamber. Sir Thomas Knyvet with his retinue approaches unseen. The stars and the beams from the lantern show that it is the middle of the night.

Discovery of the Gunpowder Plot (p. 136).

From a print in the Guildhall Library.

Catesby, Faukes, and Garnet (the latter in what is apparently meant for the Jesuit habit) stand in the middle of the street conspiring secretly. Through the open door of the "cellar" the powder barrels are seen.

This illustration (without the coins) stands at the head of Book XVIII. of M. Rapin de Thoyras' *History of England*, translated by N. Tindal.

"*Guy Faukes' Lantern*" (p. 139).

Drawn by H. W. Brewer.

This object, the authenticity of which is not unquestionable, is exhibited in the Ashmolean Museum, Oxford. It bears the inscription, " Laterna illa ipsa qua usus est, et cum qua deprehensus Guido Faux in crypta subterranea ubi domo Parliamenti difflandæ operam dabat. Ex dono Robti Heywood nuper Academiae Procuratoris, Ap. 4°, 1641."

It will be remembered that the honour of having arrested Faukes has been claimed for one of the name of Heywood.

The history of the famous lantern has not escaped the variations which we are accustomed to meet with on other points. Faukes is generally said to have been found with it in his hands, and it has consequently become an inseparable adjunct in pictures of him. On the other hand, we are told, " In a corner, behind the door, was a dark lantern containing a light " (Brayley and Britton, *Palace of Westminster*, p. 377).

Thomas Percy (p. 149).

From Grainger.

Around the portrait are four small engravings representing:

1. The arrest of Guy Faukes, who is here called "Thomas Ichrup."
2. The presentation of Thomas Ichrup to the King of Jerusalem (*i.e.*, the British Solomon).
3. The assault and bombardment of the "citadel" to which Percy has fled.
4. Percy killed by an arrow.

Thomas Winter's Confession (p. 168).

A portion of the copy of Winter's confession, in the handwriting of Levinus Munck, Lord Salisbury's private secretary, and dated November 23rd. In the margin is a note in the handwriting of King James, objecting to a certain "uncleare phrase," which has been altered in accordance with the royal wish. In the printed version it appears in the amended form.

Signatures exemplifying the Effects of Torture (p. 173).

Three signatures of Faukes (November 9th, 1605), and three of Father Edward Oldcorne (March 6th, 1605-6), at different stages of the same examination.

Guy Faukes' Confession of November 9th, 1605 (p. 199).

A portion of this confession, in which Faukes speaks of the oath taken by the conspirators and of their reception of the sacrament at the hands of Father John Gerard, adding, however, that "Gerard was not acquainted with their purpose." The last clause has been marked for omission by Sir Edward Coke who has written in the margin *hucusq*. ("thus far").

The letter B in the margin is also inserted by Coke,

APPENDIX A. 243

who habitually indicated by such letters which portions of the depositions were to be read in court and which omitted, all being always suppressed which told in any way in favour of the accused.

The document is written by a clerk, and signed by Faukes at the foot of each page.

The Powder Plot. III. (p. 215).

This is taken from a large plate [British Museum, *Political and Personal Satires*, i. 67], of which only the lower portion is here reproduced. At the top is the inscription:

THE POWDER TREASON, Propounded by Sathan, Approved by Anti-Christ, Enterprised by Papists, Practized by Traitors, Reveled by an Eagle, Expounded by an Oracle.—Founded in Hell, Confounded in Heaven.

Beneath are many emblematical devices.

In the portion here exhibited, King James is seen on his throne with Lords and Commons before him. Under the floor is a diminutive figure of Faukes with an ample store of barrels. At the bottom, in the left hand corner, some of the conspirators receive the sacrament from Father Gerard: on the right they are executed. On a lunette are the thirteen conspirators, with the arch-traitor Garnet in the centre, the band being described as "The Pope's Saltpeeter Saints." Within the lunette are the Jesuits in Hell.

The Powder Plot. IV. (p. 227).

This is the portion on the left of a composite picture [British Museum, *Political and Personal*

Satires, 63], on the right being represented the catastrophe known as the "Blackfriars Downfall." On Sunday, October 26th, 1623, many Catholics having assembled in an upper room of the French ambassador's house, in Blackfriars, to hear a sermon from the Jesuit, Father Drury, the floor collapsed, and many, including the preacher, were killed. As October 26th, O.S., corresponded to November 5th, N.S., it was ingeniously discovered that the accident was meant to signalize Gunpowder Plot day, though this fell on November 5th, O.S., or November 15th, N.S.

In our illustration the Parliament House is represented by a nondescript edifice, the wall of which is partially removed, showing King James and some of the Peers. An oven-like vault beneath represents the "cellar," well stored with barrels, which Faukes is preparing to light with a torch fanned by a crowned fiend with a pair of bellows. A company of halberdiers approaches under the guidance of an angel. In the background is a royal funeral procession.

A Latin inscription is attached which runs thus:

"Anno 1623, Quinto Novembris, eo scripto die quo Angliæ Parliamentum, aº 1605, proditione et insidiis Jesuitarum, pulvere nitreo inflammari et in æthera spargi debuit, Jesuitarum conventus Londini, . . . ad missam et conciones audiendas congregatus, fatali providentia, ædium ruina præcipitatus et dissipatus est, oppressis centum et plus totidem vulneratis.

> Loiolides sanctos efflare volebat ad astra;
> Astra repercutiunt fulmine Loiolidem.
> Loiolides, sine te penetrabit astra fidelis:
> Tu fato ad Stygias præcipitaris aquas."

The Powder Plot. V. (p. 229).

This is an edition of Samuel Ward's print described above, improved and embellished by a "Transmariner" in 1689. [British Museum, *Political and Personal Satires*, i. 43.]

The tent in which the council table stands is ornamented at the four corners with figures of a wolf, a parrot, an owl, and a dragon : a cockatrice is on the table ; on the top lie a gun, a sword, and a brace of pistols. A demon, bearing behind him a Papal Bull, accompanies Faukes, beneath whose lantern, as a play on his name, is written *Fax*. At the door of the cellar are scorpions and a serpent. On the top of the barrels within are seen the " yron barres," placed there to make the breach the greater.

APPENDIX B. (p. 33).

Sir Everard Digby's letter to Salisbury.

IT seems to have been always assumed that this celebrated letter, which is undated, was written after the failure of the Gunpowder Plot, and the consequent arrest of Sir Everard, and doubtless to some extent internal evidence supports this view, as the writer speaks of himself as deserving punishment, and of " our offence." It is, moreover, clear that the letter, which is undated, cannot have been written before May 4th, 1605, the date of Cecil's earldom. On the other hand, the whole tone of the document appears utterly inconsistent with the supposition that it was written by one branded with the stigma of such a crime as the Powder Plot. Some of the expressions used, especially in the opening sentence, appear, likewise, incompatible with such a supposition, and the letter bears the usual form of address for those sent in ordinary course of post, "To the Right Hon. the Earl of Salisburie give these"; it has moreover been sealed with a crest or coat-of-arms; all of which is quite unlike a document prepared by a prisoner for those who had him under lock and key. It is noteworthy, too, that at the trial, according to the testimony of the official account itself, on the very subject of the treatment of Catholics, Salisbury acknowledged "that Sir E. Digby was his ally."

It seems probable, therefore, that the letter was written before Digby had been entangled by Catesby in the conspiracy (*i.e.*, between May and September, 1605). If so, what was the "offence" of which he speaks? The answer to this question would throw an interesting light on this perplexed history. The following is Sir Everard's letter:

"Right Honourable, I have better reflected on your late speeches than at the present I could do, both for the small stay which I made, and for my indisposition that day, not being very well, and though perhaps your Lordship may judge me peremptory in meddling, and idle in propounding, yet the desire I have to establish the King in safety will not suffer me to be silent.

"One part of your Lordship's speech (as I remember) was that the King could not get so much from the Pope (even then when his Majesty had done nothing against Catholics) as a promise that he would not excommunicate him, so long as that mild course was continued, wherefore it gave occasion to suspect, that if Catholics were suffered to increase, the Pope might afterwards proceed to excommunication, if the King would not change his religion. But to take away that doubt, I do assure myself that his Holiness may be drawn to manifest so contrary a disposition of excommunicating the King, that he will proceed with the same course against all such as shall go about to disturb the King's quiet and happy reign; and the willingness of Catholics, especially of priests and Jesuits, is such as I dare undertake to procure any priest in England (though it were the Superior of the Jesuits) to go himself to Rome to negotiate this business, and that both he and all other religious men (till the Pope's pleasure be known) shall take any spiritual course to stop the effect that may proceed from any discontented or despairing Catholic.

"And I doubt not but his return would bring both assurance that such course should not be taken with the King, and that it should be performed against any that should seek to disturb him for religion. If this were done, there could then be no cause to fear any Catholic, and this may be done only with those proceedings (which as I understood your lordship) should be used. If your Lordship apprehend it to be worth the doing, I shall be glad to be the instrument, for no hope to put off from myself any punishment, but only that I wish safety to the King and ease to Catholics. If your Lordship and the State think it fit to deal severely with Catholics, within brief there will be massacres, rebellions, and desperate attempts against the King and State. For it is a general received reason amongst Catholics, that there is not that expecting and suffering course now to be run that was in the Queen's time, who was the last of her line, and last in expectance to run violent courses against Catholics ; for then it was hoped that the King that now is would have been at least free from persecuting, as his promise was before his coming into this realm, and as divers his promises have been since his coming, saying that he would take no soul money nor blood. Also, as it appeared, was the whole body of the Council's pleasure, when they sent for divers of the better sort of Catholics (as Sir Thos. Tressam and others) and told them it was the King's pleasure to forgive the payment of Catholics, so long as they should carry themselves dutifully and well. All these promises every man sees broken, and to thrust them further in despair, most Catholics take note of a vehement book written by Mr. Attorney, whose drift (as I have heard) is to prove that the only being a Catholic is to be a traitor, which book coming forth, after the breach of so many promises, and before the ending of such a violent parliament, can work no less effect in men's minds than a belief that every Catholic will be brought within that compass before the King and State have done with them. And I know, as the priest himself told me, that if he had not hindered there had somewhat been attempted, before our offence, to give ease to Catholics But being so safely prevented, and so necessary to avoid, I doubt not but your Lordship and the rest of the Lords will think of a more mild and undoubted safe course, in which I will undertake the performance of what I have promised and as much as can be expected, and when I have done, I shall be as willing to die as I am ready to offer my service, and expect not nor desire favour for it, either before the doing it, nor in the doing it, nor after it is done, but refer myself to the resolved course for me. So, leaving to trouble your Lordship any further, I humbly take my leave. Your Lordship's poor bedesman, EV. DIGBY."

Addressed "To the Right Honourable the Earl of Salisburie give these."

Sealed.
[P. R. O. *Dom. James I.* xvii. 10.]

APPENDIX C. (p. 34).

The Question of Succession.

FATHER PARSONS' well-known book on this subject, written under the pseudonym of Doleman, was denounced by Sir Edward Coke as containing innumerable treasons and falsehoods. In fact, as may be seen in the work itself, it is an exhaustive and careful statement of the descent of each of the possible claimants, and of other considerations which must enter into the settlement. Sir Francis Inglefield wrote that it was necessary to take some step of this kind, to set men thinking on so important a question which would soon have to be decided, for that the anti-Catholic party had made it treason to discuss it during the queen's life, with intent to foist a successor of their own selection on the nation, when the moment should arrive, trusting to the ignorance universally prevalent as to the rights of the matter; but that such lack of information could not help the people to a sound decision. [Stonyhurst MSS., *Anglia*, iii. 32.]

The Spanish sympathies of Parsons and his party were afterwards made much of as evidence of their traitorous disposition. On this subject it must be noted (1) the Infanta of Spain was amongst those whose claim was urged on genealogical grounds; (2) the project was to marry her to an English nobleman. As Parsons tells us, when she married and was endowed with another estate, English Catholics ceased to think of her. [*Ibid.* ii. 444.] (3) Father Garnet notes that, "since the old king of Spain died [1598], there hath been no pretence ... for the Infanta, or the King [of Spain], or any of that family, but for any that should maintain Catholic religion, and principally for His Majesty" [James I.]. [*Ibid.* iii. n. 41.]

A remark of Parsons' on this point, which at the time was considered almost blasphemous, will seem now almost a truism, viz., that the title of particular succession in kingdoms is founded only upon the positive laws of several countries, since neither kingdoms nor monarchies are of the essence of human society, and therefore every nation has a right to establish its own kings in what manner it likes, and upon what conditions. Wherefore, as each of the other great parties in England (whom he designates as Protestants and Puritans) will look chiefly to its own political interests, and exact from the monarch of its choice pledges to secure them, it behoves Catholics, being so large a part of the nation, to take their proper share in the settlement, and therefore to study betimes the arguments on which the claims of the competitors are severally based.

APPENDIX D. (p. 36).

The Spanish Treason.

THE history of the alleged treasonable negotiations with Spain, conducted by various persons whose names were afterwards connected with the Gunpowder Plot, appears open to the gravest doubt and suspicion. It would be out of place to discuss the question here, but two articles on the subject, by the present writer, will be found in the *Month* for May and June, 1896.

APPENDIX E. (p. 60).

Site of Percy's lodging [*see* View, p. 56, and Plan, p. 59.]

THAT the lodging hired by Percy stood near the south-east corner of the old House of Lords (*i.e.* nearer to the river than that building, and adjacent to, if not adjoining, the Prince's Chamber) is shown by the following arguments.

1. John Shepherd, servant to Whynniard, gave evidence as to having on a certain occasion seen from the river "a boat lye cloase to the pale of Sir Thomas Parreys garden, and men going to and from the water

through the back door that leadeth into Mr. Percy his lodging." [*Gunpowder Plot Book*, 40, part 2.]

2. Faukes, in his examination of November 5th, 1605, speaks of "the windowe in his chamber neere the parliament house towards the water side."

3. It is said that when digging their mine the conspirators were troubled by the influx of water from the river, which would be impossible if they were working at the opposite side of the Parliament House.

[It has always been understood that Percy's house stood at the south end of the House of Lords, but Smith (*Antiquities of Westminster*, p. 39) places it to the south-west instead of the south-east, saying that it stood on the site of what was afterwards the Ordnance Office.]

APPENDIX F. (p. 64).

Enrolment of Conspirators.

The evidence on this point is most contradictory.

1. The Indictment, on the trial of the conspirators, mentions the following dates.

May 20th, 1604. [Besides Garnet, Greenway, Gerard, "and other Jesuits,"] there met together T. Winter, Faukes, Keyes, Bates, Catesby, Percy, the two Wrights, and Tresham, by whom the Plot was approved and undertaken.

March 31*st*, 1605, R. Winter, Grant, and Rokewood were enlisted.

[No mention is made of Digby, who was separately arraigned, nor in his arraignment is any date specified.]

2. According to Faukes' confession of November 17th, 1605, Percy, Catesby, T. Winter. J. Wright, and himself were the first associates. Soon afterwards C. Wright was added. After Christmas, Keyes was initiated and received the oath. At a later period, Digby, Rokewood, Tresham, Grant, and R. Winter were brought in. Bates is not mentioned.

[In this document the names of Keyes and R. Winter have been interchanged, in Cecil's writing, and thus it was printed : the latter being made to appear as an earlier confederate.]

3. According to T. Winter's declaration of November 23rd, 1605, Catesby, J. Wright, and himself were the first associates, Percy and Faukes being presently added. Keyes was enlisted before Michaelmas, C. Wright after Christmas, Digby at a later period, and Tresham " last of all." No others are mentioned.

4. Keyes—November 30th, 1605—says that he was inducted a little before Midsummer, 1604.

5. R. Winter and Grant (January 17th, 1605-6) fix January, 1604-5, for their introduction to the conspiracy, and Bates (December 4th, 1605) gives the preceding December for his. Neither date agrees with that of the indictment in support of which these confessions were cited.

6. There is, of course, no evidence of any kind to show that Father Garnet and the "other Jesuits" ever had any conference with the conspirators, nor was such a charge urged on his trial.

7. Sir Everard Digby's case is exceptionally puzzling. All the evidence represents him as having been initiated late in September, or early in October, 1605. Among the Hatfield MSS., however, there is a letter addressed

to Sir Everard, by one G. D., and dated June 11th, 1605, which treats ostensibly of a hunt for "the otter that infesteth your brooks," to be undertaken when the hay has been cut, but has been endorsed by Cecil himself, "Letter written to Sir Everard Digby— *Powder Treason ;*" the minister thus attributing to him a knowledge of the Plot, more than three months before it was ever alleged that he heard of it.

APPENDIX G. (p. 94).

Henry Wright the Informer.

1. *Letter to Sir T. Challoner, April,* 1604. [*Gunpowder Plot Book,* n. 236.]

Good Sir Thomas, I am as eager for setting of the lodgings as you can be, and in truth whereas we desired but twenty, the discoverer had set and (if we accept it) can set above three score, but I told him that the State would take it for good service if he set twenty of the most principal Jesuits and seminary priests, and therewithal I gave him thirteen or fourteen names picked out of his own notes, among the which five of them were sworn to the secresy. He saith absolutely that by God's grace he will do it ere long, but he stayeth some few days purposely for the coming to town of Tesmond [Greenway] and Kempe, two principals; their lodgings are prepared, and they will be here, as he saith for certain, within these two days. For the treason, Davies neither hath nor will unfold himself for the discovery of it till he hath his pardon for it under seal, as I told you, which is now in great forwardness, and ready to be sealed so that you shall know all. . . . Your worship's most devoted,

HEN. WRIGHT.

[A pardon to Joseph Davies for all treasons and other offences appears on the Pardon Roll, April 25th, 1605, thus supplying the approximate date of the above letter.]

2. *Application to the King.* [*Gunpowder Plot Book*, n. 237.]

If it may please your Majesty, can you remember that the Lord Chief Justice Popham and Sir Thomas Challoner, Kt., had a hand in the discovery of the practices of the Jesuits in the powder, and did from time reveal the same to your Majesty, for two years' space almost before the said treason burst forth by an obscure letter to the Lord Mounteagle, which your Majesty, like an angel of God, interpreted, touching the blow, then intended to have been given by powder. The man that informed Sir Thomas Challoner and the Lord Popham of the said Jesuitical practices, their meetings and traitorous designs in that matter, whereof from time to time they informed your Majesty, was one Wright, who hath your Majesty's hand for his so doing, and never received any reward for his pains and charges laid out concerning the same. This Wright, if occasion serve, can do more service."

[*Addressed*, "Mr. Secretary Conway."

Headed, "Touching Wright and his services performed in the damnable plot of the Powder treason."]

APPENDIX H. (p. 119).

Lord Monteagle to King James. (British Museum MSS. Add. 19402, f. 146.)

"MOST gracious Soveraine.—Your maiestyes tender and fatherly love over me, In admonishinge me heartofore, to seake resolution In matter of religion, geves me both occasion, and Incouragement, as humbly to thanke your maiestye for this care of my soules good, so to crave leave of gevinge into your maiestyes hand this accompt, that your wisdome, seinge the course and end of my proceadinges, might rest assured that by the healp of god, I will [live and] dye, In that religion which I have nowe resolved to profes.

"It may please your maiestye therfore to knowe, that as I was breed upp In the Romish religion and walked in that, because I knew no better, so have I not sodainely or lightly made the chaunge, which nowe I desire to be seane In, for I speake, Sir, as before him that shall Judg my soule, I have by praier, for god his gidance, and with voues to him, to walk in that light he should shew me, and by longe carefull and diligent readinge, and conference with lerned men, on both sides, and impartiall examination of ther profes and argumentes, come to discerne the Ignorance I was formerly wrapped In, as I nowe wonder that ether my self, or any other of common understandinge, showld bee so blynded, as to Imbrace that gods trewth, [*sic*] which I nowe perseyue to be grounded uppon so weake foundations. And as I never could digest all poyntes therin, wherof not few seamed to bee made for gaine and ambition, of the papacye, so nowe I fynde that the hole frame and bodye of that religion (wherin they oppose us) difereth from the platforme, which god him self hath recorded In the holy scriptures, and hath In length of tyme, by the Ignorance and deceiptfulness of men, bene peaced together, and is now maintayned by factious obstinacye, and certain coulerable pretences, such as the wittes and learninge of men, are able to cast uppon any humaine errors, which they list to uphowld. Nether have I left any thinge I doubted of untried or unresolued, becawse I did Intend and desire to so take up the trewth of god, once discouered to me, as neuer to suffer yt to bee questioned any more In my owne consienc. And In all this, Sir, I protest to your maiestye, before almightye god, I have simply and only propounded to my self the trew seruise of god, and saluation of my owne soule, Not gaine, not honor, no not that which I doe most highly valew, your maiestyes fauour, or better opinion of me. Nether on the other side am I affraide of those censures of men whether of the partye I have abandoned, or of others which I shall Incur by this alteration, howldinge yt contentment Innough to my self, That god hath in mercye enlightened my mynde to see his sacred trewth, with desire to serue [the paper here is mutilated] . . And rest, your maie[styes] most loyall and obedient servant W. Mownteagle."

Addressed, "To the Kinge his most excellent Maiestye."

From the absence of any allusion to the Powder Plot and its "discovery," it appears certain that this letter must have been written previously to it.

On August 1st, 1609, Sir Wm. Waad wrote to Salisbury that the disorders of Lord Monteagle's house were an offence to the country. At this period he appears to have been suspected of concealing Catholic students from St. Omers. [*Calendar of State Papers.*]

APPENDIX I. (p. 140).

Epitaph in St. Anne's, Aldersgate. [Maitland, London (1756), p. 1065.]

"*Peter Heiwood*, younger son of *Peter Heiwood*, one of the Counsellors of *Jamaica*, . . . Great Grandson to *Peter Heiwood* of *Heywood* in the County Palestine of *Lancaster;* who apprehended *Guy Faux* with his dark Lanthorn; and for his zealous prosecution of Papists, as Justice of Peace, was stabbed in *Westminster-Hall* by *John James*, a *Dominican* Friar, An. Dom. 1640. Obiit *Novem.* 2. 1701.

> Reader, if not a Papist bred
> Upon such Ashes gently tread."

It is to be presumed that the person who died in 1701 is not the same who was stabbed in 1640, or who discovered Guy Faukes in 1605.

The Dominican records contain no trace of any member of the Order named John James, nor does so remarkable an event as the stabbing of a Justice of Peace in Westminster Hall appear to be chronicled elsewhere.

Peter Heywood, J.P. for Westminster, was active as a magistrate as late as December 15th, 1641. [*Calendar of State Papers.*]

APPENDIX K. (p. 173).

The Use of Torture.

THERE can be no doubt that torture was freely employed to extract evidence from the conspirators and others who fell into the hands of the government.

The Earl of Salisbury, in his letter to Favat, of December 4th, 1605, clearly intimates that this was the case, when he complains " most of the prisoners have wilfully forsworn that the priests knew anything in particular, and obstinately refuse to be accusers of them, *yea, what torture soever they be put to.*"

About the middle of November, Lord Dunfermline wrote to Salisbury [*Dom. James I.* xvi. 81] recommending that the prisoners should be confined apart and in darkness, that they should be examined by torchlight, and that the tortures should be slow and at intervals, as being thus most effectual.

There is every reason to believe that the Jesuit lay-brother, Nicholas Owen, *alias* Littlejohn, actually died upon the rack. [*Vide* Father Gerard's *Narrative of the Gunpowder Plot*, p. 189.]

Finally we have the king's instructions as to Faukes [*Gunpowder Plot Book*, No. 17]. " The gentler tortours are to be first usid unto him, *et sic per gradus ad ima tenditur*,[1] and so God speede your goode worke."[2] Guy's signature of November 9th is sufficient evidence that it was none of the "gentler tortours" which he had endured.

In the violently Protestant account of the execution of the traitors,[3] we read: " Last of all came the great Devil of all Faukes, who should have put fire to the powder. His body being weak with torture and sickness, he was scarce able to go up the ladder, but with much ado, by the help of the hangman, went high enough to brake his neck with the fall."

APPENDIX L. (p. 227).

Myths and Legends of the Powder Plot.

AROUND the Gunpowder Plot has gathered a mass of fabulous embellishment too curious to be passed

---

[1] "And so by degrees to the uttermost."

[2] These instructions furnish an interesting specimen of the king's broad Scotch, *e.g.*, "Quhat Gentlewomans Letter it was y^t was founde upon him, and quhairfor doth she give him an other Name in it y^n he giues to himself. If he was ever a papiste; and if so, quho brocht him up in it. If otherwayes, hou was he convertid, quhair, quhan, and by quhom."

The following passage is very characteristic of the writer:

"Nou last, ye remember of the crewellie villanouse pasquille y^t rayled upon me for ye name of Brittanie. If I remember richt it spake something of harvest and prophecyed my destructiō about y^t tyme. Ye may think of y^s, for it is lyke to be by ye Laboure of such a desperate fellow as y^s is."

[3] *The Arraignment and execution of the late traitors*, etc., 1606.

over in silence. This has chiefly attached itself to Guy Faukes, who, on account of the desperate part allotted to him has impressed the public mind far more than any of his associates, and has come to be erroneously regarded as the moving spirit of the enterprise.

One of the best authenticated facts regarding him is that when apprehended he was booted and spurred for a journey, though it is usually said that he was to have travelled by water.

There is, however, a strange story, told with much circumstantiality, which gives an elaborate but incomprehensible account of a tragic underplot in connection with him. This is related at considerable length in a Latin hexameter poem, *Venatio Catholica*, published in 1609, in the *History of the Popish Sham Plots*, and elsewhere. According to this tangled tale the other conspirators wished both to get rid of Faukes, when he had served their purpose, and to throw the suspicion of their deed upon their enemies, the Puritans. To this end they devised a notable scheme. A certain Puritan, named Pickering, a courtier, but a godly man, foremost amongst his party, had a fine horse ("Bucephalum egregium"). This, Robert Keyes, his brother-in-law, purchased or hired, and placed at the service of Faukes for his escape. The steed was to await him at a certain spot, but in a wood hard by assassins were to lurk, who, when Guy appeared, should murder him, and having secured the money with which he was furnished, should leave his mangled corpse beside the Bucephalus, known as Mr. Pickering's. Thus Faukes would be able to tell no tales, and—though it does not appear why—suspicion would be sure to fall on the

Puritan, and he would be proclaimed as the author of the recent catastrophe.

> "Hoc astu se posse rati convertere in hostes
> Flagitii infamiam, causamque capessere vulgo
> Qua Puritanos invisos reddere possent,
> Ut tantæ authores, tam immanis proditionis.
> Cognito equo, et facta (pro more) indagine cædis,
> Aulicus hic sceleris tanquam fabricator atrocis
> Proclamandus erat, Falso (ne vera referre
> Et socios sceleris funesti prodere possit)
> Sublato."

Many curious circumstances have likewise been imported into the history, and many places connected with it which appear to have no claim whatever to such a distinction.

Thus we hear (*England's Warning Peece*) that the Jesuit Cresswell came over from Spain for the occasion "to bear his part with the rest of his society in a victorial song of thanksgiving." Also that on November 5th, a large body of confederates assembled at Hampstead to see the House of Parliament go up in the air.

In the *Gentleman's Magazine*, February, 1783, is a remarkable description of a summer house, in a garden at Newton Hall, near Kettering, Northamptonshire, in which the plotters used to meet and conspire, the place then belonging to the Treshams; "and for greater security, they placed a conspirator at each window, Guy Faukes, the arch villain, standing in the doorway, to prevent anybody overhearing them."

According to a wide-spread belief Guy Faukes was a Spaniard.[1] He has also been called a Londoner, and

[1] See, for instance, *London and the Kingdom* (mainly from the Guildhall Archives), by Reginald R. Sharpe, ii. 13.

his name being altered to Vaux, has been said to have a family connection with Vauxhall. He was in fact a Yorkshireman of good family, though belonging to a younger branch of no great estate. His father, Edward Faukes, was a notary at York, where he held the office of registrar and advocate of the cathedral church. Guy himself was an educated man, more than commonly well read. He is always described in the process as "Guido Faukes, Gentleman."

Another most extraordinary example of an obvious myth, which was nevertheless treated as sober history, is furnished by the absurd statement that the astute and wily Jesuits not only contrived the Plot, but published its details to the world long before its attempted execution, in order to vindicate to themselves the credit of so glorious a design. Thus Bishop Kennet, in a fifth of November sermon, preached at St. Paul's before the Lord Mayor, in 1715, tells us:[1]

"It was a general surmise at least among the whole Order of Jesuits in foreign parts: or else one of them could hardly have stated the case so exactly some four or five years before it broke out. Father Del-Rio, in a treatise printed An. 1600, put the case, as if he had already looked into the Mine and Cellars, and had surveyed the barrels of powder in them, and had heard the whole confessions of Faux and Catesby."

This "general surmise" does not appear to have been confined to the Jesuits themselves. Another ingenious writer, nearly a century earlier,[2] tells a wonderful story concerning the sermon of a Dominican,

[1] P. 9.
[2] Lewis Owen, *Unmasking of all popish Monks*, etc. (1628), p. 49.

preached in the same year, 1600, wherein it was related how there was a special hell, beneath the other, for Jesuits, so thick and fast did they arrive as to need extra accommodation. The preacher avowed that he had, in his vision of the place, given warning to the demon in charge of it, "to search them with speed, for fear that they had conveyed hither some gunpowder with them, for they are very skilfull in Mine-workes, and in blowing up of whole States and Parliament-houses, and if they can blow you all up, then the Spanyards will come and take your kingdom from you."

Another notable specimen of the way in which reason and probability were cast to the winds is afforded by two letters written from Naples in 1610, one to King James and the other to Salisbury, by Sir Edwin Rich,[1] who announced that Father Greenway —who of all the Jesuits was said to be most clearly convicted as a traitor—intended to send to the king a present of an embroidered satin doublet and hose, which, being craftily poisoned, would be death to him if he put them on.

APPENDIX M.

Sir William Waad's Memorial Inscriptions.

IN a room of the Queen's House in the Tower, in which the conspirators are supposed to have been examined by the Lords of the Council, Sir William

[1] *Dom. James I.* lvii. 92-93, October 5th.

APPENDIX M. 265

Waad has left a series of inscriptions as memorials of the events in which he played so large a part. Of these the most noteworthy are the following:

I.

Jacobus Magnus, Magnæ Britanniæ
rex, pietate, justitia, prudentia, doctrina, fortitudine,
clementia, ceterisq. virtutibus regiis clariss'; Christianæ
fidei, salutis publicæ, pacis universalis propugnator, fautor
auctor acerrimus, augustiss', auspicatiss'.
Anna Regina Frederici 2. Danorum Regis invictiss' filia sereniss[a],
Henricus princeps, naturæ ornamentis, doctrinæ præsidiis, gratiæ
Muneribus, instructiss', nobis et natus et a deo datus,
Carolus dux Eboracensis divina ad omnem virtutem indole,[1]
Elizabetha utriusq. soror Germana, utroque parente dignissima
Hos velut pupillam oculi tenellam
providus muni, procul impiorum
impetu alarum tuarum intrepidos
conde sub umbra.

[This is evidently intended for a Sapphic stanza, but the last two words of v. 3 have been transposed, destroying the metre.]

II.

Robertus Cecil, Comes Sarisburiensis, summus et regis
Secretarius, et Angliæ thesaurarius, clariss' patris
et de repub. meritissimi filius, in paterna munera
successor longe dignissimus;
Henricus, comes Northamptoniæ, quinq. portuum præfectus et
privati sigilli custos, disertorum litteratissimus, litterato-
rum disertissimus;
Carolus comes Nottingamiæ, magnus Angliæ admirallus
victoriosus;
Thomas Suffolciæ comes, regis camerarius splendidissimus,
tres viri nobilissimi ex antiqua Howardorum familia, ducumq.
Norfolciæ prosapia;

---

[1] At the time of the Plot Charles was not quite five years old.

Edwardus Somersetus, comes Wigorniæ, equis regiis præfectus ornatissimus ;
Carolus Blunt, comes Devoniæ, Hyberniæ prorex et pacificator,
Joannes Areskinus,[1] illustris Marriæ comes, præcipuarum in Scotia arcium præfectus ;
Georgius Humius, Dunbari comes, Scotiæ thesaurarius prudentiss'
omnes illustriss' ordinis garteri milites ;
Joannes Popham, miles, justiciarius Angliæ capitalis, et justitiæ consultissimus :

Hi omnes illustrissimi viri, quorum nomina ad sempiternam eorum memoriam posteritati consecrandam proxime supra ad lineam posita sunt, ut regi a consiliis, ita ab eo delegati quæsitores, reis singulis incredibili diligentia ac cura sæpius appellatis, nec minore solertia et dexteritate pertentatis eorum animis, eos suis ipsorum inter se collatis responsionibus convictos, ad voluntariam confessionem adegerunt : et latentem nefarie conjurationis seriem, remq. omnem ut hactenus gesta et porro per eos gerenda esset, summa fide erutam, æterna cum laude sua, in lucem produxerunt, adeo ut divina singulari providentia effectum sit, ut tam præsens, tamq. fœda tempestas, a regia majestate, liberisq. regiis, et omni regno depulsa, in ipsos autores eorumq. socios redundarit.

III.

Conjuratorum Nomina, ad perpetuam ipsorum infamiam et tantæ diritatis detestationem sempiternam.

Monachi salutare Jesu nomē ementiti { Henry Garnet
John Gerrard
Oswald Tesond
Hamō
Baldwī }

Thomas Winter
Robert Winter
John Winter
Guy Fawkes
Thomas Bates
Everard Digby, K.
Am' Rookewood
John Graunt
Robert Keyes
Henry Morgā

Thomas Percy
Robert Catesby
John Wright
Christopher Wright
Francis Tresham
Thomas Abbington
Edmond Baineham, K.
William Stanley, K.
Hughe Owen.

[1] Erskine.

IV.

Besides the above there is a prolix description of the Plot, devised against the best of sovereigns, "a Jesuitis Romanensibus, perfidiæ Catholicæ et impietatis viperinæ autoribus et assertoribus, aliisq. ejusdem amentiæ scelerisq. patratoribus et sociis susceptæ, et in ipso pestis derepente inferendæ articulo (salutis anno 1605, mensis Novembris die quinto), tam præter spem quam supra fidem mirifice et divinitus detectæ."

There is, moreover, a sentence in Hebrew, with Waad's cipher beneath, and a number of what seem to be meant for verses. The following lines are evidently the Lieutenant's description of his own office :

> " Custodis Custos sum, Carcer Carceris, arcis
>   Arx, atque Argu' Argus ; sum speculæ specula ;
> Sum vinclum in vinclis ; compes cum compede, clavū
>   Firmo hærens, teneo tentus, habens habeor.
> Dum regi regnoq. salus stet firma quieta,
>   Splendida sim Compes Compedis usque licet."

This is considerably more metrical and intelligible than some of the rest.

In 1613 Waad was dismissed from his post, one of the charges against him being that he had embezzled the jewels of Arabella Stuart.[1]

In Theobald's *Memoirs of Sir Walter Raleigh* (p. 16), Waad is described as "the Lieutenant of the Tower, and Cecil's great Creature."

[1] *Dom. James I.* lxxii. 129.

APPENDIX N.

THE PUBLISHED CONFESSION OF GUY FAUKES. A.

The draft, November 8th, 1605 (G. P. B. 49).

*** Passages between square brackets have been cancelled. Those marked * have been ticked off for omission.

The Confession of Guy Fawkes, taken the 8 of November, 1605.

HE confesseth that a Practise in generall was first broken unto him, agaynst his Majesty, for the Catholique cause, and not invented or propounded by himself, and this was first propounded unto him about Easter last was twelvemonth, beyond the seas in the Low countreyes, by an English Lay-man, and that English man came over with him in his company into England, and they tow and three more weare the first five mencioned in the former examination. And they five resolving to do some thinge for the Catholick cause, —a vowe being first taken by all of them for secrecye, —one of the other three propounded to perform it with Powder, and resolved that the place should be,— where this action should be performed and justice done,—in or neere the place of the sitting of the Parliament, wherein Religion had been uniustly suppressed. This beeinge resolved the manner [of it] was as followeth.

The Published Confession of Guy Faukes. B.

As signed by Faukes, November 17th, 1605
(G. P. B. 101).

⁎⁎⁎ Square brackets indicate an erasure. Italics an addition or substitution.

THE [deposition] *declaration* of Guy Fawkes prisonner in the Tower of London *taken the* 17 *of Nov.* 1605, *acknowledged before the Lords Commissioners.*[1]

A. I confesse that a practise in generall was first broken unto me against his Majestie, for releife of the Catholique cause, and not invented or propounded by my self.

And this was first propounded unto me about Easter last was twelvemonth, beyond the Seas, in the Low countries of the Archdukes obeysance by Thomas Wynter, who came thereupon with me into England," and there wee imparted our purpose to three other Englishmen more, namely Robt Catesby, Thos Percy, and John Wright, who all five consulting together of the meanes how to execute the same, and taking a vowe among our selves for secresie Catesby propounded to have it performed by Gunpowder, and by making a myne under the upper house of Parliament, which place wee made choice of the rather,

---

[1] Alterations and additions (in italics) made by Sir Edward Coke.

[*A. The draft.*]

First they hyred the Howse at Westminster of one Ferris,[1] and havinge the howse they sought to make a myne under the upper howse of Parliament, and they begann to make the myne in or about the xi of December, and they five first entered into the worke, and soone after toke an other unto them, havinge first sworne him and taken the Sacrament, for secrecye. And when they came to the wall,—that was about three yards thicke,—and found it a matter of great difficultie, they tooke to them an other in like manner, with oath and Sacrament as afore sayd. All which seaven, were gentlemen of name and bloode, and not any man was employed in or about that action,—noe not so much as in digginge and myning that was not a gentleman. And having wrought to the wall before Christmas, they reasted untill after the holydayes, and the day before Christmas,—having a masse of earth that came out of the myne,—they carryed it into the Garden of the said Howse, and after Christmas they wrought on the wall till Candlemas, and wrought the wall half through, and sayeth that all the tyme while the others wrought he stood as Sentynell to descrie any man that came neere, and when any man came neere to the place, uppon warninge given by him they rested untill they had notyce to proceed from hym, and sayeth that they seaven all lay in the Howse, and had shott and powder, and they all resolved to dye in that place before they yeilded or weare taken.

[1] This name has seemingly been tampered with.

[*B. The Confession as signed.*]
because Religion having been uniustly suppressed there, it was fittest that Justice and punishment should be executed there.

B. This being resolved amongst us, Thomas Percy hired a howse at Westminster for that purpose, neare adjoyning the Parl^t howse, and there wee beganne to make a myne about the xi of December 1604. The fyve that entered into the woorck were Thomas Percye, Robert Catesby, Thomas Wynter, John Wright, and my self, and soon after we tooke another unto us, Christopher Wright, having sworn him also, and taken the Sacrament for secrecie.

C. When wee came to the verie foundation of the Wall of the house, which was about 3 yeards thick, and found it a matter of great difficultie, we took to us another gentleman Robert [Wynter] *Keys*[1] in like manner with our oathe and Sacrament as aforesaid.

D. It was about Christmas when wee brought our myne unto the Wall, and about Candlemas we had wrought the Wall half through. And whilst they were a working, I stood as sentinell, to descrie any man that came neare, whereof I gave them warning, and so they ceased untill I gave them notice agayne to proccede. All wee seaven lay in the house, and had shott and powder, being resolved to dye in that place before we should yeild or be taken.

[1] Changed by Cecil; but on November 14th, writing to Edmondes, he included Keyes amongst those that "wrought not in the myne," and R. Winter amongst those who did.

[*A. The draft.*]

And as they weare workinge, they heard a rushinge in the cellar which grew by *one*[1] Brights selling of his coles whereuppon this Examinant, fearinge they had been discovered, went into the cellar and viewed the cellar, and perceivinge the commoditye thereof for their purposs, and understandinge how it would be letten his maister, Mr Percy, hyred the Cellar for a yeare, for 4 pounds rent. And confesseth that after Christmas 20^ty barrells of Powder weare brought by themselves to a Howse which they had on the Banksyde in Hampers, and from that Howse removed the powder to the sayd Howse, neere the upper Howse of Parliament. And presently upon hyringe the cellar, they themselfs removed the powder into the cellar, and couvered the same with faggots which they had before layd into the sellar.

After, about Easter, he went into the Low Countryes,—as he before hath declared in his former examination,—and that the trew purpos of his goinge over was least beinge a dangerous man he should be known and suspected, and in the meane tyme he left the key [of the cellar] with Mr Percye, whoe in his absence caused more Billetts to be layd into the Cellar, as in his former examination he confessed, and retourned about the end of August or the beginninge of September, and went agayne to the sayd howse, nere to the sayd cellar, and received the key of the cellar agayne of one of the five. And then they brought in five or six barrells of powder more into the cellar, which all soe they couvered with billetts, saving fower little barrells covered with ffaggots, and then this examinant went into the Country about the end of September.

[1] Interlined.]

APPENDIX N.

[*B. The Confession as signed.*]

E. As they were working upon the wall, they heard a rushing in a cellar of removing of coles ; whereupon wee feared wee had been discovered, and they sent me to go to the cellar, who fynding that the coles were a selling, and that the Cellar was to be lett, viewing the commoditye thereof for our purpose, Percy went and hired the same for yearly Rent.

Wee had before this provyded and brought into the house 20 barrells of Powder, which wee removed into the Cellar, and covered the same with billets and fagots, which we provided for that purpose.

F. About Easter, the Parliament being proroged tyll October next, wee dispersed our selfs and I retired into the Low countryes, *by advice and direction of the rest, as well to acquaint Owen with the particulars of the plot, as also*[1] lest by my longer staye I might have grown suspicious, and so have come in question.

In the meane tyme Percy, having the key of the Cellar, layd in more powder and wood into it.

I returned about the beginning of September next and then receyving the key againe of Percy, we brought in more powder and billets to cover the same againe.

[1] The words italicised are added in the published version.

[*A. The draft.*]

* It appeareth the powder was in the cellar, placed as it was found the 5 of November, when the Lords came to proroge the Parliament, and sayeth that he returned agayne to the sayd Howse neare the cellar on Wednesday the 30 of October.

[He confesseth he was at the Erle of Montgomeryes marriage, but as he sayeth with noe intention of evill, havinge a sword about him, and was very neere to his Majesty and the Lords there present.]

Forasmuch as they knew not well how they should come by the person of the Duke Charles, beeinge neere London, where they had no forces,—if he had not been all soe blowne upp,—He confesseth that it was resolved amonge them, that the same day that this detestable act should have been performed, the same day should other of their confederacye have surprised the person of the Lady Elizabeth, and presently have proclaimed her queen [to which purpose a Proclamation was drawne, as well to avowe and justify the Action, as to have protested against the Union, and in no sort to have meddeled with Religion therein. And would have protested all soe agaynst all strangers] and this proclamation should have been made in the name of the Lady Elizabeth.

* Beinge demanded why they did not surprise the Kinges person and draw him to the effectinge of their purpose, sayeth that soe many must have been acquaynted with such an action as it could not have been kept secrett.

He confesseth that if their purpose had taken effect untill they had power enough they would not have avowed the deed to be theirs; but if their power,—for their defence and safetye,—had been sufficient they themselfes would have taken it upon them.

[*B. The Confession as signed.*]

And so [I] went for a tyme into the country, till the 30 of October.

G. It was farther resolved amongst us that the same day that this action should have been performed some other of our confederates should have surprised the person of the Lady Elizabeth the Kings eldest daughter, who was kept in Warwickshire at the Lo. Harringtons house, and presently have proclaimed her for Queene, having a project of a Proclamation ready for the purpose, wherein we made no mention of altering of Religion,———

——— nor would have avowed the deed to be ours untill we should have had power enough to make our partie good, and then we would have avowed both.

[*A. The draft.*]

* They meant all soe to have sent for the Prisoners in the Tower to have come to them, of whom particularly they had some consultation.

* He confesseth that the place of Rendez-vous was in Warwickshire, and that armour was sent thither, but the particuler thereof he knowes not.

He confesseth that they had consultation for the takinge of the Lady Marye into their possession, but knew not how to come by her.

And confesseth that provision was made by some of the conspiracye of some armour of proofe this last Summer for this Action.

* He confesseth that the powder was bought of the common Purse of the Confederates.

L. Admyrall
L. Chamberlayne
Erle of Devonshire
Erle of Northampton
Erle of Salisbury
Erle of Marr
L. cheif Justice
} attended by Mr Attorney generall.

[*Endorsed*] Examination of Guy Fauks, Novr 8th, 1605.

APPENDIX N.

[*B. The Confession as signed.*]

H. Concerning Duke Charles, the Kings second son, we hadd sundrie consultations how to sease on his person, but because wee found no meanes how to compasse it,—the Duke being kept near London,—where we had not forces enough, wee resolved to serve ourselves with the Lady Elizabeth.

J. The names of other principall persons that were made privie afterwards to this horrible conspiracie.
                  [*Signed*] GUIDO FAUKES.
    Everard Digby, Knight
    Ambrose Ruckwood
    Francis Tresham
    John Grant
    Robert [Keys] *Wynter*
[*Witnessed*] Edw. Coke   W. Waad.
[*Endorsed*] Fawkes his [deposition] *declaration 17 Nov. 1605.*[1]

---

[1] Words in italics added by Coke.

INDEX.

Abbot, Robert, Bishop of Salisbury, his version of the missing confessions of Faukes, 192 seq.
Acton, Robert, 113.
Alabaster, Thomas, a priest in government employ, 204 note.
Andrew, William, servant to Sir E. Digby, evidence of, 78 note.
Annals of England, cited, 48.
Answere to Scandalous papers (Cecil's manifesto), 44, 219 seq.

Babington's Plot, 14.
Baldwin, Father William, S. J.; allegations against him, 185, 187 seq.; which are not substantiated, 195; correspondence with Father Schondonck, 201, 222.
Bancroft, Richard, Archbishop of Canterbury, 46, 147.
Barlow, Thomas, Bishop of Lincoln, 62, 70 note.
Barnes, a government agent, 112.
Bartlett, George, servant to Catesby, his evidence reported, 160.
Bates, Thomas, servant to Catesby, his introduction to the Conspiracy, 3, 178; his alleged evidence against Greenway, 178-183; trial and execution, 6. See also Conspirators.

Batty, Matthew, evidence regarding Monteagle, 78 note.
"Blackfriars Downfall," the, 242.
Blount, Father Richard, S.J., on government intelligence, 77; on Suffolk's proposal of toleration, 224; on Cecil's "new stratagem," 224, 225.
Brayley and Britton (*Palace of Westminster*), 79 note.
Brewer, Rev. John Sherren, on the fate of Parry, the conspirator, 14; on government devices, 15; on Cecil's knowledge of the Plot, 48; on the Monteagle letter, 117.
Bromley, Sir Henry, Sheriff of Worcestershire, 167 note.
Buck, Mr., alleged warning given to, 51 note, 106.
Burnet, Gilbert, Bishop of Salisbury, 46.
"Bye," the, 15 note.

Camden, William, the historian, 36 note.
Capon, William, on the old Palace of Westminster, 79, 86; on traces of the mine, 87.
Carleton, Dudley, afterwards Viscount Dorchester, patronized by Cecil, 62; assists Percy to hire

the house at Westminster, 61 ; reports the French version of the Plot, 140 ; and its contradiction, 141 ; his mysterious connection with the Conspiracy, 150 *note;* his opinion of Percy, 150.

Castlemaine, Earl of (Roger Palmer), on State plots, 14, 48 ; on Osborne's qualifications as an historian, 44 *note;* on the fate of decoy ducks, 152.

Carte, Thomas (*General History of England*), 46.

Carey, ———, evidence regarding Percy, 150.

Catesby, Robert, a ringleader in the Conspiracy, 9, 64; his character and antecedents, 35 *seq.*; persuades his associates not to reveal their project to priests, 179 ; undertakes to proclaim the new sovereign, 83; his death, 4, 152 *seq.*; suspicions concerning him, 156, 160. *See also* Conspirators.

Catholics, their numbers, 28 ; their condition under Elizabeth, 29 ; their hopes from James, 31, 33, 247, 248; his promises to them, 29 ; they welcome his accession, *ibid*, 34 ; temporary relief at his hands, *ibid;* their consequent increase, 28, 30 ; Cecil's hostility, 28, 30, 47, 48, 51, 105 ; attempt to charge them with the Plot, 4-6, 107, 108 ; legislation against them on account of it, 212 *seq.*; its lasting effects in their regard, 209, 225.

Cecil, Robert, first Earl of Salisbury, his character, 19 *seq.*; dignities conferred by James I., 19 *note;* and nicknames, 19 *note;* his unpopularity, 21 *seq.*; difficulties and dangers of his position, 26 *seq.*; in the pay of Spain, 21 ; and probably of France, 22 *note;* his secret correspondence with King James, 21 ; his intrigues against Northumberland and Raleigh, 26, 198, 216; hostility to the Catholics, 27, 95, 105 ; anxiety on account of the king's attitude, 28; and dealings with Pope Clement VIII., 104 ; endeavours to commit James to a policy of intolerance, 105; his political methods, 44, 111; employs the services of forgers, 112 *note*, 203; his knowledge of the Plot, 94 *seq.*; alleged secret dealings with Percy, 15 ; Tresham, 158 ; and Catesby, 160 ; contradicts himself concerning the "discovery," 123 *seq.*; his inexplicable delay in making it, 132 ; and conduct afterwards, 137 ; was not taken by surprise, 210 ; at once turns the Plot to his advantage, 213 ; his determination to incriminate priests, 4 *seq.*, 130 ; advantages reaped by him, 30, 213 *seq.*; his Manifesto, 218 *seq.*; suspected of having originated or manipulated the Conspiracy, 43 *seq.*; alleged attempt to float a second Plot, 225.

Cecil, Thomas, first Earl of Exeter, 19 *note*, 160 *note*.

Cecil, William, second Earl of Salisbury, his testimony reported, 160.

Cecil, William, a priest in government employ, 45 *note*.

INDEX. 281

"Cellar," the, its situation and character, 58, 79 *note;* hired by the conspirators, 69 *seq.*; problems concerning it, 87 *seq.*; its after history, 137; accompanies the migrations of the House of Lords, 80 *note.*

Challoner, Sir Thomas, information addressed to, 94, 95.

Chamberlain, John, M.P., on Cecil's death and character, 23, 24; account of the "discovery," 128; on the King's lucky day, 231; on Percy's character, 150.

Charles, Duke of York, afterwards Charles I.; plans of the conspirators regarding him, 81 *seq.*

Chichester, Sir Arthur, Deputy in Ireland, 4, 108, 124.

Coal, Father Greenway's description of, 71 *note.*

Cobham, eighth Lord (Henry Brooke), his charge of forgery against Waad, 202.

Cobham, ninth Lord (William Brooke), his evidence reported, 45.

Coke, Sir Edward, Attorney-General, his falsification of evidence, 200; Cecil's instructions to him, 116 *note;* his assertions, 85, 88; interrogatories prepared by him, 176; his humour, 63 *note;* proofs against Owen, 190; witnesses Thomas Winter's declaration, 169; and that of Faukes, 172; his treatment of Raleigh and Northumberland, 217.

Coleridge, Lord Chief Justice, on the English penal laws, 29 *note.*

Conspirators, the, list of, 2, 3; their character and antecedents, 35-41; their enrolment, 9, 64, 252; their plans and proceedings, 9-11, 60 *seq.*; mining operations, 10, 63; incredibilty of the story, 65 *seq.*, 76 *seq.*, 141; they hire the "cellar," 69 *seq.*; purchase and store gunpowder, 78; difficulties concerning it, 78, 132, 134-137; further designs, 11, 80-82; alarmed by the prorogation, 114, 230; flight and attempted rebellion, 2; their fate, 4-6.

Cope, Sir Walter, on the character of Cecil, 27 *note.*

Cornwallis, Sir Charles, English Ambassador in Spain, on the character of the conspirators, 40; letter to Father Cresswell, 195; on the Catholic design to murder Cecil, 221 *note.*

Cresswell, Father Joseph, S.J., allegations concerning him, 195; Cornwallis' letter to him, *ibid.*

Dacre, Francis, titular Lord, efforts to connect him with the Plot, 177.

Darnley, Henry, Lord, father o James I., the victim of a gunpowder plot, 37, 50.

Davenport, Father Christopher, O.P. (Francis à S. Clara), 145 *note.*

Davies, Joseph, a government "discoverer," 94.

De Beaumont, M., French Ambassador, 119 *note.*

De la Boderie, M., French Ambassador, on Cecil's insecurity, 26; on the ruin of Northumberland, 23.

Del-Rio, Father Martin, S.J., said

to have described the Plot A.D. 1600, 263.

Derby, Earl of (William Stanley), attempt to incriminate him, 198.

De Ros, Lord, on Faukes' plan of escape, 144 *note*.

Devonshire, Earl of (Charles Blount), 168 *note*, 170 *note*, 211, 266.

Digby, Sir Everard, joins the Conspiracy, 10, 253; difficulties and contradictions regarding him, 79 *note*, 253; his letter to Salisbury, 33, 245; part assigned to him, 78 *note*; his fate, 6. See also Conspirators.

Digby, Sir John, English Ambassador in Spain, 22 *note*.

Digby, Sir Kenelm, his evidence reported, 160.

Digby, Sir Robert, 38 *note*.

Dixon, Hepworth (*Her Majesty's Tower*), on government intelligence, 111 *note*.

Dodd, Rev. Charles, on the origin of the Plot, 18, 51.

Dorset, Earl of (Thomas Sackville), his esteem for Cecil, 21.

Dunbar, Earl of (George Hume), 168 *note*, 172, 266.

Dunfermline, Earl of (Alexander Seaton), on the effective use of torture, 259.

Dunsmoor Heath, projected hunting match on, 11.

Edmondes, Sir Thomas, English Ambassador at Brussels, account of the "discovery" sent to him, 108, 124; version of Faukes' confession sent to him, 186; proofs against Owen sent to him, 190, 191; his negotiations with the archdukes, 186 *seq.*; letters of, 102, 187, 188, 189; letters to, 85, 106, 113, 154, 186, 187, 188, 189, 190.

Elizabeth, Princess, daughter of James I., designs of the conspirators regarding her, 81.

England's Warning Peece, 195, 262.

English Protestants' Plea, 40, 51, 108 *note*, 195 *note*.

Eudaemon-Joannes, Father Andrew, S.J., 204.

Faukes, Guy or Guido, *alias* John Johnson, his position and character, 39, 262; his Spanish mission, 36; introduced to the Conspiracy, 9, 64; passes as Percy's servant, 71, 77; keeps guard while the others work, 66; discovers the "cellar," 70; has charge of the premises, 77, 89, 142; visits Flanders, 91, 162; appointed to fire the powder, 1; plans for his escape, 144; arrest, 123-128; published confession, 169 *seq.*, 268 *seq.*; evidence falsified, 200; missing depositions, 191; tortured, 172, 200, 260; trial and execution, 6, 260; fables respecting him, 261. See also Conspirators.

Favat, Mr., Cecil's letter to, 5, 182.

Ferrers, Henry, sub-lets the house at Westminster to Percy, 61.

Fifth of November, a propitious day for the "discovery," 231; the day solemnized, 5.

Floyde, Griffith, a government spy, 49.

INDEX. 283

French historians on the Plot, 141 *note*.
French official accounts of the Plot, 140, 141.
Fuller, Mr., M.P., 132 *note*.
Fuller, Thomas (*Church History of Britain*), 46, 225.
Fulman MSS., 169.

Gardiner, Professor Samuel Rawson, his favourable estimate of Cecil's character, 20; on the Spanish pension, 22 *note*; repudiates imputations against the government, 18; on the conspirators' plans, 82; on the Monteagle letter, 117; on the king's interpretation, 132 *note*; on the desire to incriminate priests, 4 *note*.
Garnet, Father Henry, S.J., proclaimed as a principal conspirator, 5; his capture, 7, 166; lack of evidence, 7; trial and execution, *ibid.*; his account of the conspirators' proceedings, 208; his evidence against Catesby, 157; on the accession of James, 29 *note*.
Gentleman's Magazine, 52 *note*, 262.
Gerard, Col. John, 160 *note*.
Gerard, Father John, S.J., proclaimed as a principal conspirator, 5; exonerated by historians, 237; his history of the Plot, 205; his experiences in the Tower, 202; on the persecution of Catholics, 32; opinion of the "discovery," 49; and of the official narrative, 129; on the death of Percy and Catesby, 156 *note*.
Goodman, Godfrey, Bishop of Gloucester, on the origin of the Conspiracy, 44; on the king's promises to Catholics, 29 *note*; on the persecution of Catholics, 32; on the "discovery," 134 *note*; on the death of Whynniard, 92 *note*; on Percy's intercourse with Cecil, 151; on the death of Percy and Catesby, 154; his religious views, 145 *note*.
Gowrie Conspiracy, the, 231, 232.
"Great Horses," 2 *note*.
Grange, Justice E., 148 *note*.
Grant, John, 37. *See also* Conspirators.
Green, Mrs. Everett, wrongly describes Owen as a Jesuit, 185 *note*.
Green, John Richard (*History of the English People*), 30.
Greenway, *alias* Tesimond, Father Oswald, S.J., proclaimed as a principal conspirator, 5; Bates' alleged evidence against him, 178-183; his history of the Plot, 206; opinion of the official narrative, 134; on the effects of an explosion, 133; on government despatches concerning Percy, 155; his visit to the rebels at Huddington, 206 *note*; fables respecting him, 264.
Gregory, Arthur, a forger employed by government, 203.
Grene, Father Martin, S.J., notes on the Plot, 45.
Gunpowder, amount procured by the conspirators, 78; difficulties concerning it, 132 *seq.*

Hagley Hall, R. Winter and S. Littleton captured there, 4.
Hallam, Henry (*Constitutional History*), repudiates imputations

against the government, 18; on Father Garnet's capture, *ibid.*, *note;* on King James's title to the crown, 34.

Harington, Sir John, 4.

Hawarde, John (*Les Reportes del Cases in Camera Stellata*), 165 *note.*

Heiwood, or Heywood, Peter, 139 *note*, 258.

Hendlip House (Thomas Abbington's), the scene of Father Garnet's capture, 18 *note*, 166 *note.*

Henry, Prince of Wales, anticipations concerning him, 33; the conspirators' plans in his regard, 80, 81, 176.

Herring, Francis (*Pietas Pontificia*), 27 *note*, 143 *note.*

Higgons, Bevil (*English History*), 47.

Hoby, Sir Edward, on the death of Percy, 154.

Holbeche House (Stephen Littleton's), the conspirators there slain or captured, 2, 4.

House of Lords, its situation and subsequent migrations, 55 *seq.*; never represented in pictures of the Plot, 228.

House, Percy's, at Westminster, its position, 60, 251; circumstances of the bargain for it, 60; difficulties concerning it, 62, 64, 67, 88.

Howes, Edmund (continuation of Stowe's *Chronicle*), 127.

Huddington House (Robert Winter's), 206 *note.*

Ichrup, Thomas, name given to Faukes, 149, 244.

Inglefield, Sir Francis, 249.

James I., King of Great Britain, his claim to the succession, 34; circumstances of his accession, 34, 35; hopes of the Catholics, 28; who support his cause, 34; his policy at first favourable to them, 29; soon reversed, 31; his dealings with Pope Clement VIII., 104; his supposed interpretation of the letter, 128, 131; Tuesday his lucky day, 230; his speech to Parliament, 211; accuses Catholics in general and the Pope, 4; suspected of previous knowledge of the Plot, 46; anxiety for evidence against priests, 182; letter to the Archdukes, 187 *note;* alleged subsequent opinion of the Plot, 45; instructions for the torture of Faukes, 259; his Scotch dialect, 260 *note;* gives his royal word against Owen and Baldwin, 187; his policy permanently affected, 209.

James, John, a supposed Dominican, 139 *note*, 258.

Jardine, David, on the character ot the official narrative, 129, 163; on the falsification of evidence, 199; on the Monteagle letter, 117; on the king's interpretation, 132 *note;* on the established facts of the case, 12; not perfectly impartial, 161, 207; on the results of the Plot, 213.

Jessopp, Augustus, D.D., on the value of money, 36 *note*, 117 *note;* on Father Gerard's innocence, 207.

Jesuits, efforts to incriminate, 177

note; Cecil on their "insolencies," 106.

Kennet, White, Bishop of Peterborough, 45 *note*, 46, 263.
Keyes, Robert, contradictions respecting him, 84 *note*, 183. See also Conspirators.
"King's Book," the, its character, 108; Cecil's description of it, 219, 220.
Knyvet, or Knevet, Sir Thomas, leads the party which captures Faukes, 124 *seq.*; receives a peerage, 139 *note*; the Countess of Suffolk his sister, 224 *note*.

Lake, Sir Thomas, 19, 232.
Lenthal, William, Speaker of the Long Parliament, his evidence reported, 160.
Lindsay, Sir James, conveys messages between King James and Pope Clement VIII., 104.
Lingard, John, D.D., 68 *note*, 231.
Littleton, Humphrey, 167 *note*.
Littleton, Stephen, 2, 4, 156.
Lodge, Edmund, F.S.A. (*Illustrations of British History*), 98.
Lopez' Plot, 14.

"Main," the, 15 *note*, 26, 216.
Mar, Earl of (John Erskine), 168 *note*, 172, 266.
Mary, Princess, daughter of James I., 81, 176.
Milton, poems on the Plot, 226.
Mine, the, story told respecting it, 63 *seq.*; difficulties respecting it, 84 *seq.*
Mischeefe's Mystery, 72, 115, 121, 123, 153 *note*, 159.

Money, value of, 36 *note*, 117 *note*; amount raised by conspirators, 39.
Monteagle, Lord (William Parker), his character and antecedents, 118; relations with the king and court, 34, 119; letter to the king, 119, 256; connection with the conspirators, 118; communicates the warning letter to Cecil, 120-123, 160; attends parliament on the day of the "discovery," 137 *note*; devices of the government on his behalf, 116; rewards conferred, 116; subsequent conduct, 258.
Moore, Sir Francis, his evidence reported, 151.
Moore, Sir Jonas, 138.
More, Father Henry, S.J., 49.
Morgan, Harry, 81 *note*.
Morgan, Thomas, 157 *note*, 193 *note*.

Naunton, Sir Robert, on Cecil's character, 19.
Northampton, Earl of (Henry Howard), a nominal Catholic promoted by King James, 29; Cecil's agent in his secret correspondence, 26 *note*; on Cecil's death, 23; on the history of the "cellar," 58 *note*; not admitted to all Cecil's secrets, 112.
Northumberland, Earl of (Henry Percy), a rival of Cecil's, 26; who secretly traduces him, 26 *note*, 215, 216; the Plot turned to his ruin, 26, 107, 216-218; which is attributed to Cecil, 26 *note*, 218, his sentiments in return, 218.
Nottingham, Earl of, Lord Admiral (Charles Howard), 170 *note*, 265.

Oates, Titus, 46, 138.
Oath taken by the conspirators, 9.
Oldcorne, *alias* Hall, Father Edward, S.J., captured along with Garnet, 7 ; never accused of complicity *ib.* ; Catholic demonstration at his execution, 28 *note ;* tortured, 173.
Oldmixon (*Royal House of Stuart*), 25 *note*, 46.
Osborne, Francis, on Cecil's unpopularity, 25 ; on the "discovery," 44 ; on the 5th of August celebration, 232 *note* ; on Northumberland and Cecil, 218 ; his qualifications as an historian, 44.
Owen, Captain Hugh, falsely described as a Jesuit, 173 *note*, 185 *note ;* particularly obnoxious to the government, 173, 185 ; evidence fabricated against him, 174 ; Cecil's instruction respecting him, 116 *note ;* efforts made to secure him, 185 *seq.;* his intercourse with Phelippes, 112, 185 *note.*
Owen, Lewis, 263.

Paris, Henry, 162.
Parliament, its successive adjournments, 67, 70 *note*, 91, 114, 230 ; meets on the day of the "discovery," 136 ; activity against Catholics, 5, 212 *seq.*
Parry, Sir Thomas, English Ambassador at Paris, instructions given to, 28 *note ;* intelligence supplied by, 98, 101, 102 ; account of the discovery furnished to, 126 *seq.*
Parry, Dr. William, his Plot, 14, 153.

Parsons, Father Robert, S.J., letters to, 29 *note*, 77, 223 ; his views as to the succession, 249 ; on Walsingham's "spyery," 77.
Percy, Sir Charles, 192 *note.*
Percy, Thomas, one of the first and principal conspirators, 9, 64 ; his antecedents, 36, 37, 148 ; house hired by him, 60; and "cellar," 75 ; strange conduct in both transactions, 88 ; conduct afterwards, 88, 91 ; undertakes to seize Duke Charles or Princess Elizabeth, 82; his death, 4, 152 *seq.* ; profession of religious zeal, 148; bigamy, *ibid*; Catholics suspicious of him, 150 ; alleged secret dealings with Cecil, 151 ; the case against him, 148-156. *See also* Conspirators.
Phelippes, Thomas, the "decipherer," employed by the government, 111 ; their devices against him, 112 ; correspondence with Hugh Owen, 185 *note.*
Pickering, Mr., and his horse, 261.
Plain and Rational Account of the Catholick Faith, 49.
Plots under Elizabeth and James I., 14, 15, 153, 157 *note*, 193 *note ;* their common feature, 13.
Polititian's Catechism, 51 *note*, 106, 137 *note.*
Pope Clement VIII., interchanges communications with James I., 104.
Pope Paul V., represented as an accomplice in the Plot, 5, 239.
Popham, Sir John, Lord Chief Justice, 170 *note*, 197, 266.

Raleigh, Sir Walter, Cecil's enmity

towards him, 26 *note*, 48 *note*, 198; his ruin, 26, 216; attempt to implicate him in the Powder Plot, 197, 198.
Ratcliffe, Ralph, a government spy, 95, 96, 191.
Rich, Sir Edwin, 264.
Richardot, President, 189.
Rogers, Professor Thorold, on the value of money, 117 *note*; on James's title to the throne, 34.
Rokewood, Ambrose, 179 *note*. See also Conspirators.

Salisbury, first Earl of. *See* Cecil, Robert.
Salisbury, second Earl of. *See* Cecil, William.
Sanderson, Sir William, 46.
Schondonck, Father Giles, S. J., Rector of St. Omers, on the innocence of the Jesuits, 201; on Cecil's manifesto, 222.
Scott, Sir Walter, 132 *note*.
Shakespeare, never alludes to the Plot, 226 *note*.
Sharpe, Dr. R. R., 262 *note*.
Shepherd, John, evidence of, 251.
Smith, John Thomas (*Antiquities of Westminster*), 58 *note*, 79 *note*, 89 *note*.
Soane, Sir John, 238.
Southwaick, or Southwell, a government spy, 99-102.
Speed, John (*Historie*), 62, 63 *note*.
Squires, Edward, his plot, 14.
Stanley, Sir William, 185, 192 *note*.
Strange, Father Thomas, S. J., 96 *note*.
Streete, John, pensioned for killing Percy and Catesby, 155.
Strype, John (*Annals*), 28 *note*.

Suffolk, Earl of, Lord Chamberlain (Thomas Howard), his venality, 224.

Talbot, John, of Grafton, 38 *note*.
Talbot, Peter, Archbishop of Dublin. *See Polititian's Catechism*.
Theobald, Lewis, 267.
Topcliffe, Richard, priest-hunter, 202.
Torture, use of, 4, 5, 172, 173, 201 *note*, 259, 260.
Tresham, Francis, enlisted in the enterprise, 10, 252 *seq*.; his previous record, 35, 36; his action on behalf of King James, 34; suspected of writing the warning letter, 147, 158; and of collusion with Cecil, *ibid*.; his conduct after the "discovery," 3, 158; his death in the Tower, 6 *note*, 158. See also Conspirators.
Tresham, Sir Thomas, proclaims King James, 34; summoned to Court, 248.
True and Perfect Relation, character of the narrative, 43, 163.
Tytler, Patrick Fraser, 112.

Usher, James, Archbishop of Armagh, his evidence reported, 45.

Venatio Catholica, 261.
Vetusta Monumenta, 79, 86.
Villeroy, M., on Cecil's duplicity, 23.
"Vinegar House," 60 *note*.
Vowell, Peter, evidence reported, 160.

Waad, Sir William, lieutenant of the Tower, charged by Cobham with forgery of evidence, 202; dismissed from his post, 203 *note*, 267; his inscriptions in the Tower, 264, 267; letters to Cecil, 168, 258.

Walsh, Sir Richard, sheriff of Worcestershire, 4, 154 *note*.

Ward, Samuel, preacher and artist, 239.

Webb, John, evidence reported, 160.

Weldon, Sir Anthony, on Cecil's unpopularity, 25.

Welwood, James (*Memoirs*), 46.

Westmoreland, titular Earl of (Henry Neville), attempt to implicate him, 197.

Whynniard, Mr., landlord of Percy's house, 61 *note*, 89; his sudden death, 92 *note*.

Whynniard, Mrs., evidence of, 61, 67, 72, 88, 142.

Willaston, William, intelligence supplied by, 99.

Wimbledon, Viscount (Edward Cecil), his evidence reported, 160.

Windsor, Lord, his house plundered by the conspirators, 2.

Winter, Robert, introduced to the conspiracy, 10; captured at Hagley, 4; evidences of foul play in his regard, 183, 184; trial and execution, 6. *See also* Conspirators.

Winter, Thomas, one of the first conspirators, 9, 64; character, 35; Spanish mission, 36, 118; brings Faukes from Flanders, 9; attends the prorogation, Oct. 3rd, 74 *note*, 230; captured at Holbeche, 4; his published confession, 167 *seq.*; probably tortured, 169; trial and execution, 6. *See also* Conspirators.

Wood, Anthony à, notes addressed to, 159.

Worcester, Earl of (Edward Somerset), 168 *note*, 266.

Wotton, Sir Henry, 160.

Wren, Sir Christopher, 138.

Wright, Christopher, his introduction to the Conspiracy, 9, 64; character, 35, 37; previous employment in Spain, 36; killed at Holbeche, 4, 152. *See also* Conspirators.

Wright, Henry, his informations, 94, 95, 254.

Wright, John, one of the first conspirators, 9, 64; character, 35, 37; killed at Holbeche, 4, 152. *See also* Conspirators.

CHISWICK PRESS:—CHARLES WHITTINGHAM AND CO.
TOOKS COURT, CHANCERY LANE, LONDON.

www.ingramcontent.com/pod-product-compliance
Lightning Source LLC
Chambersburg PA
CBHW030818230426
43667CB00008B/1276